DAT

SIGNS
OF THE
ZODIAC

SIGNS
—— OF THE ——
ZODIAC

A REFERENCE GUIDE
TO HISTORICAL, MYTHOLOGICAL,
AND CULTURAL ASSOCIATIONS

Mary Ellen Snodgrass

Illustrated by Raymond Miller Barrett, Jr.

GREENWOOD PRESS
Westport, Connecticut • London

Library of Congress Cataloging-in-Publication Data

Snodgrass, Mary Ellen.
  Signs of the zodiac : a reference guide to historical,
mythological, and cultural associations / Mary Ellen Snodgrass ;
illustrated by Raymond Miller Barrett, Jr.
      p.   cm.
  Includes bibliographical references and index.
  ISBN 0–313–30276–6 (alk. paper)
  1. Zodiac.   2. Astrology.   I. Title.
  BF1726.S66   1997
  133.5′2—dc21   97–5598

British Library Cataloguing in Publication Data is available.

Library of Congress Catalog Card Number: 97–5598
ISBN: 0–313–30276–6

First published in 1997

Greenwood Press, 88 Post Road West, Westport, CT 06881
An imprint of Greenwood Publishing Group, Inc.

Printed in the United States of America

The paper used in this book complies with the
Permanent Paper Standard issued by the National
Information Standards Organization (Z39.48–1984).

10 9 8 7 6 5 4 3 2 1

For Pattie Tyndall

It is true, without falsehood, certain and very real,
That that which is on high is that which is below,
And that which is below is as that which is on high,
In order that the miracle of Unity may be very perpetual.

Hermetic Writings from the Emerald Table
Twelfth Century A.D.
(Shulman 1976, 41)

God is the light of the heavens and of the earth. His light is like a
niche in which is a lamp—the lamp encased in glass—the glass, as it
were, a glistening star. From a blessed tree it is lighted, the olive neither from the East nor of the West, whose oil would well nigh shine
out, even though the fire touched it not. It is light upon light. God
guideth whom he will to his light, and God setteth forth
parables to men.

Koran 24:35

CONTENTS

PREFACE

The purpose of *The Signs of the Zodiac* is to supply the student, researcher, historian, amateur astronomer or astrologer, teacher, or librarian with the background of zodiacal lore and its application to current culture. The opening chapters introduce the concept of an identifiable star path and a pervasive human interest in the cyclical appearance of constellations. Among the questions implicit in this study are these universal queries:

- Why do the stars appear and disappear in a regular cycle?
- What power does this cyclical movement have over Earth?
- How do the heavens influence human life and character?
- What part do the constellations play in government?
- What is the appropriate response of worshippers to the god who made the heavens?
- What is the difference between astronomy and astrology?
- How much of traditional lore is superstition and how much science?
- What is the purpose of horoscopes?

Following a discussion of superstitions and religious beliefs that have evolved worldwide from centuries of star study, this book presents a detailed history of early star gazers with particular attention to Babylon, Egypt,

Arabia, the Orient, Greece, and Rome and sages such as Berossus, Alexander the Great, Hippocrates, Euclid, Galen, St. Augustine, and the Zoroastrians. Subsequent star wisdom from the post-Christian era centers on philosophical differences over the power of the zodiac over history and human fate. This section concludes with scientific advancements such as the astrolabe and telescope, which have subsumed early philosophies and interpretations of star movements and replaced them with detailed physical analysis and mathematical calculations.

The final chapters present the twelve signs of the zodiac in their traditional order, Aries through Pisces. Each segment introduces a sign, its physical components, the origin of star and cluster names, and the correspondences that have accrued to each pattern. Detailed commentary on literature, the arts, and advertising note the influence of zodiacal lore on creativity and commerce. Application of each sign's stereotypical qualities uncovers possible ties with famous people, including singers, painters, humanitarians, military leaders, royalty, and scientists. Appendices list more detailed information about constellation size, distance, and intensity and correspondences to minerals, precious and semi-precious stones, plants, colors, shapes, and human pathology.

On the whole, *The Signs of the Zodiac* systematizes star lore and zodiacal wisdom alongside citations from a variety of scriptures and great writers. The work focuses on descriptions of classic art and architecture and on a panorama of astrological details that render the subject fascinating and universally applicable to human endeavors. The index enables the reader or researcher to access particular facets of zodiacal lore, for example, zodiacal healing, star size and intensity, heavenly bodies mentioned in the Bible, or famous people born under specific sun signs who display stereotypical characteristics. For whatever purpose, serious inquiry or curiosity, *The Signs of the Zodiac* presents the history of human interest in constellations, their cycles, and their time-honored significance.

INTRODUCTION

The star-flecked sky has intrigued, baffled, and delighted humankind for as long as there have been eyes to see and minds to contemplate the heavens. Early nomads set their itineraries over sand and ridge to the shift of stars above the azimuth. To specify segments of the far-flung celestial map, these wandering people resorted to naming star patterns, much as children point out camels and bears and dragons in the clouds. With definite names for segments of their star maps, they could trade information, question fellow travelers, and ennoble the guideposts that brought them safely to their destinations.

When the nomads settled down to become farmers, they continued the practice of calibrating their daily lives and seasonal work by familiar, dependable astral timepieces. Seafarers and surveyors also drew on star positions as way markers. Worldwide, navigators felt confident in leaving port when they were certain of the moon, Polaris, Venus, and Orion, the most familiar heavenly signposts. In Thomas Hood's words:

> The stars are with the voyager,
> Wherever he may sail,
> The moon is constant to her time,
> The sun will never fail.
> But follow round the world
> The green earth and the sea . . .

And so the night is never dark,
And day is brighter day. (Hood, 1959, 2)

From these anonymous stargazers, the more than 200 billion stars and billions of galaxies acquired sets of names that conferred personalities, legends, symbolism, and powers on constellations. The atavistic mythology of demons, monsters, and vengeful gods spread over the skies a pastiche of recognizable symbols, all pacified into lights that resided in a civil, nonviolent structure. The nightly shift of the sidereal mosaic has supplanted the boisterous stories of Chiron and Hercules with a resplendent serenity, which Babylonians worshiped as the pulsating heart of the world and the Romans identified with eternity. The blend of nomenclature from primitive societies with Roman theology established one universal truth: star lore forms a slender, yet enduring tether between the heavens and destiny, a religious, pseudo-scientific, and cult interpretation that spans all peoples.

The most familiar family of constellation terminology in the Western world is called by its Greek name, the zodiac. Taking its place outside the realm of Western empirical science, the study of the zodiac carries no value as a fixed discipline. Unlike the science of astronomy (which systemizes the movements of heavenly bodies) or astrometry (which measures their progress across the night sky), astrology is a personalized contemplation of reality through analogies to planetary motion. As the etymology of the words "star-crossed" and "disaster" indicate, disunion in the stars bodes ill for earthlings. Human rationalization tends to blame the heavens for catastrophes. Because the study of astrology relies on judgment and intuition, astrological knowledge carries a subjective or human element of prediction. Thus, its validity depends on the faith of millions of believers who trust seers, crystal ball viewers, and stargazers to calculate and interpret the conjunctions of planets and their influence on weather, crops, healing, and the lives, character, fortunes, and decisions of individuals.

Architectural monuments of past civilizations mirror human compulsions to apply heavenly phenomena to vicissitudes in daily affairs. Around 1000 B.C., the Zapotec built Monte Alban in central Mexico to help them keep tabs on the stars. They constructed a central courtyard and inscribed around the walls a calendar based on a fifty-two-year cycle. Likewise, second-century Mesoamericans living thirty miles north of Mexico City constructed Teotihuacan, a notable, pleasing city based on an astral plan. The ruins contain pyramids to the sun and moon. Archaeoastronomers believe that the geometric pattern of Teotihuacan's streets and temples coincides with the predawn rise of the Pleiades, one of the most familiar star patterns in history.

Two centuries after Teotihuacan took shape, the Maya of the Yucatan Peninsula began massive excavations for Chichen Itza. A ceremonial city intended to propitiate the gods, it honored Venus, the nation's patron planet. Mayan codices served the populace as an almanac to coordinate ritual sacrifice with the rise of the planet in the sky. When the Toltecs overthrew the Maya in 987 A.D., they kept Chichen Itza and added Castillo, a stepped pyramid that ripples with shadows shortly before the equinox sunset. The visual effect is so stunning, so evocative, that visitors still gather to view it.

Farther north, prehistoric Indians created worship centers that corresponded with astral patterns. Around 700 A.D., late woodland Indians constructed the Cahokia Mounds near what is now Collinsville, Illinois. Cahokia's axial orientation served as a predictor of solstices and equinoxes, both considered beneficent times. In the Southwest at Four Corners—the convergence of Utah, New Mexico, Arizona, and Colorado—the Anasazi built a stone complex between 900 and 1115 A.D. A major settlement, Casa Rinconada is a kiva or underground ceremonial chamber that follows two exactly perpendicular north-south and east-west diameters. On nearby Fajada Butte, these same aborigines marked midsummer's day by inscribing spirals on the rock outcroppings. Similar reverence for the heavens motivated the Inca to design Machu Picchu, a temple complex built astride the Andes Chain in Peru, and Cuzco, an Incan worship center that venerates the Milky Way and Alpha Crucis, the brightest star in the Southern Cross and a source of cosmic power from prehistory.

Eastern and Mideastern systems of star study—including the Hebrew, Babylonians, Chaldeans, Assyrians, Greeks, Chinese, Japanese, Korean, and Tibetan—are less architectural and more metaphoric in their contemplations of the heavens. Housed in the Victoria and Albert Museum in London, for example, is a cartouche of Indian astrology that pictures the paths of the nine planets—Sun, Moon, Mars, Mercury, Jupiter, Venus, Saturn, Ketu the comet, and Rahu the bringer of eclipses—as the routes of chariots. The mideastern system of astrology, which derived from a convergence of Chaldean, Babylonian, Egyptian, and Greek lore, based astral calculations on the zodiac. Priests allied a star-centered belief system with sacred or canonical geometry, which derived from observations of heavenly movements. One truth sets the Mideastern heavenly study apart from the Toltec, Incan, Mayan, and Anasazi cosmologies: Mesoamerican and Amerindian star systems vanished with the people. The Mideastern system of astrology still thrives. Throughout history, this long-lived theory of star power has bobbed in and out of fashion, at times trounced to dust, then rising like the fabled phoenix to a new and glorious ascendance.

THE ZODIAC

The zodiac, which is based on the solar calendar, is an imaginary belt that encircles the heavens about eight degrees on each side of the ecliptic, (the orbital path the earth makes around the sun). The zodiac's path is the fixed cyclic or series of planetary orbits, which parallel the earth's equator. The circle bears the name "zodiac" from the Greek *zoidiakos* plus *kyklos* meaning "life wheel" or "circle of little animals," possibly derived from a society in prehistory who venerated bestial totems. This band subdivides into the twelve constellations or star clusters. The appearance of these constellations coincides with the position of the sun, which moves behind them in turn and illuminates them to observers on earth. Each month, as the circle completes one-twelfth of a rotation, a separate constellation is visible from Earth. Observers can view each cluster on a limited hemisphere that rests on the horizon and shifts westward at the rate of about one degree daily.

Individual constellations bear a two-fold Latin name: one form is plain, its alternate form indicates possession, as in Leo (Leonis) and Virgo (Virginis). In use, the forms function as they do in Latin sentences. For example, Virgo has a star labeled gamma. Scientists refer to the star as gamma Virginis, which means the "gamma star of Virgo." There is a constellation name and possessive form for each month (note that only two are plural—Pisces and Gemini):

Constellation	Possessive Form and Its Meaning
Taurus	Tauri (of Taurus)
Gemini	Geminorum (of Gemini)
Cancer	Cancri (of Cancer)
Leo	Leonis (of Leo)
Virgo	Virginis (of Virgo)
Libra	Librae (of Libra)
Scorpio	Scorpii (of Scorpio)
Sagittarius	Sagittarii (of Sagittarius)
Capricorn	Capricorni (of Capricorn)
Aquarius	Aquarii (of Aquarius)
Pisces	Piscium (of Pisces)
Aries	Arietis (of Aries)

The prevalence of these twelve symbols in ancient European cultures is a common feature in art, found in the petroglyphs of Cueva de Arce in Laguna de la Jana, Cadiz; sculpture in Alvao, Portugal; and heavenly maps engraved in stone at Eira d'os Mouros, Galicia.

Metaphorically, the star belt's shape suggested to early astronomers the serpent biting its tail, a standard figure in ancient religion and mythology. Like a rolling hoop or a wedding ring, the heavenly belt and its twelve components have no identifiable beginning or end. To early poets and stargazers, the circle represented a procession of complementary forces that, like the attractive poles of magnets, are eternally linked in nature. To the philosopher, these antipathies suggested form with shapelessness, spirit with matter, action with inertia, unity with complexity, raw energy with actualized force, and potential with reality. The star belt's predictable rotations caused human observers to relate a series of common patterns in their feelings, attitudes, and frustrations. Like the stars, these shifts in human emotion had existed throughout history. Over time, the star patterns merged with their counterparts in the human psyche. From the merger arose the concept of astral prediction—the forecasting of human events derived from heavenly powers.

As though viewed in a single, unified telescopic sweep, this powerful circle of celestial forces corrals the sun, moon, and heavenly bodies—Mercury, Venus, Mars, Jupiter, Saturn, Uranus, Neptune, and most of the movements of Pluto, which continues its orbit beyond the circle. Each of the circle's twelve arcs corresponds to an arbitrary astrological sign. Astrologers use these metaphoric signs to determine the control of the stars over earthly life. By 100 B.C., the components, counting west to east from the vernal equinox, were identified by metaphoric images, beginning with Aries, the symbol of spring. The arrangement of signs along the circular band varies about one degree in 70 years. This variance reflects the imperfect shape of the earth and the slight bulge at the polar axis, which displaces the equinoxes.

The study of the twelve houses of the zodiac is complicated by additional influences on each sign. Groupings by fours determine whether the house marks the beginning of a season (cardinal), the sun firmly fixed in a season (fixed), or the decline of a season (mutable). Additional data establishes the influence of the four elements—fire, earth, air, and water, the raw materials from which all matter is made. Astrologers added an arbitrary designation of duality—the star's tendency toward masculine or feminine, which alternates every other month. The alliance of these tendencies coordinates into a single chart:

Sign and Symbol	Dates	Quality	Element	Tendency
Aries (ram)	Mar. 21–Apr. 19	cardinal	fire	masc.
Taurus (bull)	Apr. 20–May 20	fixed	earth	fem.
Gemini (twins)	May 21–June 21	mutable	air	masc.
Cancer (crab)	June 22–July 22	cardinal	water	fem.
Leo (lion)	July 23–Aug. 22	fixed	fire	masc.
Virgo (maiden)	Aug. 23–Sept. 22	mutable	earth	fem.
Libra (scales)	Sept. 23–Oct. 23	cardinal	air	masc.
Scorpio (scorpion)	Oct. 24–Nov. 21	fixed	water	fem.
Sagittarius (archer)	Nov. 22–Dec. 21	mutable	fire	masc.
Capricorn (goat)	Dec. 22–Jan. 19	cardinal	earth	fem.
Aquarius (water bearer)	Jan. 20–Feb. 18	fixed	air	masc.
Pisces (fish)	Feb. 19–Mar. 20	mutable	water	fem.

An exact natal horoscope requires more particular study calculated on the exact moment of birth. In the pseudo-science of astrology, star-watchers determine the planets' influence on human beings by placing the earth at the center of the solar system and measuring positions of the planets at a particular moment, which must be computed exactly by Greenwich Mean

Time. By establishing the geographical coordinates of longitude and latitude, the astrologer determines the horoscope (literally, "hour watch"), an objective diagram or natal chart summarizing locations of heavenly bodies at the *horoscopus* (the moment of birth).

People who believe in star power and who claim a sun sign learn the general personality type, comprised of attitude, intelligence, and behavior, that evolves from the influence of the stars. Astral divination projects for each of the twelve signs a range of positive and negative character and behavior traits. For example, meticulous concern for details, which can improve a business career, but can ruin an over-zealous housekeeper. The claim "to be born under a sign" implies that the individual knows what the sun's position was at the time of birth. Because the thirty-degree arc of each constellation varies from exact center, a person born in the center of the arc is more strongly influenced by the specific sun sign than one born at the edge of the arc, a position known as the cusp.

To study the general predictions for an individual house (sun sign) is to estimate a broad spectrum of possibilities for people occupying the same house. In the mid-seventeenth century, essayist Joseph Addison satirized these possibilities by reducing them to absurdly small parameters:

> Who works from morn to set of Sun,
> And never likes to be outdone?
> Whose walk is almost like a run?
>   Who? Aries.

> Who smiles through life—except when crossed?
> Who knows, or thinks he knows, the most?
> Who loves good things: baked, boiled, or roast?
>   Oh, Taurus.

> Who's fond of life and jest and pleasure:
> Who vacillates and changes ever?
> Who loves attention without measure?
>   Why, Gemini.

> Who changes like a changeful season:
> Holds fast and lets go without reason?
> Who is there can give adhesion
>   To Cancer?

> Who criticizes all she sees:
> Yes, e'en would analyze a sneeze?

Who hugs and loves her own disease?
   Humpf, Virgo.

Who praises all his kindred do:
Expects his friends to praise them too—
And cannot see their senseless view?
   Ah, Leo.

Who puts you off with promise gay,
And keeps you waiting half the day?
Who compromises all the way?
   Sweet Libra.

Who keeps an arrow in his bow,
And if you prod, he lets it go?
A fervent friend, a subtle foe—
   Scorpio.

Who loves the dim religious light:
Who always keeps a star in sight?
An optimist both gay and bright—
   Sagittarius.

Who climbs and schemes for wealth and place,
And mourns his brother's fall from grace—
But takes what's due in any case—
   Safe Capricorn.

Who gives to all a helping hand,
But bows his head to no command—
And higher laws doth understand?
Inventor, Genius, Superman—
   Aquarius.

Who prays and serves, and prays some more;
And feeds the beggar at the door—
And weeps o'er love lost long before?
   Poor Pisces. (Wedeck 1973, 138)

Such narrow stereotypes, which have been published in newspapers and magazines since the 1930s, are too imprecise to advise someone desiring an accurate individual horoscope. To say that all Pisceans are dreamers or that all Cancerians are difficult to love, is too general a summary to assist anyone seeking to chart destiny on the positions of the stars.

Casting of horoscopes requires a knowledge of Euclidean geometry, specifically, the arcs of a circle and the placement of two diameters, one linking the ascent of the sun at dawn and its descent in the evening. Crossing this straight line at right angles is a second diameter linking noon or *medium coeli* (middle of the sky), when the sun is at its height, with the depth of night or *imum coeli* (bottom of the sky). At each two-hour rotation of the heavenly chart, a sun sign comes into power or ascendancy. To apply the chart to an individual, the astrologer locates the sidereal or "star moment" of birth in Greenwich Mean Time (GMT) and establishes the birthplace in degrees and minutes of longitude and latitude. The exact position of the heavens at the time of birth corresponds to a position on an ephemeris, a meticulous chart that names the relationships to each sun sign moment by moment.

Horoscopy by the traditional method involves an exact numerical calculation of constellations, rising and setting sun signs, and the angles that evolve from the two diameters. The most significant placements are 60, 90, 120, and 180 degrees, which indicate the magnetic attraction of the planets. The result is a precise document stating heavenly powers that require a professional interpretation. By studying the traits of each house, a skilled astrologer locates the influences and counter-influences on the subject's personality and destiny. By applying the powers that motivate and stymie the subject, the astrologer must blend mathematical calculations with a shrewd guess at their implications for the subject's social position and educational attainment.

The symbolic code of astrology results from three sets of information—the planets, signs of the zodiac, and the twelve houses that range around the 360–degrees of the solar cycle. The planets, which bear Roman names and unique sets of factors, affect specific aspects of human life:

Sol	*type*: hot, dry, masculine, fruitful, electric the human body, life, psychic energy, masculinity, personality, early environment, honor, power, vitality, luck, creative and regenerative power, will, determination, striving, authority
Luna	*type*: cold, moist, fruitful, nocturnal, magnetic the spirit, emotions, change, knowledge, finances, expression, femininity, passion, desire, health, unconscious emotions, reflection, cooperation, adaptation
Mercury	*type*: dry and moist, androgynous, magnetic the mind, logic, movement, communication, siblings, nerves,

versatility, vivacity, judgment, competition, intellect, mediation, tradition, analysis, critical ability

Venus *type*: beneficent, nocturnal, feminine
art, attraction between the sexes, love, sex, home life, old age, pleasure, children, art, luck, wealth, idealism, energy, feelings, harmony

Mars *type*: hot, dry, barren, malefic, masculine, superior
physical energy, action, impulse, libido, aggression, war, courtship, children, speculation, pleasure, fire, courage, enthusiasm, wounds, adventure, success, vibrance, ruthlessness, brutality

Jupiter *type*: fruitful, beneficent, electric, superior
wealth, health, development and expansion, humor, service, religion, philosophy, law, science, power, ceremony, travel, optimism, dynamism, problem-solving, ownership, ethics, morality, aspiration, enlargement

Saturn *type*: cold, dry, barren, magnetic, superior
concentration, restriction, maturity, separation, delay, partnership, sternness, inheritance, death, selfishness, reticence, diplomacy, disappointment, labor, earth, constriction, perseverance, mining, principles, inhibition, gravity, taciturnity, melancholy

Uranus *type*: barren, superior
violence, rebellion, alteration, sudden changes, genius, creativity, vocation, disturbance, social status, intelligence, eccentricity, invention, spontaneity, excitability, reform, catastrophe, unexpected luck, individualism

Neptune *type*: fruitful, feminine, superior
fantasy, romanticism, the occult, hope, friends, deceit, susceptibility, psychic power, emotional genius, art, poetry, mysticism, dreams, intuition, drugs, fraud, drunkenness, personal magnetism, imagination

Pluto *type*: superior
power, despotism, rule, common people, limitations, confinement, money, sexuality, providence, invisible force, propaganda, demagoguery

The planets Pluto and Uranus are more recent discoveries and lack the thorough definition of type found in the better known heavenly bodies. The astrologer simplifies names for the planets by using a standard set of symbols to represent each. The symbol or ideograph for Mars is a shield and spear, a sign of belligerence and readiness, which is also the scientific symbol for the male sex. The corresponding female symbol is the hand mirror of Venus, which allies womanhood with vanity. Although the position of earth has slowly shifted in the heavens since ancient times, modern astrologers maintain the traditional names for the positions of the constellations.

In addition to the power of the twelve planets, the twelve signs of the zodiac carry their own influences. Archetypal personality traits and behaviors cluster around each sign:

Aries	energetic, bold, courageous, impetuous, determined, hot-tempered, impulsive, hasty, driven, adventure-loving, competitive, unable to concentrate over long periods of time
Taurus	persistent, circumspect, possessive, loyal, obstinate, patient, affectionate, sensible, stubborn, conservative, grudge-bearing
Gemini	witty, lively, verbose, intelligent, progressive, unstable, moody, restless, indecisive
Cancer	sensitive, patriotic, inspired, elusive, home-loving, emotional, instinctive, bashful, artistic, intuitive, secretive, complex, moody
Leo	powerful, pretentious, dignified, expansive, cheerful, proud, colorful, beneficent, self-absorbed, domineering
Virgo	logical, rational, exacting, modest, practical, chaste, fastidious, attentive, self-righteous, sensible, methodical, discriminating, intelligent, industrious
Libra	balanced, evaluative, detail-oriented, companionable, diplomatic, pleasant, affectionate, honorable, just, alert, sympathetic, painstaking, artistic
Scorpio	insistent, forceful, deep-thinking, secretive, lurking, passionate, intense, quick-tempered, moody, uninhibited, spiteful, opinionated, energetic
Sagittarius	mannerly, just, knowledgeable, optimistic, generous, restless, outgoing, relaxed, enthusiastic, candid, sporting, outdoorsy, curious, impulsive
Capricorn	abstract, independent, stubborn, ambitious, cautious, practical, dignified, persistent, serious, stoic, loyal, persevering, tactful, reserved, closed

Aquarius   principled, spiritual, vulnerable, curious, outgoing, inde-
           pendent, up-to-date, open-minded, serious, freedom-loving,
           capricious, logical, scientific, moderate, probing, affable, hu-
           mane, popular, honest

Pisces   tolerant, sympathetic, lazy, artistic, emotional, sensitive,
           vague, intelligent, affable, unfocused, popular, melancholy,
           gentle, unlucky, retiring, kind

Like the planets, each of these signs carries a symbol or glyph, for example, a circle topped with horns to represent Taurus the bull and an arrow set against a bowstring to symbolize Sagittarius. According to manuscripts dating to the Middle Ages, these symbols were standardized by the Greeks of Alexandria during the Hellenistic period, or the second century A.D.

To these sun sign specifics, the astrologer must add another influence— the focuses of the twelve houses or positions on the circular chart, beginning with dawn:

1. evolution of the ego, environment, childhood, physical body, appearance, personality

2. money, possessions, material goods, prosperity, changes of fortune

3. communication, travel, neighbor and family relationships

4. inherited traits, childhood, home

5. sexuality, procreation, pleasure, risks, speculation

6. health, sense of well-being, servants

7. marriage, partnership, community, personal enemies

8. accidents, death, inheritance, benefits, dowry

9. travel, philosophy, religion, spiritual life, mysticism

10. profession, public life, work, fame

11. friends, aims, wishes, social life

12. secret enemies, obscure problems, seclusion, confinement

By establishing the dominant or ruling planets in the ascendant position, the experienced astrologer can draw some exacting conclusions, such as a tendency to fool oneself with fantasies and dreams or the likelihood that the subject will succeed in business. Because this information was difficult to recall, Roman astrologers memorized the twelve focuses by linking them with corresponding mnemonic nouns: *Vita, lucrum, fratres, genitor, nati, valetudo, uxor, mors, pietas, regnum, benefactaque, carcer* (Life, money, brothers, sire, offspring, health, wife, death, duty, career, benefits, prison).

The aspects form an emerging picture as traits bolster or negate each other; for example, love with a tendency toward domination or good health compromised or threatened by accidents. Scoffers label such fortune-telling as false science, superstition, amusement, even blasphemy. Believers accept the indications for what they are—an interpretation of astral influences on human life and destiny. As novelist Henry Miller characterizes horoscopy, the study of the stars allies human life with the rhythms of the universe.

THE HISTORICAL FOUNDATION OF ASTROLOGY

THE ANCIENT WORLD

The paralogical or occult concept of evaluating planets and constellations to determine their influence on human life is the only prerational doctrine to survive from early times. Academic study of the ancient world's fascination with the zodiac—called archeoastronomy or astro-archeology—discloses a common thread in Akkadia, Sumeria, Babylonia, and Chaldea (sometimes lumped under the name Assyria, now the juncture of Iran and Iraq). Parallel strands of thought about star power is obvious in ancient ruins in the Americas, India, Judea, Persia, Egypt, Spain, Africa, and Celtic Britain. Lyrical star mythology evolved from the Akkadians, predecessors of the Babylonians, who lived in what is now southeastern Iraq. Their priests, who combined the work of magus and astrologer, employed herding metaphors to name the planets, which they called *bibbu* or wild goats, and to describe the stars, which they called the "celestial flock." To aid farmers, priestly stargazers predicted flooding along the Tigris and Euphrates, branching rivers that water the land known as the fertile crescent, which lies north of the Persian Gulf. Because these state priests reported directly to monarchs, their observations and interpretations were honored nationwide and their writings revered as divine scripture.

The first archeological evidence of symbolic analysis of stars dates to 2750 B.C., during the reign of Sargon of Agade, an Akkadian king who possessed charts that predicted solar eclipses. An apparent devotee of astral prediction, Sargon oversaw the compilation of *The Day of Bel*, an astrological handbook. To benefit his dynasty and nation, Sargon hired a team to codify and standardize zodiacal interpretation. The completed document, a collection of predictions and omens, was called the *Anu-Ea-Enlil*, which lists and explains influences of the skies on earth. Examples demonstrate the era's unsophisticated alliance of cause and effect:

- The appearance of the moon the first night of the month presaged peace.
- A haloed moon insured a strong monarchy.
- A moon on the thirtieth of the month was good for Akkad, but inauspicious for Syria, the coastal power that was Akkad's enemy.
- A large setting sun with three bluish rays spelled doom for the king.

Of weather, the *Anu-Ea-Enlil* had much to say:

- A darkly haloed moon meant a cloudy, wet month.
- Thunder during the month of Shebat preceded swarms of locusts.
- Thunder during the month of Nisannu meant a diminished barley crop.

The extremes of prognostication were arbitrary and, at times, terrifying: Jupiter entering the moon preceded a collapse of national finances; a conjunction of Mars and Gemini foretold the king's death and a power struggle of rivals. Gullible people who studied the implications of Sargon's document felt small and powerless against so great a manifestation of heavenly power as they saw in the stars.

In 1750 B.C.—a half century after the Celts constructed Stonehenge in southern England to calculate lunar and solar movements—the Babylonians made a shrewd plan to segment time into seven-day weeks, a forerunner of the modern concept of seven-day biorhythms. The Babylonians divided the year into twelve lunar months and added an intercalary month to complete the solar year. Just as Stonehenge served as a microcosm of the universe and calculated solstices and equinoxes, the Babylonian calendar charted the emergence and disappearance of constellations. Based on the belief that planetary motions were messages from gods, they evolved astral contemplation into a science of correspondence or sympathy in nature. Babylon's priests, who became the world's first official astrologers, formulated rituals and ceremonies to mark the appearance of star clusters. The number of these signs varied until the advent of mathematical astronomy, which settled the heavenly procession of star patterns on twelve arcs or sectors of thirty degrees each, which totaled 360 degrees (one rotation of the sun's annual cycle).

Not all early systems arrived at the same interpretation of star movements. In the Western Hemisphere, around the first century A.D., the Maya of Mexico and Central America evolved a cyclic system of star interpretation based on twenty objects: crocodile, wind, house, lizard, snake, death, deer, hare, water, dog, ape, grass, reed, jaguar, eagle, vulture, earthquake, stone knife, rain, and flower. The Mayan calendar, which stone engravings preserve from the third century A.D., appears to have relied more on calculation than astronomical observation.

Later Mesoamerican cultures reflect the wisdom of the Mayan calendar. According to Hernán Cortéz, the Spanish *conquistador* who reached the Yucatan Peninsula in 1520, the Aztec, who lived around Mexico City seven centuries after the Maya, recited an almost identical list of astral signs: crocodile, wind, house, lizard, snake, death, deer, hare, water, dog, ape, grass, reed, jaguar, eagle, vulture, the twisted, knife, rain, and flower. A calendar called the Tonalamah linked the signs of auspicious and inauspicious days with solstices and equinoxes. The Inca, the contemporaries of the Aztec who lived along South America's western coast and east into the Andes Mountains, drew zodiacal signs reflecting twenty days of the week.

In western Asia, Islamic and Hindu astrologers also applied a set of pictures to a distinct zodiac. To the Arabs, the sky contained six wet or northern signs and six corresponding dry or southern signs. To the east they saw three fiery shapes—Aries, Leo, and Sagittarius. To the south lay Taurus, Virgo, and Capricorn, the cold, dry signs. The west housed Gemini, Libra, and Aquarius, a hot, wet triad. The North was the home of the cold, wet trio—Cancer, Scorpio, and Pisces. The Hindu created a zodiac in the shape of a wheel of signs called the *Rasi chakra* or evolutionary dance. The sun held the center; planetary deities posed around the core, which featured Rahu and Ketu as Jupiter, who formed the head and tail of a dragon or supreme power. His satellite powers included Buddha as Mercury; Chandra as Mars, a moon figure; and Saturn and Venus as an Indian couple.

Far more complex than the Islamic and Hindu zodiacs were China's moon stations and star stations, evolved by astronomers Hsien, Shih Shen, and Kan Te. Before the Chinese system was codified, a royal astrologer named Wen Wang made rudimentary observations from a state tower before

1000 B.C. His successor, Hsien, a court shaman, cataloged the stars, which were not mapped until the collaboration of cosmologists Shih Shen and Kan Te in the fourth century B.C. These two pioneers color-coded the procession of star clusters in white, red, and black. Three centuries later, Keng Shou-Ch'ang augmented China's two-dimensional studies with a useful invention—the armillary sphere, a skeletal bronze globe formed of interconnected hoops representing planetary orbits. As visual evidence of divine order in the universe, Ch'ien Le-chieh pictured and labeled China's traditional lore on China's first star map in 790 A.D.

Star knowledge animated a variety of Asian sciences. Taoist philosophers claimed that the soul could purify itself by feeding on sunshine, moonlight, and celestial influences, which numbered sixty elements in a single cycle. Chinese imperial seers used these elements to predict harmonic convergences between earth and heaven. Calligraphers pictured the elements as twelve animal ideographs—the rat, ox, tiger, hare, dragon, snake, horse, sheep, monkey, rooster, dog, and pig. These twelve figures—six wild and six domestic or six yin and six yang—individually dominate a single solar year or Year Tree, which is based on movements of Jupiter, the Year Star.

According to Chinese cosmology, the purpose of the twelve code names was to harmonize human destiny with space and time. This long-lived zodiac extended into the thirteenth century, when the Venetian explorer Marco Polo returned from his seventeen-year trek from Hangchow with reports that 5,000 magi and clairvoyants supplied Emperor Kublai Khan with data gained from weather and star study. To assure order and positive outcomes, Chinese travelers studied the zodiac and chose propitious days for journeys. Similarly, couples selected promising times for betrothals, parents conceived children during lucky convergences, and mourners selected the favorable dates for funerals, even if they had to wait years before burying their dead. Thus, the Chinese zodiac influenced most of the mundane and festive events of human life.

Orientalists surmise that the star lore also undergirded literacy. Chinese drew individual letters of the alphabet from the twenty-eight constellations of the lunar zodiac, a calendar designed for farmers. The first letter contains six stars forming an ox head, symbol of the Chinese constellation *Niu*. The sign is the same as the Phoenician letter *aleph*, the Arabic *alif,* and Greek *alpha*. The second letter, which Phoenicians called *beth*, Arabs named *ba*, and Greeks wrote as *beta*, derives from four stars that indicate "house." One theory of the spread of this alphabet of concrete nouns places its origin in Iraq. Philologists conclude that the Sumerian letter system of 2000 B.C., along with loan words and idioms, traveled west to Phoenicia in what is now western Syria about the time that it passed east through India and Burma to the Far East. In this fashion, the literate world allied astral observations with the symbols they used to write words.

In contrast to the Chinese zodiac, the Indo-European evolution of a symbolic code required a smaller number of animal shapes. In the prehistory of India, the zodiac symbolized sun worship and a mystical eight-part cosmology: *edu* the ram, *yal* the harp, *nand* the crab, *amma* the mother, *tuk* the scales, *kani* the dart, *kuda* the pitcher, and *min* the fish. Parallels to current zodiacal figures—particularly Aries, Cancer, Virgo, Libra, Sagittarius, Aquarius, and Pisces—are unmistakable. These shapes have remained static for centuries, even during the metamorphosis of zodiacal philosophy and interpretation. Brahmin priests continue to apply these astral signs to the interpretation of the Veda, their sacred texts.

Egypt took a different path to its zodiac. About 1000 B.C., Egyptians structured mythology around Aton, the sun; Shu, the life spirit; and Tefnut, the cosmos. Shu and Tefnut produced twin offspring: Geb, the younger spirit of life, and Nut, the matriarch who presides over order. A focal myth in the Egyptian pantheon describes how the twins were separated and placed in individual spheres—Geb on earth and Nut in the sky. In a pyramid text, Geb calls to his sister:

O Great One who has become the sky!

You have the mastery, you have filled every place with
   beauty.

The whole earth lies beneath you, you have taken possession
   thereof.

You have enclosed the whole earth and everything therein
   within your arms.

As Geb shall I impregnate you in your name of sky,
I shall join the whole earth to you in every place.
O high above the earth! You are supported upon your father Shu,
   But you have power over him,

He so loved you that he placed himself—and all things beside—
   beneath you

So that you took up into you every god with his heavenly barque,
And as "a thousand souls" did you teach them
That they should not leave you—as the stars. (Leeming 1990, 97–98)

From the union of sky and earth come Egypt's durable pantheon: Osiris, god of the underworld; Isis, goddess of the moon; Seth, god of evil and darkness; Nephthys, goddess of death; and Horus, god of light. Although the early panoply of divinity lacked direct association with planets and constellations, Egypt's gods established the power of the stars over earth.

Archeological evidence of these astral shapes appear on the ceiling of the tenth chamber of the tomb of Sethos I, which was built in the valley of Biban el-Muluk near Thebes in the fourteenth century B.C. By the time the Temple of Esneh was erected in central Egypt across the Nile from Luxor some five centuries later, the Egyptians had formulated a cycle of constellations. According to figures in the portico, the celestial circle, called a denderah or zodiac, began at Virgo and ended with Leo. The union of maiden with lion produced the sphinx, a term meaning "closely united." The serene figure—a recumbent lion marked by outstretched forepaws and the uplifted head of a woman—represented the juncture of the heavenly procession from Virgo to Leo. The puzzling shape has remained so entrenched in Egyptology that it still appears in literature, opera, cinema, art, and trademarks.

Although the Egyptians created an astral cycle and maintained that human fate was determined by natal stars, they cannot be credited with inventing the zodiac. They passed basic assumptions about the denderah north to the Babylonians, the founders of horoscopy. Because the Babylonians venerated the external world as divine or as a god, they believed that an understanding of the heavens contributed to their knowledge of all nature, which functioned as a unit. Scientists and priests of both the Egyptian and Babylonian cultures became adept at interpreting dreams, which they revered as mystical messages from the gods. They faithfully observed the heavens and recorded mundane events as well as anomalies, such as star showers and comets.

Civilizations at the eastern end of the Mediterranean gained a reputation for skill in astrology. According to Cicero's *De Divinatione* (About Divination), the people of Egypt and Babylonia had a natural advantage over lands occupied by Romans and Greeks:

> [They] reside in vast plains where no mountains obstruct their view of the entire hemisphere, and so they have applied themselves to that kind of divination called astrology. (Shulman 1976, 24)

Supplied with adequate star lore, Babylonian seers cast horoscopes based on the sun, moon, and five planets—Ishtar (Venus), goddess of fertility and evening star; Nergal (Mars), the bloody-handed war-monger; Marduk (Jupiter), ill-tempered king of gods and sender of disasters; Nebo or Nabu (Mercury), a sly, shifty deity; and Ninib or Ninurta (Saturn), the "night sun," a terrible dual-natured divinity who could launch thunderstorms as well as spring zephyrs. Priests drew conclusions about the heavens, for example, that Mars, the red planet, flushed with anger and aggression or that Venus smiled on love. Babylonian kings submitted to astral readings and noted in particular the unpredictable behaviors of Ninib, the king's star. Contemplation of these heavenly bodies and their anthropomorphic behaviors evolved into a religion that associated seven planets with fate and the number seven with magic.

Growth of astrological knowledge and skill at forecasting spans most of Babylon's history. By the mid-seventh century B.C., King Ashurbanipal had expanded his royal library at Nineveh, a royal city on the Tigris river north of modern Baghdad. Among ancient texts and contemporary observations and records collected from Eridu and other Assyrian temple cities, he included the "Creation Legend," a series of clay tablets written in cuneiform, an ancient writing system. This valuable piece of sky study documented a division of the sky into three heavenly paths: the zodiacal belt, northern sky, and southern sky. Enlil's way corresponds to the Tropic of Cancer; its counterpart, Ea's way, is the equivalent of the Tropic of Capricorn. The central path, Anu's way, is a solar system that prefigures the current zodiac.

Eager to boost their reputations for accurate predictions of the future, Babylon's religious hierarchy kept vigil on the skies from square-based pyramidal towers that were built ziggurat or step style. Their location was so vital to both state and monarchy that it shared space with government offices and warehouses of emergency food and weapon supplies. Bel-u, one of Ashurbanipal's priests at Nineveh, composed a lengthy commentary on the hazards of eclipses and urged his lord to write to the monarchs of Assur, Babylon, Uruk, and Borsippa to compare notes on a predicted eclipse that may have been occluded by clouds. To make certain that no evil would befall Babylon by default, Bel-u, who appears to have worried about his own infallibility, recommended that priests perform ritual safeguards.

The area around the Tigris and Euphrates rivers was so closely linked to contemplation of the skies that disdainful Hebrew writers referred to magicians and astrologers by the pejorative "Chaldeans." No less interested in heavenly messages, Hebrew sages also studied star patterns. They called their zodiac the Mazzaroth and referred to the four brightest stars as Cherubim or the Four Brigades. According to Josephus, the authoritative Jewish historian adopted by imperial Rome, Hebrew astronomy dated to

Adam and his sons Seth and Enos, who were the first human males and the first stargazers. Identified in Josephus's *Antiquities of the Jews*, published in 94 A.D., Seth and Enos

> were the inventors of that peculiar sort of wisdom which is concerned with the heavenly bodies, and their order. And that their inventions might not be lost before they were sufficiently known, upon Adam's prediction that the world was to be destroyed at one time by the force of fire, and at another time by the violence and quantity of water, they made two pillars; the one of brick, the other of stone: they inscribed their discoveries on them both, that in case the pillar of brick should be destroyed by the flood, the pillar of stone might remain and exhibit those discoveries to mankind; and also inform them that there was another pillar of brick erected by them. Now this remains in the land of Siriad to this day. (Josephus 1960, 27)

A major difference between Hebrew sky lore and Babylonian astrology is the matter of interpretation. To the Babylonians, the heavens foretold the future; to the Hebrews, such foretellings were a sacrilege against their faith, which was founded on the worship of one god, Yahweh.

Still, ambivalent writers of the Talmud claimed that stars foretold the birth of their patriarch, Abraham, the founder of monotheism in the Western world. They contended that he was an astrologer who learned from the stars that he would be childless until late in his life. According to Genesis 15:5, God eases Abraham's worries about heirs by comparing his dynasty to the stars: "And he brought him forth abroad, and said, Look now toward heaven, and tell the stars, if thou be able to number them: and he said unto him, So shall thy seed be." An integral part of both Judaism and Islam, God's promise presages the rise of the two great religions, both of whom call Abraham their patriarch.

Differences in attitudes toward astrology perpetuated cultural differences between Hebrews and Assyrians. A contemporary of two Assyrian kings, Sargon II and Sennacherib, the Hebrew prophet Isaiah led his followers in a moral and philosophical battle against Babylonia, which in 710 B.C. warred against Jerusalem, a prize city west of the Jordan River in what is now Israel. Isaiah spoke positively of the constellations as evidence of the Creator and urged, "Lift up your eyes on high, and behold who hath created these [stars], that bringeth out their host by number: he calleth them all by names by the greatness of his might, for that he is strong in power; not one faileth" (Isaiah

40:26). Against the Babylonian practice of horoscopy, which the Hebrews considered pagan and godless, Isaiah snarled,

> Your nakedness will be exposed and your shame uncovered.
> I will take vengeance; I will spare no one.
> Our Redeemer—the Lord Almighty is his name—
> Is the Holy One of Israel. . .
> [Destruction] will come upon you in full measure,
> In spite of your many sorceries and all your potent spells.
> You have trusted in your wickedness
> And have said, "No one sees me."
> Your wisdom and knowledge mislead you when you say to yourself,
> "I am, and there is none besides me."
> Disaster will come upon you,
> And you will not know how to conjure it away.
> A calamity will fall upon you
> That you cannot ward off with a ransom.
> Keep on, then, with your magic spells
> And with your many sorceries,
> Which you have labored at since childhood . . .
> Let your astrologers come forward,
> Those stargazers who make predictions month by month,
> Let them save you from what is coming upon you.
> (Isaiah 47:3–4, 9–13)

Struggling to reclaim Israel from its decline, the visionary prophet castigated "the lady Babylon" for venerating idols, cult objects, and zodiacal symbols. In anger at their effrontery toward Jehovah, Isaiah taunted that a heavenly flame would devour them like wheat stubble, but his harsh mouthings railed fruitlessly against the widespread practice of divination.

According to the *MulAlpin* (Plough Star), a series of tablets dating to 700 B.C. and compiling six centuries of observations, Babylonian astrologers assigned metaphoric names to star clusters, for example, En Gonasin, the Kneeler, now called Hercules and Draco. Observations of the clusters caused astronomers to believe that the appearances and disappearances of heavenly signs indicated either favor or disapproval of the attendant god. The viewers made up stories to account for the shifts in heavenly bodies and for such idiosyncrasies as color, magnitude, and configuration. There are two possible interpretations for the astronomers' stories: they were either simple nature lore explaining these complex phenomena or, like the teachings of Christ and Aesop, they were parables meant to upgrade the nation's morality. As celestial guideposts, the symbols also offered practical information; for example, a weak glow in Pisces foretold a year of low-grade spawning among sea creatures.

The Babylonian circle of constellations matches classical mythology in poetic imagery—the hairbrush for the Pleiades, the furrow for Spica, the great swallow for Pegasus, the sickle sword for Auriga, and Anu's true shepherd for Orion. Figures include a flying pig, dragon, winged lion, tethered bird, charioteer, and mermaid. Priests derived names for these Mesopotamian star clusters from mythology. They connected their twelve *berous* or zodiacal houses to familiar images: the twins, bull, crab, lion, a maiden holding an ear of grain, scales, scorpion, a hippo-centaur, goatfish, gula, and two-tails (the fish). The resulting cosmology varies from later nomenclature in three houses: it refers to Aquarius as Gula; it lacks the current figure of Aries, which the Babylonians supplanted with the laborer; and it omits the bow in the hand of the hippo-centaur, which developed into Sagittarius.

Archeological evidence of a written star code derives from the translation of the tablet of Cambyses from the sixth century B.C. Further proof of a star system comes from Babylonian art, which features crescent moons and eight-pointed stars, Ishtar's symbols. Still attractive and in remarkable repair, artist models of a zodiac cover a vivid teal brick facade decorated with 575 ceremonial bulls. Similar signs mark the Ishtar gate of Nebuchadnezzar's fabled city, Babylon, which lay on a bend of the Euphrates river south of modern-day Baghdad. It was in Nebuchadnezzar's court around 590 B.C. that Daniel, the Old Testament visionary, bested a team of royal astrologers, priests, and magicians and fled a den of lions. Parallel histories of Daniel's ordeal appear in the Torah (the first five books of the old testament) and in Josephus's *Antiquities of the Jews*. Josephus states that Nebuchadnezzar took four noble Jewish children into his court to be trained by Chaldean savants. The staunchest of the four, Daniel, was quick-witted when threatened and impressed the king by interpreting his dreams of the clay-footed statue and the giant tree laden with fruit. Nebuchadnezzar's successor, Belshazzar or Baltasar, saw indecipherable handwriting on the wall, reading "Mene, mene, tekel uparsin." Alarmed, he called his astrologers and diviners and promised, "Whoever reads this writing and tells me what it means will be clothed in purple and have a gold chain placed around his neck, and he will be made the third highest ruler in the kingdom" (Daniel 5:7). Daniel translated the words to "Numbered, numbered, weighed, divided" and interpreted the phrase as an omen that the kingdom would fall to Belshazzar's enemies, the Medes and Persians. In old age, Daniel was honored for his prophecy and bore the title of "king's savant."

This period of intense interest in the zodiac and prophecy extended into the east to India and Arabia. Early in the fifth century B.C., the Indian mathematician Gautama Siddhartha, founder of Buddhism, published an astrological almanac. About this same time in Arabia, Caliph Ma'mun built an observatory and discovered uncharted stars to add to the Arabian zodiac. His Muslim contemporaries viewed the sky from the clear, uncluttered desert landscape and named these new stars Algol, Betelgeuse, Aldabaran, and Vega. The Eastern nomenclature remains in use, interspersing Babylonian, Egyptian, Greek, and Roman terms with Arabic designation for stars and nebula.

During the next century, Babylonian star knowledge expanded. A cuneiform document dated 419 B.C. augmented the list of twelve identifiable constellations to Aries, Gemini, Leo, Libra, Scorpio, Sagittarius, Capricorn, Aquarius, and Pisces plus the Pleiades, Praesepe, and Spica, which were later changed to Taurus, Cancer, and Virgo. The invention of these images served astronomers as an organizing pattern by which they could identify celestial observations. To basic metaphors describing the heavens, the third-century Babylonian astronomer Kiddinu theorized how heavenly gyrations produced equinoxes. Using the *clepsydra* (water clock) and *gnomon* (sundial), he calculated the lunar month as 29 days, 12 hours, 44 minutes, and 3.3 seconds. His unsophisticated math scarcely overshoots the current calculation of 29 days, 12 hours, 44 minutes, and 2.87 seconds.

Over the centuries, the Babylonian analysis of celestial powers grew more sophisticated and inventive in applying astrology to human fate. Around 600 B.C., their mode of prediction became the passion of rulers, who sought guidance from seers or wisemen known in the gospel of Matthew and among Zoroastrian astrologers as magi (the plural of magus or sorcerer). The astral relationships they interpreted were simplistic: a rising planet was positive, a setting planet negative. In general, a strong moon was the forerunner of stability. Ishtar brought serenity. Marduk's dominance indicated wealth and longevity. A rising Marduk and setting Ishtar boded well for a man, but indicated that his wife would desert him. An ascendant Nergal and descendant Marduk presaged capture by an enemy. A rising Ishtar and setting Marduk predicted that the woman would be stronger than her mate. A child born with rising Nergal and setting Marduk could expect happiness and the decline of personal enemies. After 539 B.C., the predictive power of the zodiac extended to commoners and linked birth dates to destiny and character. For example, predictions for a Babylonian man are precise and professional:

> Year 77 of the Seleucid era, month Siman, from the 4th day, in the last part of the night of the fifth day, Aristocrates was born.
> That day: Moon in Leo. Sun in 30° Gemini. The moon set its face from the middle toward the top; [there will ensue] destruction.
> Jupiter in 18° Sagittarius. The place of Jupiter means: [his life will be] regular, well; he will become rich, he will grow old, [his] days will be numerous.
> Venus in 4° Taurus. The place of Venus means: wherever he may go, it will be favorable [for him]; he will have sons and daughters.
> Mercury in Gemini, with the Sun. The place of Mercury means: the brave one will be first in rank, he will be more important than his brothers.
> Saturn: 6° Cancer. Mars: 24° Cancer. (Gauquelin 1967, 43–44)

Although Aristocrates's horoscope ends abruptly, it models the Babylonian style of horoscopy, which characterized the future of a commoner as well as it had once foretold the fortunes of the lord of the land.

ASTROLOGY AND THE GREEKS

The zeitgeist, or spirit of the times, replaced the Babylonians with the Greeks, an emerging, open-minded culture whose energized intellectualism welcomed knowledge from all quarters. Crossfertilization of sky observations from adjacent civilizations—Persian, Hindu, Chaldean, Phoenician— brought an upsurge of pan-Babylonism to the Greeks, a pragmatic people who had already imported Assyrian weights and measures, monetary system, water clock, and sun dial. As early as the ninth century B.C., Greeks had gained astronomical principles, instruments, records, and star names and tables from Babylonia. In their own cosmology, Greek astronomers rejected veneration of the planets, which the Chaldeans had called "interpreters," or revelations of the gods' will, and which the Babylonians had worshipped as deities.

Eclectic Greek scientists retained Assyria's cosmology, but rejected cosmic fatalism. They applied a secular nomenclature to identifiable constellations and heavenly bodies, which they called *planetes* or wanderers. Around the end of the ninth century, Homer, believing Venus to be two entities, had given two names to the planet—"herald of dawn" at sunrise and "Vespertine" at sunset. His contemporaries knew Mercury as "Twinkle Star," Jupiter as "Luminous Star," Mars as "Fiery Star," and Saturn as "Brilliant Star." In addition to planets, in the *Iliad* and *Odyssey*, Homer named six constellations—the Pleiades or Seven Sisters, Hyades or Rainmaker, Ursa Major or the Great Bear, Boötes the Plowman, Orion the Hunter, and Sirius or Orion's Dog, all of which guided Odysseus during his ten-year journey home from the Trojan War. As the hero takes his leave of the enchanting Calypso in Book V of the *Odyssey*, he follows her directions explicitly:

> Glorious Odysseus, happy with the wind, spread sails and taking his seat artfully with the steering oar he held her on her course, nor did sleep ever descend on his eyelids as he keeps his eye on the Pleiades and late-setting Boötes, and the Bear, to whom men give also the name of the Wagon, who turns about in a fixed place and looks at Orion, and she alone is never plunged in the wash of the Ocean. For so Calypso, bright among goddesses, had told him to make his way over the sea, keeping the Bear on his left hand. (Homer 1967, 95)

The astral reading is so exact that, in the mid-twentieth century, navigator Ernle Bradford was able to calculate Odysseus's position and determine where he would have arrived within eighteen days, the time it took Odysseus to sail from Calypso's isle to Phaeacia.

Several generations after Homer, Hesiod, the mythographer and moralist of the eighth century, used these same star designations in his *Theogony* and *Works and Days*. To the farmer he promised,

> At the time when the Pleiades, the daughters of
>   Atlas, are rising,
> Begin your harvest, and plow again when they
>   are setting.
> The Pleiades are hidden for forty nights and
>   forty days, and then, as the turn of the year
>   reaches that point
> They show again, at the time you first sharpen
>   your iron. (*Hesiod* 1973, 65)

Ever the dour, frugal farmer, Hesiod felt no compulsion to delight in stars. To him, nature meant work: when Arcturus, the bear watcher, arose, Hesiod pruned vines; after the Pleiades set, he honed his sickle and hired helpers for the harvest. Winnowing and grain storage began when Orion rose; the hunter at its height initiated the grape harvest and wine-making. When Orion disappeared along with the Hyades and Pleiades, Hesiod fertilized his vineyard and broke ground for the next season. His attitude toward stars was purely utilitarian: if the heavens could ease his burden and deflect agricultural losses, then they were worth knowing.

After the Greeks advanced from star myths to sidereal science, their cosmology centered on the physical structure of the universe. About 600 B.C., a Greek merchant, astronomer, and political adviser named Thales of Miletus, a coastal city in what is now Turkey, followed the Mediterranean shore south to Egypt, where he learned Chaldean astronomy. From journeys along Phoenician colonies on Africa's northern coast, he absorbed their cosmology and was so rapt in observing star motions that he fell into a ditch. Aristotle reports that Thales recovered his dignity by proving to contemporaries that stargazing had its practical side:

> Thales, perceiving by his skill in astrology that there would be great plenty of olives that year, while it was yet winter hired at a low price all the oil presses in Miletus and Chios, there being no one to bid against him. But when the season came for making oil, many persons wanting them, he all at once let them upon what terms he pleased; and raising a large sum of money by that means, convinced them that it was easy for philosophers to be rich if they chose it. (Durant 1939, 136)

Thales introduced the Ionian Greeks to mathematics and astronomy and surprised Ionia by correctly predicting an eclipse on May 28, 585 B.C. Unlike Thales and his belief that the universe was made of water and governed by its dynamics, Anaximander, a philosopher and mapmaker who flourished around 550 B.C., supplied a mechanistic description of the universe. He saw the earth as a floating cylinder and the sun as the hub of a massive wheel, a forerunner of Galileo's geocentric universe. Anaximander's contemporary, the philosopher Anaximenes of Miletus, challenged Thales by picturing the heavens as a crystal layer rotating above the earth. Nailed to the surface were fixed stars.

The preliminary theories of Thales, Anaximander, Anaximenes, and others helped the Ionian Greeks synthesize a stable zodiac through rigorous logic, which ruled out faulty or romanticized concepts. According to Pliny and Hyginus, two first-century Roman encyclopedists, Cleostratus of Tenedos, an island off Turkey's Asian coast, imported the Babylonian sidereal code and other advancements in astral study around the second half of the sixth century B.C. At the beginning of the fifth century B.C.—a period known as the Greek Enlightenment—astronomers profited from Mesopotamian calculations of equinoxes and phases of the moon, which they first accessed in Anatolia, now in Asian Turkey. Oenopides, a Greek astronomer, set the stage for constellation study by identifying the ecliptic. With his advancement in celestial contemplation, the raw materials were in place for exciting breakthroughs.

At last major players in the world of astrology, Greek stargazers adapted these foreign explanations of heavenly mechanics to their observations of the sky. They shunned mythology and superstition as their calculations moved closer to pure mathematics. The most numerical explanation of the universe was made about 530 B.C. by a renowned scholar and world traveler, Pythagoras of Samos, an island off Turkey's western coast. He was the first to call himself a philosopher, the first to use the word *cosmos* to name the world, and the first academic to claim that the earth is round. He voluntarily exiled himself from his native Samos to Croton, Italy, where he established a learned community. While teaching disciples about vegetarianism, numerology, and transmigration of souls, he hypothesized that planetary movements produced sound:

> Around [earth] the sun, moon, and planets revolve in concentric circles, each fastened to a sphere or wheel. The swift revolution of each of these bodies causes a swish, or musical hum, in the air. Evidently each planet will hum on a different pitch, depending on the ratios of their respective orbits—just as the tone of a string depends on its length. Thus the orbits in which the planets move form a kind of huge lyre whose strings are curved into circles. (Gauquelin 1967, 47)

Pythagoras characterized a harmony of heavenly bodies that corresponded to musical intervals. Stated in numerical ratios, these intervals—the octave, fifth, and fourth—epitomized a new way to explain divinity.

Released from old superstitions, the Greeks embraced the Pythagorean concept of the universe and its workings and expanded science with a burst of discoveries and enhancements. Around 475 B.C., Eustemon or Euctemon of Athens wrote a weather almanac. In it he linked weather forecasting with Aquarius and other constellations. Forty years later, the astronomer Meton and the philosopher Democritus used star movements to improve the calendar, which the Roman scientist Lucretius admired and adopted. Meton upgraded sidereal notation by formulating a dating system for astronomical observations. His system of intercalation, or evening out of the calendar, is called the *enneakaidekaëteris* or Metonic cycle, a nineteen-year period which synchronizes lunar and solar cycles. Greeks so appreciated Meton's system that they referred to his calculation as the Golden Number and in 432 B.C. engraved it in gold in the Agora, Athens's marketplace.

Although progress answered questions about nature, the conundrum of forecasting fate by zodiacal movements was no closer to settlement. Like Pythagoras and Meton, the philosopher Plato echoed his era's upbeat enthusiasm for the sun, moon, fixed stars, and planets in *Timaeus*, a dialogue in which the speaker, Socrates, explains creation and formalizes harmony between the soul and the sky. To his listeners, he championed objective inquiry:

> The sight of day and night and the months and the revolutions of the years have created numbers and have given us a conception of time and the power of enquiring about the nature of the universe; and from this source we have derived philosophy, than which no greater good ever was or will be given by the gods to mortal man. (Plato 1996, n. p.)

Plato explained the cyclical concept of history, which repeats itself every 25,000 years or one Great Year—the time it takes stars to make one revolution about the heavens and to return to their original positions. On the perfection of heavenly motion, he commented: "There is no difficulty in seeing that the perfect number of time fulfills the perfect year when all the eight revolutions . . . are accomplished together and attain their completion at the same time." (Thorndike 1964, 26)

In Book VII of the *Republic*, Plato advanced the cause of pure science by naming the five branches of mathematics necessary to education—arithmetic, plane geometry, solid geometry, astronomy, and harmonics. He cautiously legitimized a progressive attitude toward Ptolemy's harmony of the spheres and the "spindle of necessity" on which the heavenly orbits turn. Avoiding undue piety and didacticism, Plato discredited hucksters and fortune-tellers who merchandized the data. With his usual idealism, he urged that students access astrology as a gateway to truth:

> [The true astronomer] will believe that the great architect of the heavens has framed the skies and all that is in them as beautiful as such works can possibly be; and when he reflects how night and day are fitted together, and these with month and month with year, and the

other stars with these and one another, will he not consider it absurd to believe that these things, which both have bodies and are visible, exist as they are forever without any change, and absurd to seek with all his power to grasp reality in these? (Plato 1956, 329)

Unable to refute astral projection or to embrace it wholeheartedly, he concluded poetically that astronomy was a means to know God: it forced the soul to gaze upwards and led humanity from earth to the divine.

THE FIRST FORMALIZED HOROSCOPES

A few decades after Plato, astrologers developed the concept of heavenly power over life into formal zodiacal statements called horoscopes. The earliest extant horoscopes date to 409 B.C. By 400 B.C., zodiacal analyses reached Egypt and took on an abstract meaning based on mathematical calculation of the constellations' positions. Military superiority advanced the Greeks' knowledge by placing at their disposal the wisdom of Assyrian astrologers. In 331 B.C.—during Alexander the Great's subjugation of eastern states—the Greek military subsumed Chaldea, the southern portion of Babylonia from the Persian Gulf northwest along the Euphrates River. After this shift in power, Greek astrology supplanted primitive patterns established by Eastern seers.

From simple beginnings, the Greeks pressed on toward fuller understanding of star movements. Heracleides Ponticus, a philosopher and revolutionary astronomer from the coastal city of Heraclea on the Black Sea, drew a two-dimensional planetary guide hypothesizing that the earth rotates, the planets move about the sun, but the stars remain fixed. His contemporary, Eudoxus from the peninsula of Cnidus on the southern coast of modern-day Turkey, was a graduate of the Socratic school. He studied astronomy and geography with the priests of Heliopolis, a sacred Egyptian city at the base of the Nile delta. He taught his students that fortune-telling by the stars bastardized science. After setting up an observatory in Cnidus, he wrote an extended poem, *Phenomena*, the first work in the ancient world to describe forty-four constellations. Eudoxus explained how heavenly bodies moved in uniform homocentric spheres around different axes.

Following Eudoxus's example and echoing his title, the poet Aratus of Cilicia, the coastal kingdom northwest of Syria, detailed the stars with his eloquent verse cosmology, *Phenomena*, a translation of Eudoxus's work commissioned by King Antigonus Gonatas of Macedonia in northeastern Greece. Composed about 250 B.C., Aratus's volume broke new ground by explaining the zodiac and weather signs and accounting for the system of naming star groups as a method of simplifying and standardizing astral notation. He credited Zeus with setting zodiacal signs and advised:

> Make light of none of these warnings. Good rule it is to look for sign confirming sign. When two point the same way, forecast with hope; when three, with confidence. . . . Study all the signs together throughout the year and never shall thy forecast of the weather be a random guess. (*Aratus* 1989, 297–299)

Aratus's *Phenomena* was so useful that it became Rome's standard textbook and influenced the orator Cicero and poets Manilius, Lucretius, and Virgil. For this brilliant exploration of the heavens, the poet Leonidas proclaimed, "Let us count him second to Zeus, in that he made the stars brighter" (Hadas 1954, 297).

Formal shift in planetary study from astrology to the precise science of astronomy occurred in Egypt, where Greek scholars based their operations at the learning center of Alexandria. A coastal city on the western tip of the delta crest, Alexandria drew from all parts of the Mediterranean the brightest and most open-minded thinkers and researchers. Over two centuries, astronomers had synchronized their observations with the discoveries of four scientists—Euclid, Eratosthenes, Hypsicles, and Hipparchus. In 300 B.C., Euclid, the Alexandrian mathematician and father of plane geometry, had applied his axioms to astronomy. By the late third century B.C., Eratosthenes, a respected scholar who lived in Cyrene, a Greek colony on the African coast due south of Greece, had authored a seventeen-volume encyclopedia. After being named director of Alexandria's library, he calculated the earth's circumference. A versatile authority on geography, education, literature, theater, and history, Eratosthenes referred to himself as a *philosophos*, a lover of learning. In addition to writing an epic on Hermes, commentary on comedy, and a chronology of major world events, he became a knowledgeable geographer and cartographer. His *Catasterisms* (Star Events), a mythological handbook completed about 225 B.C., collected forty-four sidereal myths, which elucidate the significance of the Milky Way, Ursa Major, and the signs of the zodiac.

In the next century, two learned Greeks—Hypsicles and Hipparchus of Nicaea—placed a stronger mathematical basis under Chaldean astrology, which they learned from Kidenas, Nabourianos, and Soudines, the triad of hellenized Assyrian priests who maintained close academic ties with Greek academics. Around 150 B.C., Hypsicles of Alexandria composed *On Rising*

Times, an arithmetic formula for computing the appearance of zodiacal figures. A generation later, Hipparchus of Nicaea, an inland city south of the Bosporus Strait in Turkey, acquired a reputation as an astronomer and the father of trigonometry. Pliny the Elder, the Roman encyclopedist, later declared in his *Historia Naturalis* (Natural History) that Hipparchus would never reap the praise he had earned "since no one has better established the relationship between man and the stars, or shown more clearly that our souls are particles of heavenly fire" (Pliny n.d., 95).

After patient scanning of the skies, Hipparchus observed Scorpio's comet in 136 B.C. and plotted its course by polar longitudes. From these charts, he constructed a globe of the sky and mapped sidereal positions by a new technique—applying the degrees of a circle as a measure and establishing star locations in the latitude and longitude used for land measure. Around 120 B.C., he followed Eratosthenes's example and wrote texts on the heavens, the most notable being *A Commentary on the Phenomena of Eudoxus and Aratus*, a three-volume work. In addition to compiling a sine table, he cataloged 1,080 heavenly bodies, 48 constellations, and the relative magnitude of major stars, which he divided into six classes of brightness. Hipparchus was the first to explain the precession of the equinoxes, a gradual shift to the west caused by two simultaneous movements—the slow rotation of the earth as it spins. The earth's turn within a turn accounted for a phenomenon that had teased astronomers since the beginning of time—the migration of constellations in a steady pattern about the zodiac.

Employing this body of revolutionary advancements, the Egyptians—who are sometimes erroneously credited with inventing the zodiac and astrology—developed a late-blooming expertise in star study. They fine-tuned the science of astrology and assigned priests to make calendars and to locate auspicious days. Egyptian seers regrouped sidereal knowledge in charts called *sphera barbarica* (foreign spheres). Educated Greeks and Romans, who had grown pompous and over-confident, discounted Egyptian calculations as fascinating, but spurious. Temple keepers etched the star charts on courtyard pillars for general reference. The symmetry and precision of Egyptian sidereal cycles impressed Hindu and Arab astrologers. Inclined to doubt foreign calculations, the Greco-Roman astrological community admired the pillars as art, but dismissed them as unscientific.

At this point in the development of zodiacal study, critical research allied astrology with medicine. A contemporary of Aratus and historian of Sennacherib, Berosus (or Berossus), the most illustrious of Babylon's hellenized priests, wrote in Greek the three-volume *Babyloniaca*, an encyclopedia of Assyrian lore in which he applied star knowledge to the diagnosis and healing of human ills. A priest once in service to Marduk, Berosus emigrated to Cos, the island home of Hippocrates, who had founded medicine during the fifth century B.C. In *Against Apion*, the historian Josephus displays his respect in a lengthy entry beginning, "Berosus shall be witness to what I say; he was by birth a Chaldean, a man well known by the learned, on account of his publication of the Chaldean books of astronomy and philosophy among the Greeks (Josephus 1960, 613)." The thriving medical colony accepted Berosus's astrological knowledge and added local herbalism and medical techniques. The Stoics expanded Berosus's learning to a cosmology based on sympathetic forces that derived from the stars.

ASTROLOGY COMES TO ROME

The fall of the Babylonian and Greek civilizations introduced a major chapter in the development of the zodiac after Romans applied their skill to zodiacal study and interpretation. After the Roman general Titus conquered Greece in 196 B.C., Romans were in turn captivated by Eastern sidereal lore. They didn't learn it from teachers, textbooks, or scientific research—it was Greek slaves who cast horoscopes. They thrived on city boulevards and collected outside the Circus Maximus to advise avid gamblers on the outcome of horse races. Unscrupulous con artists of many nationalities who claimed to be Egyptian necromancers, hawked to the unwary a phony astrology manual called *The Revelations of Nechepso and Petosiris*, a purported sacred tome named for a fabled king and his court priest. The influx of pseudo-Babylonian rivals infuriated the entrenched Roman priesthood. Their elite corps of aristocrats comprised a sizeable public hierarchy:

- sixteen augurs to determine the will of the gods
- fifteen *pontifices* or calendar supervisors
- six Vestal Virgins to tend Rome's sacred altar
- fifteen *flamines* or priests of the three major gods—Jupiter, Mars, and Quirinus
- fifteen superintendents of foreign cults
- a college of twenty *fetiales* or regulators of public treaties
- a board of fifteen men to take charge of the Sibylline books and to interpret oracular sayings

- quasi-official *haruspices* to study lightning, earthquakes, animal entrails, and other prodigies to settle matters of prophecy left in doubt by the augurs

- a *pontifex maximus*, the figurehead at the top, who was more political appointee than religious leader.

Such high-ranking, well-paid state jobs were at risk if the Chaldean tradition supplanted Roman augury.

Rival methods of reading signs and portents developed into a power struggle over orthodoxy. Claiming to protect Rome from dangerous foreign influence, augurs clung to the ancient Etruscan dissection of livers, which were removed from freshly slaughtered birds and beasts and analyzed to determine the *auspicia* or religious sanction of the gods. A bronze model of an ox's liver dating to the third century B.C., now housed in the Piacenza City Museum, shows thirty-five positions that correspond to a pantheon of gods, which the augurs used to predict the future. A separate faction of astrologers and stargazers undermined the priesthood by offering the Roman commoner a skill once reserved for patricians. The priestly caste of purple-robed liver-readers unified in outrage at interlopers from the East and demanded the expulsion of suspect Chaldeans, whom they rated on a par with fakirs, mesmerists, and marketplace palm readers.

The tug of war between augury and astrology spanned four centuries. Several forces worked in tandem to discredit the Etruscan tradition and to legitimize Eastern Mediterranean astrology. The college of auguries temporarily ousted the hated *Chaldei* in 139 B.C., but the old-school priests lost permanently to Babylonian astrologers as Rome became more cosmopolitan. In addition to populist sentiments, science also favored star study over the perusal of animal entrails. Around 100 B.C., Roman marble workers sculpted the Farnese Globe, one of the most valuable astronomical artifacts from ancient times. The globe is a copy of a Greek original, which was painted to show the positions of the constellations. Thirty years later, Geminus, an obscure mathematician and scientist active about 70 B.C., strictly delineated star study and fortune-telling in his *Introduction to Astronomy*, a factual description of planets and constellations. Spokesman Cato, a noble Roman statesman and public censor of morals, hastened augury's decline with his sneer at soothsayers: "I cannot see how one liver-diviner can meet another without laughing in his face" (MacKendrick 1960, 55).

The life of Cicero, Republican Rome's venerated orator and political essayist, exemplifies academia's ambivalence toward divination about the time that the Republic crumbled. He had been the pupil of a learned but obscure Syrian scholar named Poseidonius of Orontes, who sided with the *Chaldei*. An enthusiastic syncretist, Poseidonius had correlated Semitic traditions with Greek philosophy and passed to his disciples a rich ecumenical body of religious wisdom that proclaimed the heavens eternal and humanity the heir of generous gods. A year after Cicero was appointed augur in 53 B.C., he composed *De Legibus* (Concerning Laws), which supported state-mandated augury and portents. He followed with an early theological treatise, *De Natura Deorum* (Concerning the Nature of the Gods), a thoughtful centrist essay that credits Zeno, the fourth-century B.C. founder of stoicism, with calling stars a *vis divina* (divine power). Overall, Cicero displays the influence of his teacher by respecting both pro-astrology and anti-astrology points of view and by balancing the pros and cons of divination. Near the end of the Republic, which received a death blow on March 15, 44 B.C., debate over astrology rose to a clamor in the aftermath of astral portents of Julius Caesar's death, including the appearance of a ghostly owl and dead men walking the city's streets. After a comet blazed the heavens the night before the grisly assassination on the Senate floor at the base of Pompey's statue, citizens believed that the heavens were exalting their leader and welcoming him among the ranks of the divine.

In the chaotic months before his own execution in 43 B.C., Cicero abandoned his original stance. He countered the earlier treatise with *De Divinatione* (About Divination), a detailed essay that contended that astrology is ignorant superstition, as are beliefs in omens, prodigies, sybils, portents, auspices, and prophetic dreams. That same year, he completed *De Fata* (Concerning Fate), which debated the existence of free will. He lambasted superstition as obvious silliness and asked, "Were all those who perished at the battle of Cannae born under the same star?" (Shulman 1976, 42). Cicero's ultimate fillip was a snicker at astrologers who claimed that celestial influence over all living things must extend to animals as well. He questioned rhetorically, "Can anything more absurd be said?" (Shulman 1976, 45).

In spite of Cicero's substantive essays on Roman theology, popular opinion gravitated to the pro-astrology side. As the government shifted from the fallen empire to Octavius's nascent empire, the majority of Rome's citizens became devout believers in astral powers, called "Babylonian numbers." The demand for horoscopes preceded standardization of the names for the twelve constellations. Eventually, the zodiacal houses derived their titles from concrete nouns designating the scorpion, lion, maiden, fish, twins, water-carrier, ram, bull, archer, scales, and crab. All but Capricorn are pure Latin words, unchanged in spelling and meaning from their inception.

Into the first quarter of the second century A.D., feisty contention still raged between the pro-astrology Stoics and the anti-deterministic disciples of Carneades of Cyrene, an empiricist and head of the Academy in Athens, whose erudition had impressed Rome's intelligentsia during a year-long visit in 156 B.C. For two-and-a-half centuries, these vocal Carneadites debated whether free will outweighed zodiacal influence on human fate. Although philosophers on both sides of the issue dominated the academic arena, Roman plebeians had long before adopted Babylonian assumptions about Mars. They worshipped him as their patron divinity and honored the first of March, the month of Mars, as the first day of the year. Rome's famous quartet of Republican leaders—Octavius, Marius, Pompey, and Julius Caesar—sought detailed horoscopes, each Mars based. Yet, in an era that demanded zodiacal signs on medals, doorways, and trinkets, Rome's most respected philosophers, Lucretius and Cicero, continued to oppose the zodiac.

THE ZODIAC FROM THE FIRST CENTURY TO THE TWENTIETH CENTURY

The dawn of the first millennium A.D. brought no consensus on the issue of the zodiac's influence over fate. The instability of astrology's validity paralleled the political and social upheaval that jostled post-Republican Rome. According to the biographer Suetonius, Augustus temporarily banned horoscopy in 33 B.C. to restore the faith of the fathers and bolster tradition. However, after Augustus became emperor, he sought astrological counsel during crises when the emerging Empire needed heavenly guidance. The shift of imperial attitude toward astrology preceded a deluge of sidereal obsessions. Seneca quotes the rhetorician Arellius Fuscus in a dramatic paean to astrology:

> If the pretensions of astrology are genuine, why do not men of every age devote themselves to this study: Why from our infancy do we not fix our eyes on nature and on the gods, seeing that the stars unveil themselves for us, and that we can live in the midst of the gods? Why exhaust ourselves in efforts to acquire eloquence, or devote ourselves to the profession of arms? Rather let us lift up our minds by means of the science which reveals to us the future, and before the appointed hour of death let us taste the pleasures of the blessed. (Cumont 1960, 82)

A devotee of the zodiac by 19 B.C., Augustus had silver coins struck with the profile of Capricorn, his natal sign, clutching the world's rudder. After he ended the post-assassination revolution, quelled Mark Antony's threats, named himself Augustus Caesar, and firmed up the *Pax Romana* (Roman peace), citizens relaxed once more and settled into familiar habits, which included horoscopy. Subsequent emperors studied their own sun signs and emulated Asian rulers in demanding accurate prognostication from court astrologers. Analysts surmise that the imperial court may have been less gullible than shrewd: they may have broadcast zodiacal divination for propaganda to bolster public relations, especially when forecasts lauded the government, justified the caesaristic autocracy, and predicted beneficent outcomes. Whatever their reason in courting the stars, the imperial hierarchy ended the controversy: augury was out, the zodiac was in.

To the end of its five-century rule, the Roman Empire never lacked astrologers. Cicero's friend Nigidius Figulus, an Etruscan mystic, wrote comprehensively on theology, Pythagorean astronomy, and magic. An erudite supporter of the pro-astrology elite, he was too obtuse to suit the needs of the average reader of his time and died in exile in 45 A.D. According to the biographer Plutarch, a more appealing scholar gained popularity with the public around 110 A.D. Lucius Tarrutius, a *mathematicus* skilled in casting horoscopes, boosted the reputation of astrologers by charting the natal signs of Romulus, Rome's legendary founder. To assess star power in prehistory, Tarrutius overturned the usual pursuit of the future by moving backward to prehistory. According to Plutarch's *Lives of the Noble Romans*, "it was possible for the same science that predicted man's life from the time of his birth, to infer the time of his birth from the events of his life" (Thorndike 1964, 209). Plutarch also deduced from Tarrutius's work that astral prediction could cast a city's fortune the same as that of a person by calculating the astral configuration that ruled the heavens when the city began.

Augustus Caesar's personal counsellor, Thrasyllus, was more successful and better known than Nigidius Figulus or Tarrutius. He informed the emperor of innately insidious court upstarts and influenced imperial advisers by charting their futures. The emperor's architect, Vitruvius, began to seek heavenly direction by applying astrological principles. He demonstrated how he mapped out floor plans on four equilateral triangles inscribed in a circle "as the astrologers do in a figure of the twelve signs of the zodiac, when they are making computations from the musical harmony of the stars" (Thorndike 1964, 184). Versed in a broad range of disciplines, Vitruvius proclaimed that the zodiac's influence was properly discerned by such Chaldean specialists as Berosus, the Babylonian astrologer, and by his followers, to whom belongs the art of casting nativities, which enables them to declare the past and the future by means of calculations based on the stars. . . . Their learning deserves the admiration of mankind; for they were so solicitous as even to be able to predict, long beforehand, with divining minds, the signs of the weather which was to follow in the future. (Thorndike 1964, 185)

As the actions of Augustus and Vitruvius indicate, Thrasyllus grew powerful among the emperor's courtiers. The astrologer's consultancy extended to Tiberius, Rome's second emperor. Tiberius valued his learning and advice over that of envious priests. As a result, Rome's second emperor abandoned the state religion and tossed from a cliff seedy fortune-tellers and obvious hangers-on and crackpots.

The symbiotic relationship between astrologer and ruler continued in the third and fourth reigns, which brought the emperors Claudius and Nero under the influence of Balbillus, Thrasyllus's son and apprentice. During a period of doubt in 52 A.D., Claudius temporarily evicted soothsayers, but Nero returned wholeheartedly to zodiacal divination. In Suetonius's *De Vita Caesarum* (On the Lives of the Caesars), Rome's most incisive collection of biographical data from the era, the author remarked:

The sun was rising and his earliest rays touched the newly-born boy almost before he could be laid on the ground, as the custom was, for his father either to acknowledge or disavow. Nero's horoscope at once occasioned many ominous predictions; and a significant comment was made by his father in reply to friendly congratulations: namely, that any child born to himself and Agrippina was bound to have a detestable nature and become a public danger. (Hale n. d., 334)

The father was right. Nero's turbulent reign brought serious threats to the empire, violent death to his mother, near annihilation to Christians, and disorder to Rome. Under these circumstances, it is not surprising that emperors of the Julio-Claudian line depended on astral influence to sustain their dynasty.

In general, where the emperor led, the intelligentsia followed. By the midpoint of Augustus's long reign, astrology had become Patrician Rome's obsession. Fed by differing points of view, a public wrangle arose: poets lauded the night skies and the stargazers who described them; caviling satirists reviled the whole business. On the one hand, Pliny the Elder identified in *Historia Naturalis* (Natural History) a cosmic sovereignty, which he called *principale naturae regimen ac numen* (the chief rule and divinity of nature) (Cumont 1960, 73). In rebuttal, Juvenal, Rome's chief satirist, ridiculed sidereal study as a secular fad. In his caustic, misogynistic sixth satire, written about 127 A.D., the aphorist characterized dependence on horoscopes as a failing of vapid females:

> An even greater trust is placed in Chaldaeans; whatever
> An astrologer says, they fondly believe is drawn from the
>   fount
> Of Ammon, now that the Delphic oracle speaks no more . . .
> Your Tanaquil inquires about her mother who is dying of
>   jaundice:
> How long will she last? (Already she has a report on *you*!)
> When will she bury her sister and uncles? Will her lover
>   survive
> When she is gone? (What greater boon could the gods
>   vouchsafe?)
> Yet she at least cannot tell what the gloomy planet of
>   Saturn
> Portends, or under what sign joyful Venus emerges,
> Which months of the year are assigned to loss, and
>   which to profit.
> Be sure to keep out of the way of that type, too; you
>   will see her
> Carrying round in her hands, like a ball of scented amber,
> A well-thumbed Almanac. She no longer consults, but
>   rather
> She herself is consulted. When her husband is leaving
>   for camp
> Or home, she will not go too, if Thrasyllus and his sums
>   detain her.
> When she decides to travel a mile, a suitable hour
> Is produced from her book; if there's an itch in the corner
>   of her eye
> When she rubs it, she studies her horoscope before sending
>   for ointment.
> Suppose she is ill in bed, there is one right time and one
>   only,

> It seems, for taking food—the time Ptosiris lays down.
> If she is less well off, she will wander between the pillars
> At the racetrack, drawing cards for her fortune and letting
>   the seer
> Inspect her palm and forehead, while popping her lips as
>   instructed. (Juvenal 1992, 56–57)

Keen on ridiculing women, Juvenal tweaked the flaunted sophistication of the Roman Empire by associating female followers of astrology with the underside of the Circus Maximus, the gathering place of racetrack touts, grifters, and coaxing streetwalkers. By association, Juvenal's unsubtle dig maligned all practitioners and followers of astrology.

Such lethal ridicule railed in vain at the immersion of Romans in the zodiac and its prognostications. Because Roman astrologers derived technology and theory from skilled Mediterranean artisans and improved the accuracy of astral readings, their predictive powers improved. In the first century A.D., the Greek Strabo wrote a geography text that proclaimed the accuracy of the Chaldean zodiac, which its founders revered as a gift from the god Bel. Around 15 A.D., a contemporary of Strabo, the poet Marcus Manilius, composed the *Astronomicon*, a five-volume, 4,200-verse summation of the mystical star lore of his day. Profound in its vision and daring in its themes, the work parallels the Christian concept of eternity:

> Thrones have perished, peoples passed from dominion to slavery, from captivity to empire, but the same months of the year have always brought up on the horizon the same stars. All things that are subject to death are also subject to change, the years glide away, and lands become unrecognizable, each century transforms the features of nations, but Heaven remains invariable, and preserves all its parts; the flight of time adds nothing to them, nor does age take aught from them. It will remain the same forever, because forever it has been the same. Thus it appeared to the eyes of our forefathers, thus will our descendants behold it. It is God, for it is unchangeable throughout the ages. (Cumont 1960, 60)

In his masterly verse theology, Manilius challenged pagan notions of creation, star configurations, zodiacal signs, body parts governed by each constellation, and astral projection. In opposition to simplistic mythology, he noted that, if the stars were as powerful as they are numerous, they would have scorched Olympus and devoured the earth in flame.

In addition to introducing the eternal as a religious entity, Manilius rescued astrology from didacticism or superficiality with an injunction:

No sign nor planet serves itself alone,
Each blends the other's virtues with its own,
Mixing their force, and interchanged they reign,
Signs planets bound, and planets signs again. (Gauquelin 1967, 53)

The implications are clear: analyzing behavior or character via sun signs is a chancy business. According to Manilius's view of the heavens, divination requires judgment and observation of more than the natal constellation.

Another confirmation of a more erudite view of zodiacal study came from an unlikely source—Manilius's contemporary, the ambassador and scholar Philo Judaeus, a Jewish philosopher who flourished around 40 A.D. and who used astral signs to interpret the Torah. Sent to Rome as a government liaison from Alexandria, he parried the question of divination by proclaiming that all star worship is sinful because it trivializes God. However, he insisted that humankind should respect the stars as God's emissaries. In his *De Mundi Opificio* (Concerning the Creator of the World), Philo wrote, "Before now some men have conjecturally predicted disturbances and commotions of the earth from the revolutions of the heavenly bodies, and innumerable other events which have turned out most exactly true" (Thorndike 1964, 354).

Citing Genesis, Philo proclaimed that God created the heavenly bodies on the fourth day, two days before he formed Adam and Eve. Philo surmised that the stars are virtuous elements that determine events, just as the Bible indicates in its opening verses. Although he held the heavens in awe, he believed that propitiating stars violated the first commandment of Moses' decalogue: "Thou shalt have no other gods before me." For these reasons, Philo felt compelled to upbraid the Chaldeans for idol worship. From his perspective, they strayed from orthodoxy by venerating creation instead of the creator.

In the second century, literary and scientific support of zodiacal lore proved that star study was more substantial than a craze or a hobby. Around 120 A.D., the Greek satirist Lucian, a native of Samosata, Syria, wrote *Deorum Diologi* (A Dialogue of the Gods), which reinterpreted mythology as a form of astrology. By characterizing Orpheus's lute as a seven-stringed instrument corresponding to the planets, Lucian made a strong case for an astral interpretation of the Orphica, a revered body of priestly myths. Lucian developed his theory with numerous examples of Bellerophon, Phaëton,

Daedalus, and Icarus. He claimed that Bellerophon and Phaëton utilized star knowledge to enable them to soar to the skies. He described the inventor Daedalus as educating his son Icarus on astrology before testing the wings he designed to fly them out of bondage in Crete. Furthermore, Lucian claimed that Aeneas was not Venus's son, nor was Aesculapius the son of Mars: rather, their genealogies establish the two planets under which they were born, thus proving the power of heavenly bodies to direct and enhance human life.

A generation after Lucian, healer and anatomist Galen, a native of Pergamum in present-day Turkey, became court physician to the emperors Marcus Aurelius, Commodus, and Septimius Severus. After Galen retired from practice, he wrote treatises on medical issues that he knew firsthand. His *Prognostication of Disease by Astrology* favors the ancient belief that the moon in the twelve zodiac signs triggers disease and responds to appropriate treatments favoring astral healing. His writings have remained in circulation and are still cited by astral physicians today.

In 140 A.D., Claudius Ptolemy, Alexandria's greatest mathematician and geographer, greeted the heavens with an enthusiasm and awe that surpassed that of Lucian and Galen. Buoyed by an ecstasy of sidereal glory, he confided:

> Mortal as I am, I know that I am born for a day, but when I follow the serried multitude of the stars in their circular course, my feet no longer touch the earth; I ascend to Zeus himself to feast me on ambrosia, the food of the gods. (Gauquelin 1967, 204)

A scholar as well as an astral worshipper, Ptolemy became the first astronomer to categorize stars by magnitude and the first to describe the parameters of the Milky Way. His cosmology pictured the universe as a series of concentric circles floating in crystal-clear ether. He developed a rationale for astrology, which he published in his *Tetrabiblos* (Four Books), didactic treatises on star power that defended horoscopy and legitimized the link between the zodiac and human character.

One of the great minds of the classical era, Ptolemy pondered obscure points of science. One philosophical question he wrestled was the moment when life began, at conception or birth, a conundrum that bedeviled later centuries. His conclusion draws on universal power:

> Conception is regarded as the natural beginning of life. But the moment of birth, though subordinate to the other, is endowed with a

> greater energy, since this energy is brought to bear on a complete
> human being and not a seed, and is added to a similar influence already
> brought to bear on the embryo. (Shulman 1976, 37)

Ptolemy's conclusion eludicates the question of personality, which he declares is molded by celestial energies both at conception and at the time of birth. His subsequent works clearly defined astrological elements. In *Centrilocus* he collected sayings related to heavenly bodies, for example, that people born when planets are at their height grow tall or attain subnormal height if they are born when planets are descending. He also stated that beauties owe their physical perfection to the influence of Venus on their natal houses, just as generals receive military acumen from the ascendence of Mars at their births.

Overall, Ptolemy's work, which defined astronomy throughout Semitic and Western civilizations for fifteen centuries, came to be known as the Ptolemaic system. His thirteen-book astronomy text, *Almagest*, which remained in use until the end of the Middle Ages, formalized zodiacal study with exacting descriptions and locations of 1,022 stars. A classical master-work, it standardized signs of the zodiac, changing Chelae to Libra, the name it still bears. Only two minor advancements eclipsed the *Almagest*. In the next decade, an anonymous cartographer produced the *Planisphere of Geruvigus*, a constellation map as seen from earth. Also, Muslim astronomers classified stars of the first three magnitudes, which still carry Arabic names. Caliph Harun Al-Rashid, a Ptolemy fan, so admired the master's scholarship that he had the *Almagest* translated into Arabic. The data influenced Arab cosmographer Al-Sufi, who produced atlases that, centuries later, were accurate enough to guide Hispanic explorers to the New World. The Mongol king Ulush Beg, grandson of Tamerlane, was the first oriental observer to duplicate Ptolemy's observations, but Beg's work was not completed until 1437. By that date, Ptolemy's cosmology was passé.

In the third century, the Mediterranean's perpetual ambivalence toward astrology again favored skeptics and naysayers. A stringent voice, Alexander of Aphrodisias, warned that stargazers were losing touch with logic and declared that their blend of omenism, fatalism, and prayer proved that star-based theology was a failed, inconsistent human invention founded on "pitiful sophisms" (Cumont 1960, 87). The aftermath of Rome's fall in the fifth century A.D. propelled to power a debauched mob of barbarian invaders. Unschooled in Ptolemy's refinements, they gave up astronomy and horoscopy and restored pagan sun worship. At the juncture of Rome's decline and fall, Saint Augustine of Hippo, a scholarly Catholic bishop of North Africa and zealous proselytizer, warned in his *Confessions*:

> The astrologers say: "it is from the heavens that the irresistible cause of sin comes, it is due to the conjunction of Venus with Mars or Saturn." Thus man is absolved of all his faults, he who is only proudly rotting flesh. The blame is indeed given to the creator and ruler of the heavens and of the stars. (Gauquelin 1967, 51)

Augustine's charge of heresy silenced church savants who were attempting to cast a horoscope for Christ. He stood against these and four prestigious Christian astrologers: the zoologist Horapollo, author of *Hieroglyphics*; geographer Gaius Julius Solinus, who wrote *Collectanea Rerum Memorabilium* (A Collection of Memorable Things) on the origins of the world; Julius Firmicus Maternus, author of the *Mathesis* (Learning); and Bishop Synesius of Cyrene, a Neoplatonist and follower of the occult who believed that the Star of Bethlehem was a pivotal example of a celestial message.

Against all suspect practices, Augustine made an irrevocable stand for orthodox Christianity. Drawing on polemics, he leveled question after question at the inconsistencies of the poet Varro, who had produced *Res Divinae* (On Religion) around 30 B.C.:

- How could the biblical twins, Jacob and Esau, have shared the birth moment, but lived remarkably different lives?
- Why are stars and other inanimate objects considered separate deities when the entire universe is divine?
- How could pagans erect altars to a handful of stars without angering all the gods of heaven, who also demand sacrifice and propitiation?
- How can God be reduced to mere numbers or tones, as Pythagoras tried to prove?
- How can heavenly deities shift and change when God is ever the same, possessing neither past, present, nor future?

One by one, Augustine battered the proponents of star lore and astral healing—Pythagoras, Thales, Anaximander, Anaximenes, Aesculapius, Hermes Trismegistus, the Stoics. Calling on the wisdom of Origen, Hippolitus, and Lactantius, early Christian dogmatists and anti-cultists, Augustine thundered his rejection of the occult and fatalism, which he called pernicious and fatuous. In his magnum opus, *The City of God*, published in

410 A.D., he demanded, "Those who hold that stars manage our actions or our passions, good or ill, without god's appointment are to be silent and not to be heard . . . for what doth this opinion but flatly exclude all deity" (MacNiece 1964, 76).

Under strict Catholic doctrine, post-Augustine prelates blasted the zodiac as un-Christian, even heresy against God's divinity. In place of the pagan metaphors of twelve zodiacal signs, Christian apologists saw the universe as an emblem of the human relationship to God. According to Church interpretation, the universe was a divine metaphor: earth, the center of the heavens, represented humanity; heaven and God's throne reposed on the planets' outer edge. Fixed orbits exemplified the creator's control of nature. Without success, dogmatists tried to extirpate the twelve zodiacal houses and replace them with an unrelated and artificial substitute—Christ's twelve apostles. For the western Mediterranean, the rise of Christianity spelled the demise of seers and horoscopes.

As a serious study, astronomy flourished in Muslim and Hindu strongholds—Turkey, Syria, Arabia, and India. Sages and astrologers counseled clients on heavenly influences; for instance, advising them that dreams came true under certain signs, but misled and confused under other signs. Persian encyclopedist, court physician, and pharmacologist Ibn Sina, called Avicenna in Latin, recorded astral calculations and zodiacal medical treatments in Arabic from 1000 to 1037. European scientists translated into Latin *Khitab ash-Shifa* (Healing of the Soul), *Qanun fi at-tibb* (Canon of Medicine), and other of his 170 books on philosophy, medicine, mathematics, and astronomy. They also published the star studies and a letter on astrology composed by Moses Maimonides, a Jewish philosopher and court physician of Saladin, sultan of Egypt and Syria. In addition to theory and texts, this pro-science era produced numerous models of the astrolabe, a two-dimensional star plotter that guided navigators and enabled Arab astrologers to cast horoscopes for all levels of society, from caliphs to camel drivers.

Around 1200, the term *astrology* failed to delineate the growing expanse of zodiacal writing. Because the discipline covered both orthodox and experimental spheres of interest, star study separated into specialized fields:

- *natural astrology or astronomy*. A basic charting of heavenly motions using compass, astrolabe, chronometer, and other exacting tools

- *meteorological astrology* or weather forecasting. An accounting of the astral influence on abrupt changes in weather and on agriculture, flight, shipping, the military, hunting, and fishing

- *mundane astrology*. The prognostication of the fate of kings and state governments as well as of nations

- *judicial astrology*. A study of natal signs to determine human fate and national trends and such catastrophes as the end of the world

- *medical astrology*. The application of biochemical salts to problems of health, emotional well-being, disease, or nutrition

- *electional astrology*. The application of the zodiac to an expedition, enterprise, or monument; for example, the laying of the cornerstone on a cathedral or the launching of a fleet of ships

- *retrospective astrology*. The examination of lives and events from history and their alliance with conjunctions of stars

- *physiognomical astrology*. The study of small areas of the human face and their implications for human personality, character, or fate

- *horary or genethliacal astrology*. The plotting of each day's horoscope and application of sun signs to current questions.

An example of specialization comes from Roger Bacon, a Franciscan monk who composed the *Speculum Astronomiae* (The Mirror of Astronomy), a scientific text that draws on Kabbala, alchemy, and astronomy to justify astral prediction. On the popular side of astrology, during the Middle Ages, people hired electional astrologers to assist in family decisions. Prospective parents often sought soothsayers to chart influences on a child at conception and birth and to foretell talents, abilities, and tastes. These calculations also indicated propitious moments when parents should name an infant, begin a child's education, negotiate an apprenticeship, or arrange a betrothal. The electional astrologer became as essential to family well-being as a physician, attorney, or parish priest.

In the late-thirteenth century, astronomy and the study of the zodiac progressed in steady increments. Johannes Campanus systematized the twelve zodiacal houses and issued astrological tables to facilitate the preparation of horoscopes. An open-minded German theoretician and Dominican friar, Albertus Magnus, produced *Metaphysica Naturalia* (Natural Metaphysics) and *De Coelis et Mundi* (Concerning the Heavens and Earth), learned treatises that synthesized knowledge of the universe by drawing on a wide range of tenets derived from ancient Arabs, Babylonians, and Greeks. In *The Secrets of Women*, he allied the progression of nine zodiacal houses with the nine months of human gestation and blamed inauspicious planets for stillbirths and mental and physical retardation. Because of his open-

minded approach to knowledge, Magnus anticipated the surge in humanism
that buoyed fourteenth-century Italian universities and laboratories. His
willingness to learn from seers of early times earned him the title *doctor
universalis.*

Magnus's positive attitude toward the zodiac influenced his pupil
Thomas Aquinas, a Dominican friar. However, after considering the pros
and cons of astral projection, Aquinas abandoned divination. One of the
orthodox Renaissance churchmen, he pursued instead the Augustine philosophy, which thoroughly denounced horoscopy and damned as heretics
all who sought guidance from the stars. Although Aquinas believed that the
heavens control the tides, seasons, and human bodies, he declared in his
Summa Theologia (Highest Theology) that free will overrules any power
that threatens choices and consequences.

Aquinian stringency preceded a necessary shift in astrology—its divorce
from religion and its establishment as a pseudo-science. Popularized in the
Renaissance, Western astrology dropped its traditional ties to God and
religion and developed into an adjunct to mathematics and science. A
practical aid to the surveyor, builder, midwife, sailor, farmer, and herder,
astrology concentrated on lunar cycles, seasons, and weather prediction. A
demand for translations of ancient Greek, Egyptian, Arabic, and Babylonian
texts and horaries sparked a flourishing business in zodiac calendars,
almanacs, and astral handbooks. In 1540, Alessandro Piccolomini of Amalfi
printed the first collection of astral charts in *De le Stelle Fisse* (Concerning
the Fixed Stars), a practical compendium that introduced a lettering system
to identify individual stars in the constellations. Followers standardized
divination, a series of procedures that predicted the best time for planting,
signing a contract, arranging a marriage, building a house, or attacking an
enemy. In Italy, Guido Bonatti earned a devout following for his *Liber
Astronomicus* (Book of Astronomy), a manual that amalgamated traditional
and Arabic astrology. Martin Luther supported *Prognosticatio in Latino*
(Prognostication in Latin), the work of astrologer Johannes Lichtenberger,
by declaring that heavenly signs are the work of God and angels. Despite
criticism from poets Dante and Petrarch, humanist Pico della Mirandola,
and John Calvin, the French evangelist who railed against "devilish superstition," advisers and nobles read daily horoscopes and cast their children's
futures as faithfully as they attended to Catholic baptism, confirmation,
mass, feast days, and confession.

A factor of court life throughout Europe, horoscopy was a job for the
royal astrologer, who often wielded power over royalty and courtiers and
over the Pope and his bishops as well. A long-suffering example, geographer

and magician John Dee, served Queen Elizabeth I as counselor during a nervous era that saw the rise of Philip II as an empire builder and of Spain as a competitive sea power. While advising the Queen on international matters, Dee was alternately lauded, rewarded, castigated, interrogated, and imprisoned, depending on the outcome of affairs and his ability to project what people wanted to hear. To his benefit, Elizabeth outmaneuvered Spain in 1588. The defeat of Philip and his Spanish Armada restored Dee's freedom and reputation.

Apart from politics, astrology was the focus of crucial research in the late Renaissance. Paracelsus, a Swiss physician, experimented on the unconscious mind by coordinating medical lore with alchemy and astrology. Geronimo Cardano, an Italian physician, collected horoscopes of famous people in *Genitarum Exempla* (Examples of Birth Signs). An enigmatic genius, Michel de Nostre-Dame, better known as Nostradamus, was prognosticator and physician to King Charles IX and Queen Catherine de Medici of France. His uncanny accuracy provoked both admiration and fear in the French. Because Nostradamus doubted that humanity was ready to possess its future, he forecast in cryptic quatrains such as this:

> By night shall come through the forest of Reines,
> Two parts Voltorte Herne, the white stone,
> The black monk in grey within Varennes,
> Elected captain, causeth Tempest, fire, blood running.
> (MacNiece 1964, 15)

Interpreters link this vivid, surreal vision with Louis XVI's capture in 1791. Pursued by murderous rebels, the French king disguised himself as a monk and fled from Paris to Varennes. The pack at his heels brought him down along with his disdainful queen, Marie Antoinette. Nostradamus's bloody image correctly foretokened the guillotine, a sharp-bladed executioner that rid France of its parasitic aristocracy. According to favorable analysis, Nostradamus's *Centuries*, a collection of grim, unsettling predictions, foretold the rise of Hitler, two world wars, and calamities of nature, including volcanic eruptions, earthquakes, comets, solar storms, magnetic fields, and floods.

Less flamboyant was Nostradamus's contemporary, Johann Müller, a German astronomer known as Regiomontanus. He translated Ptolemy's *Almagest* as the basis of his *Ephemerides 1475–1506*, scientific tables that determined planetary positions by spherical trigonometry, a formulation that calculates angles and distances on ball-shaped objects such as the earth.

Improvements to the printing press, invented in Germany around 1450, resulted in widespread copies of Nostradamus's predictions, Müller's tables, and other astrology textbooks and almanacs. As a result of technology that replaced the labor-intensive job of hand-copying texts, low-cost printing broadened the reach of astrology from an exclusive royal science to a thriving cottage industry that appealed to the reading public at large. At the same time, astrologers altered their vocabulary and selected common terms in place of Greek and Latin phrases.

Just as the rise of Christianity separated astrology from religion, the late Renaissance reclassified astronomy as pure science and demoted astrology from "the queen of the sciences" to pseudo-science. The scholar Francis Bacon, polemicist and creator of the modern essay, was a noted fence-sitter on the issue of zodiacal validity. At first, he boldly sneered "that astrology was unsound and full of superstition." To cover any possibility that he might be wrong, Bacon later amended his denunciation with a quibble: "I would rather have [astrology] purified than altogether rejected" (MacNiece 1964, 15). This era in the history of stargazing demanded a full accounting of astrological method and an explanation of interpretations of heavenly phenomena. The public shunned guesswork and mumbo-jumbo and demanded technological accuracy through telescopy, earth and star measure, and computation and analysis.

Artistic representation of Renaissance astrologers illustrates the abandonment of pagan star-charters. Sketches, mosaics, and arrases dropped the stereotypical black robe dotted with moon and stars and the uplifted wand in favor of the scholar's gown and the compass and astrolabe. Merlin's pointed black hat gave way to the telescope pointed upward. Navigators charted the southern skies and added the stellar figures of Indus the Indian, Tucana the Toucan, Pavo the Peacock, Dorado the Goldfish, and Apus the Bird of Paradise. By 1536, Peter Bienewitz, known in Latin as Petrus Apianus, executed an elegant woodcut of forty-eight constellations. On a voyage to the East Indies, Dutch navigator Pieter Dircksz Keyser enhanced zodiacal drawings by appending twelve constellations to the southern star map. In 1603, Johann Hondius placed Keyser's discoveries on a celestial globe. Attorney Johann Bayer improved on the heavenly layout with his star atlas, *Uranometria* (Uranus Measure). Employing data from Keyser, he cataloged 1,300 stars and 60 constellations, grouped stars in the southern horizon into new constellations, and assigned Greek letters to individual stars—both named and undesignated—within a grouping; for example, alpha Tauri, or the alpha of Taurus, is another name for Aldebaran.

The sire of the modern science of astronomy was the Polish mathematician Nicholas Copernicus. In 1543, he completed a major document, *De Revolutionibus Orbium Caelestium* (On the Motions of Heavenly Bodies), which invalidated 4,000 years' worth of theories and practice based on a geocentric universe. His calculations proved that the sun, not the earth, was the center of the universe. A disciple, Tycho Brahe, a Danish astronomer and inventor, streamlined Copernicus's calculations and determined precise planetary orbits. Well situated in an island observatory that Danish King Frederick II built for him at Uraniborg, Brahe studied star movements night by night. By 1596, he had measured the positions of 777 stars, proved that their orbits were elliptical, and issued a catalog that served astronomers for centuries.

The chain of interconnected discoveries continued from Copernicus and Brahe to Brahe's brilliant associate, Johannes Kepler, who published his master's observations in the *Rudolphine Tables*, named for his patron, Prince Rudolph. Kepler expanded Brahe's research by improving the telescope and by formulating laws governing planetary motion. He disdained the role of fortune-teller with a taunt directed at charlatans: "Like a stubborn mule, a mind trained in mathematic deductions will resist for a long time when confronted with the erroneous foundations of astrology; only a hail of curses and blows will force it to step in that mire" (Gauquelin 1967, 59). Absorbed in serious stargazing, he downgraded astrology as the "foolish little daughter of the respectable, reasonable mother astronomy" and declared that no star in the heavens broadcasts evil (MacNiece 1964, 340).

The scientific community embraced Kepler as warmly as they had welcomed the work of Copernicus and Brahe. In 1596, his *Mysterium Cosmographicum* (Cosmographic Mystery) demonstrated five planetary orbits. By 1619, Kepler had risen to prominence from the publication of two prestigious works, *Astronomia Nova* (The New Astronomy) and *Harmonice Mundi* (World Harmonics), which states: "The square of a planet's periodic time is proportional to the cube of its mean distance from the sun" (Magnusson 1990, 821). Kepler's triad of laws proved that planets orbit in elliptical patterns equidistant from the sun. These patterns follow a mathematical formula by which astronomers can substantiate the relationships of heavenly bodies at any given time in the past or future and can duplicate the harmony of the planets, which Kepler notated on staff paper in chord progressions.

The explosion of scientific advancement moved on to new territory in Lincolnshire, England, and the laboratory of alchemist and mathematician Isaac Newton, the founder of differential calculus. Working from Kepler's laws, Newton produced *Motu Corporum* (The Motions of Objects) in 1684. Three years later, he published his masterwork, *Philosophiae Naturalis Principia Mathematica* (The Mathematical Principles of Natural Philosophy), which states the laws of universal gravitation. These objective studies of the heavens joined Copernicus's laws in eradicating medieval concepts. For his expertise, Newton was lauded throughout Europe, knighted by Queen Anne, and, at his death, honored with burial among England's laureates in Westminster Abbey.

One iconoclast belied any notion that scientific advancement is easy. In this same post-Renaissance period of fervent scientific inquiry, Galileo Galilei conducted experiments in physics that preceded the invention of reliable telescopes. In 1610, he published *The Starry Messenger*, a slim volume that described the Milky Way as a vast carpet of thousands of stars. A skilled mathematician and astronomer, he declared that the universe

stands continually open to our gaze, but it cannot be understood unless one first learns to comprehend the language and interpret the characters in which it is written. It is written in the language of mathematics, and its characters are triangles, circles, and other geometrical figures, without which it is humanly impossible to understand a single word of it. (Blitzer 1967, 101)

By increasing the acuity of the Dutch telescope to a power of thirty, Galileo was able to chart Jupiter's moons, Saturn's rings, sunspots, and moon craters. These discoveries formed the substance of his revolutionary dissertation.

Galileo's work shook the established church to its foundations. Against adversaries, he maintained that truth depends not on dogma or tradition, but on observation and objective analysis. Church apologist Christopher Clavius denounced the new cosmology as defiant of God. Pope Paul V sent for Galileo and questioned his premise that the sun is the center of the universe. For nearly twenty years, Galileo remained silent. In 1632 he published *Diologo sopra i due massimi sistemi del monto* (Dialogue on the Two Chief Systems of the World), a witty exchange that prompted the church to try him for heresy. The Inquisition found him guilty. Forced into submission, Galileo recanted:

I, Galileo, son of the late Vincenzio Galilei, of Florence, . . . must wholly forsake the false opinion that the sun is the center of the world and moves not, and that the earth is not the center of the world and moves, and that I might not hold, defend, or teach the said false doctrine in any manner. (Blitzer 1967, 104)

Under his breath, the feisty astronomer muttered, *"Eppur si muove!"* (And yet, it does move). Sentenced to prison, he bided his time. Pope Urban eventually commuted the sentence to house arrest in Siena and later in Florence, where Galileo continued his research despite diminished sight and hearing.

Because empirical science had determined that the earth did not stand at the center of the solar system and that stars did not attract each other, the Babylonian suppositions about the zodiac and heavenly motions sank to the level of ignorant tales. French physician Henry Cornelius Agrippa voiced the pervasive disgust with horoscopy when he stated, "At length I learned that wholly and altogether [astrology] was based upon no other foundation but upon mere trifles, and feignings of imaginations" (Shulman 1976, 14). The satirist Voltaire added his own castigation by exclaiming *"cette chimère d'Astrologie"* (this chimera of astrology) (MacNiece 1964, 34–35). Louis XIV banned astrology from the French Academy of Sciences. Other monarchs emulated his edict. Continental Europe's educated people gave up zodiacal study to street charlatans, palm readers, and sideshows. Only the English retained the complicated zodiacal lists and tables. They continued to consult Francis Moore's almanac, *Vox Stellarum* (Voice of the Stars), to cast horoscopes and interpret zodiacal implications for human lives. For healing, the faithful called on Robert Fludd, an English physician and author of *Integrum Morborum Mysterium* (The Whole Mystery of Diseases), a study of evil forces and their impact on bodily ills.

In the mid-seventeenth century, William Lilly, a medical astrologer from Leicestershire, grew wealthy from his predictions contained in twenty volumes on astrology. He affirmed, "I believe God rules all by his divine providence and that the stars by his permission are instruments" (MacNiece 1964, 34). Countering Lilly's confidence in stargazing, the satirist Samuel Butler snickered in *Hudibras* about the physician's knowledge of the moon:

> Her secrets understood so clear,
> That some believed he had been there,
> Knew when she was in fittest mood,
> For cutting corns or letting blood.
> When for anointing scabs and itches,
> Or to the bum applying leeches;

When sows and bitches may be spayed,
And in what sign best cider's made. (MacNiece 1964, 49)

To justify a pro-astrology stance, Lilly issued one of the earliest almanacs, *Merlinus Angelicus Junior* (Merlin Angelicus the Younger), and published *Christian Astrology*. In his *Astrological Predictions*, he foresaw "a strange catastrophe of human affairs in the commonwealth, monarchy and kingdom of England," which he called "so grand a catastrophe and great mutation unto [the king's] monarchy and government" unlike anything in English history (Shulman 1976, 105). Lilly's forebodings were so precise that, in 1647, he anticipated the London Fire that caused the lead roof of St. Paul's Cathedral to melt and run down the gutter. Lilly also predicted the rise of the Puritan faction, their unprecedented incarceration and decapitation of King Charles I, and the cessation of the monarchy, which occurred two years later. The accuracy of Lilly's foreknowledge precipitated his arrest and interrogation. He proved himself innocent of conspiracy against the crown and gained a release.

Contemporaneous with Lilly's work came Andreas Cellarius's *Atlas Coelestis Seu Harmonia Macrocosmica* (An Atlas of the Heavens or the Harmony of the Universe), containing splendid color drawings of constellations and winged beings. In 1729, England's Astronomer Royal, John Flamsteed, published the exacting catalog *Historia Coelestis Britannica* (A British History of the Skies) and *Atlas Coelestis* (Atlas of the Skies), which numbered 3,000 stars. These two works led the field in precision until 1800, when Johann Elert Bode introduced maps showing the shift of constellations by month. During this same period, French astronomer Nicolas Louis de Lacaille journeyed to the Cape of Good Hope to observe and measure stars, which he mapped in 1763 in his *Coelum Australe Stelliferum* (Star Catalog of the Southern Sky), a comprehensive listing of 10,000 stars and constellations, many of which he named. His work brought the list of star patterns to 88.

A resurgence of interest in the zodiac coincided with the rise of romanticism, a complex attitude toward nature and the self that emphasized mysticism, the occult, and individualism. English poet George Byron expressed the mystical beauty of the zodiac in Canto III, Stanza 88 of his verse epic, *Childe Harold's Pilgrimage*:

Ye stars which are the poetry of heaven!
If in your bright leaves we seek to read the fate
Of men and empires—'tis to be forgiven

That, in our aspirations to be great,
Our destinies o'erleap this mortal state
And claim a kindred with you: for ye are
A beauty and a mystery and create
In us such love and reverence from afar
That Life, Fame, Power and Fortune have named
    themselves a star. (Bernbaum 1948, 550)

The English reclaimed medieval zodiacal lore in the late eighteenth century, with the French following a generation later. The Germans, led by the poet Johann Wolfgang von Goethe, were the last to revive it. Throughout Europe, people were holding seances, consulting ephemerides, and studying the Kabbala, an ancient body of mystical Jewish teachings.

In 1824, astrology entered the print media. Robert Cross Smith, who predicted national disasters in his *Manual of Astrology*, introduced popular horoscopy with the publication of *Straggling Astrologer*, a weekly magazine intended for the masses. Under the pseudonym Raphael, he launched a more sophisticated version, the *Prophetic Messenger*, which remained in circulation until his death in 1832, then continued into the twentieth century as *Raphael's Almanac, Prophet Messenger and Weather Guide*. Significant to popular horoscopy was the development of theosophy, the study of God through mystical insight into divine essence, a universal unknown. In 1875, American theosophists founded a national league. Led by philosophers Henry Steel Olcott and Madame Helena Petrovna Blavatsky, author of *Isis Unveiled* and *The Secret Doctrine*, disciples gained over 100,000 followers of theosophical teachings on mysticism from China, India, and Egypt. Blavatsky's successor, Annie Besant, affirmed the zodiac in her *Autobiography*, which declared that energies from the depths of the universe impinge on humankind.

In the last quarter of the nineteenth century, Alan Leo, a modern theosophist and publisher of *Astrological Magazine*, revived medieval zodiacal texts. To solve human inequalities by instructing the world on horary astrology, he mailed pamphlets to people who wanted to see into the future. His influence rejuvenated in Germany an interest in predictions through sun signs. By winnowing out quackery, German astrologers evolved a modern system of astrology. Two German star studies—Alfred Witte's Hamburg School of Astrology and Reinhold Ebertin's method—exclude the zodiac. Witte's Hamburg School draws on an eight-part collation of tables based on the Transneptunian planets. The Ebertin method, a streamlined approach described in *Combinations of Stellar Influences*, concentrates on the mathematics of an astrological dial.

Numerous twentieth-century leaders, scholars, and artists have embraced astrology, including financier J. P. Morgan, writers Oswald Spengler and Henry Miller, poet William Butler Yeats, editor Karl Ernst Krafft, actress Shirley MacLaine, and physicist Albert Einstein. Composer Gustav Holst produced a symphony, *The Planets*, which expresses the power of heavenly influence; British choreographer Frederick Ashton created a ballet, *The Horoscope*, on the theme of sun signs and love. Psychologist Carl G. Jung, a Nobel prize-winner and pioneer of intuitive psychology, castigated skeptics for summary dismissal of centuries of ancient wisdom and celestial observation. He lauded the return of zodiacal horoscopes because they supported his theory of archetypal or original patterns of behavior. In his words, "We are born at a given moment, in a given place and, like vintage years of wine, we have the qualities of the year and of the season in which we are born. Astrology does not lay claim to anything more" (Cavendish 1970, 156).

In his 1950 treatise *Synchronicity*, Jung related the zodiac to the concept of a cosmic wheel, which turns inexorably in the heavens through a cycle of 25,920 years. These rotations alter lives via arbitrary influences, which create sounds, colors, and heavenly vibrations; for example, wind, rainbows, and ocean tides. As did other physicians and counselors, he applied the zodiac to his patients to map such physical and emotional weaknesses as susceptible hearts in people born in Leo, kidney problems in Librans, unstable ankles in Aquarians, and foot problems in Pisceans. By categorizing similar psychological susceptibilities, Jung diagnosed the faulty temperaments of unstable patients and mapped out potential cures. In *Interpretation of Nature and the Psyche*, he used astrology to assess character and to predict the success of marriages and careers.

In the last quarter of the twentieth century, astral study deviated from Babylonian determinism. Scientists linked sunspots to epidemiology, sunrise to blood serum levels, solar activity to accident frequency, planet clocks to human archetypes, and lunar cycles to the body's natural rhythms. According to Frank A. Brown, the biological clock predisposes the individual to success, frustration, or failure. Prestigious people such as Jawaharlal Nehru, Japanese trade barons, and former First Lady Nancy Reagan have sought these latter-day predictions and analyses. In France, Germaine Soleil, known as Madame Soleil, broadcast an astrology column on television from 1970 until her death in 1996. In private, she forecast for President François Mitterrand and maintained a wide sphere of influence through the

Internet. Today, newspapers in the United States, Great Britain, India, and Japan disseminate a one-size-fits-all horoscope that perpetuates wisdom accumulated over 4,500 years.

THE ZODIAC IN THE ARTS
AND SCIENCES

Zodiacal figures are pervasive in human affairs. Across cultures, the characteristics of standard astral houses imply a continuity: the Chinese red bird equates with Mexico's vulture; Egypt's hawk resembles Tibet's Garuda-vulture. Astral figures on a mirror of the T'ang dynasty produce a graceful circular motif; detailed drawings from ancient India of the figures paralleling Capricorn and Aquarius adorn a circle of shapes similar to the Greek concept of the "circle of animals." Hindu artisans adorn temple walls and lintels with Mesha the Ram, Vrisha the Bull, Mithuna the human couple, Karkata the Crab, Simha the Lion, Kanya the Virgin, Tula the Balance, Vrishika the Scorpion, Dhanus the Bow, Makara the Sea-monster, Kumbha the Waterpot, and Mina the Fish. Alterations to Gemini, Capricorn, Sagittarius, and Aquarius are slight enough to maintain connections between a human pair and the star twins, a blended animal shape and Capricorn, a bow and the heavenly archer, and a water vessel and the starry water-carrier.

ART AND ARCHITECTURE

From Mediterranean nations come the standardized twelve shapes and glyphs of the zodiac. Egyptians carved circles composed of animal and human shapes and hieroglyphs representing the twelve houses around the lids of sarcophagi and inscribed them on pyramid walls and canopi or burial urns. In a Roman funerary relief from the Empire, a procession of musicians, servants, pallbearers, and family accompany the deceased on a funeral bier. Above the reclining figure, a crescent moon and stars link the soul to the universe.

In more European and Near Eastern art and architecture, zodiacal symbolism remains a design constant. Inscribed over the doorways of Romanesque and Gothic sanctuaries, signs of the zodiac enhance universal themes and characterize the passage of time and the labors of the seasons. Representative of the first century A.D., a statue now housed in the National Museum in Naples, Italy, features Atlas supporting a globe covered in symbols of forty-eight constellations. Near his right hand, the shapes of Cancer, Gemini, Taurus, and Sagittarius stand out from the background in high relief. Two Mideastern zodiacs appear as decorations of elegant buildings—the sixth-century synagogue of Bet Alfa in northeastern Israel, which features a zodiacal motif on the mosaic floor, and the eighth-century palace of Qasr al-'amral outside Amman, Jordan, which showcases a zodiac on the ceiling of its main chamber.

During the Medieval era, the zodiac remained a popular theme. Seal rings, keys, jewelry, and family stamps sometimes preserved the sun sign of the patriarch as a modified family crest. Traveling nobles used their rings and stamps for sealing letters and legal documents and for establishing identity with banks, embassies, or mercantile houses during sojourns in unfamiliar territory. The dynastic motifs omitted family or institutional mottoes because there was not enough room. They sometimes combined a single zodiacal figure, such as the crab, along with the family initial. Less detailed than a formal shield, these insignia were still too complicated to be forged. In addition to identification, illuminations on the initial letter of the first word on parchments and religious documents incorporated sun signs, some indicating the conjunction of heavenly bodies at the time of a birth or historic event. The fact that subscribers commissioned ornate copy work to religious orders indicates that St. Augustine's frontal attack on astrology failed to quell enthusiasm for natal horoscopy, which survived to the present day with no change in form or style.

Art from the Renaissance to the present maintains zodiacal figures as celestial iconography. Nuremberg artist and engraver Albrecht Dürer produced a woodcut of a two-sided sky map in 1515. On the Southern Hemisphere, his cosmology features fanciful drawings of Orion, Cetus, and Hydra on a twelve-part circle. The facing map, which covers the Northern Hemisphere, names and depicts all twelve signs of the zodiac. The corners honor Aratus, Ptolemy, Marcus Manilius, and Al-Sufi, acclaimed early proponents of astrological study. A sidenote adds, *Ioam Stabius ordinavit;*

Conradus Heinfogel stellas posuit; Albertus Dürer imaginibus circumscripsit (Joachim Stabius arranged it; Conrad Heinfogel positioned the stars; Albrecht Dürer drew it from his imagination).

Some late Renaissance sculpture and bas-relief display a combination of earthly and zodiacal figures. For example, the fountain grouping that features Father Tiber, a mythic figure sculpted by Neopolitan Lorenzo Bernini in 1651, once graced the piazza of Rome's Campidoglio and is now housed in the Louvre Museum in Paris. The pose depicts the semi-recumbent patriarch, well muscled with full beard and abundant hair. He bears an oar in his left hand and cradles a cornucopia in his right. At the bottom right of the figure stands Rome's legendary *lupa*, the legendary wolf-mother, suckling Romulus and Remus. In addition, Bernini carved emblems of Gemini, Capricorn, and Aquarius, thus allying the twin boys with the horn of plenty in a detailed study of Father Tiber, Rome's traditional water bearer. Bernini's design honors both the earthly and astral aspects of Rome's mythic and legendary foundation.

During an era that saw the rise of feudal estates, noble houses, and aristocratic and ruling dynasties, creators of heraldry devised conventions to honor the great. Their clients included the d'Este and Medici of Italy, England's houses of York and Lancaster, France's Bourbon kings, Scottish clans, Austria's Hapsburgs, Spain's Aragonese royalty, the Vatican's Borgia popes, and the British royal lines of Plantagenet and Tudor. To aid the nonreader and to keep the rising bourgeoisie in their place, workers adapted and embellished zodiacal symbols to adorn genealogies, livery, armory, escutcheons, and crests. Artisans blazoned these grandiose designs in gilt and silk threads on throne upholstery and ceremonial robes. Woodcrafters carved them on table legs and treasury casks and fitted them into intaglio circles and shields at the entrances of baronial estates and lordly palaces. Metalsmiths pressed the devices in *repoussé* on shields, goblets, salvers, tiaras, and coronets. Calligraphers inked them on vellum and parchment and painted them on the doors of coaches, armorial cabinets, and the logos of vintners, drapers, and harness makers chosen to serve the royal family. The most familiar of these heraldic crests adorn coins minted to commemorate a monarch or event. Spent worldwide as Europeans opened markets in the New World and traded with the Orient, monies carried the arrogance of royalty to mercantile centers and obscure outposts. Failed voyages dumped whole cargoes in the sea, where divers still scour the ocean floor for crested doubloons and pieces of eight.

Heraldry

Heraldic iconography features animal shapes in dramatic poses. A common figure is the lion, which may be lunging, lying down, sleeping, sitting, squatting frontward on its haunches, walking, guarding, or standing. The minute details of European crests showcase fantastic augmentations of the beast in nature; for example, winged, robed, collared, aflame, or stylized to suggest the features of a gryphon or dragon. The hybridized lion's mane and tail may appear leafy, the feet splayed, claws abnormally flexed or barbed, tail knotted and flourished, body finned like a sea creature or scaled like a serpent, or tongue and tail elongated. The head is often crowned and forepaws grasp a sword, orb, *fleur-de-lis*, or scepter to signify the lion's eminence as the king of beasts.

Other zodiacal symbols are less common to heraldry than Leo, but no less fanciful. Fish—either alone or paired as they are in the zodiac—occupy one entire wing of natural heraldry. They appear as stylized sea creatures or in the natural shapes of dolphin, salmon, herring, whale, trout, eel, and pike. The heraldic crab and scorpion flaunt claws, pincers, and stingers to demonstrate challenge or menace. The ram, goat, and bull, with either straight or twined horns, represent their own style of defiance or independence in a family line, company logo, or university history. Groups or institutions stressing fair trade, justice, and impartiality combine Virgo and Libra with depictions of the maiden with scales in hand. The archer, human twins, and water bearer are less common among zodiacal symbols used on crests, perhaps because they represent virtues less valued to heraldry.

Not to be outdone, the underclasses formed their own heraldic conventions. Trademarks and the logos of colleges, publishing houses, religious groups, and manufacturers echo the popularity of certain figures found in heraldry. Leo in a variety of forms and poses is most common, especially in Britain and its former colonies, for which the lion is a national symbol. Painted escutcheons commonly display gold for background or highlight; the lion itself is often a bold red. For companies and financial houses wishing to appear even-handed and trustworthy, Virgo with scales in hand traditionally tops a decorated shield or entablature. A ribbon or scroll may round out the image and display a two-part motto on the theme of balance, for example, *Lux, Libertas* (Light, Liberty), *Deus et Patria* (God and Country), or *Veritas et Justitia* (Truth and Justice). Among world shipping lines, numerous fish symbols, ranging from unembellished glyph to ornate line drawings, reflect the ancient tradition pairing sea creatures with luck. As representations of good fortune, these devices had become standard notation on pub signs and the logos of oceanside bistros. As emblems of Christ, the fish appears on bumper stickers and lapel pins, denoting members of Christian fraternal organizations and sodalities. The bull and ram highlight trademarks for companies linked with strength and precision; for example, ironworks, automotive parts, tire manufacturers, and firearms.

Cinema

Historical cinema reiterates the use of zodiacal figures in past times. Classic movies about ancient Mediterranean civilizations and the rise of Christianity, such as *Cleopatra*, *Ben Hur*, *The Fall of the Roman Empire*, *Monty Python and the Holy Grail*, *Caligula*, *Quo Vadis*, and *Satyricon* incorporate planetary symbols and zodiacal glyphs in costuming, hair dressing, jewelry, drapery, and backdrops. Titles based on the Middle Ages and Renaissance—for example, *Ivanhoe*, *The Wives of Henry VIII*, *Elizabeth I*, *The Lion in Winter*, *Camelot*, and *Columbus*—emblazed heraldic devices on armor and inscribed their symbols on backdrops, costumes, and military insignia.

To a lesser degree, films on current subjects have used zodiacal figures, for instance, a made-for-TV film replicated the crimes of the notorious Zodiac killer, a stalker of lone women who picked victims according to sun signs. In the title *Capricorn One*, a 1978 adventure thriller about a space hoax, the author's connection with a sun sign echoes the use of Gemini, Mercury, and Apollo in NASA's terminology for space missions. Another zodiac-based title, *Scorpio*, names a 1970 spy flick bristling with brutality and a complex doublecross. In this case, the name suggests both the venom of the scorpion in nature and the archetypal behaviors of those born under the sign of Scorpio. Less common in title identification are Aquarius, Sagittarius, Pisces, and Cancer. The latter, which is too closely associated with an often fatal disease, creates an obviously negative connection.

Advertising

Zodiacal symbolism abounds in product advertisement and service identification. Some current examples include the Zodiac mood watch, Libratees shirts from Libra Square manufacturers, Libranet web builders, Pisces software, Scorpio Music Distributors, Aries Research, Sagittarius archery club, and Aries Natural Language Tools. Familiar logos on television and in the popular press include the Dodge Ram and Ford Taurus, Schlitz malt liquor ("Look out for the bull!"), and Wall Street's bull market.

Complementing these images of masculinity and forcefulness are genteel Virgo figures, such as Virgo, a painted china figurine in Giorgio Armani's zodiac collection. Dressed in classic beribboned hair, diaphanous chiton, and leather sandals and posed in indolent or ladylike stance, the maiden often graces vials of perfume and jewelry and the trademarks of face soap, hand cream, and shampoo, such as Cameo cleansing bars. The psychological impact of these evocative shapes from the zodiac demonstrate the universality of archetypes, particularly those that reflect gender stereotypes of the strong, resilient male and the pliant, comely female.

Space Exploration

For obvious reasons, space exploration has relied on names from mythology and history. Important segments of the U.S. space program include the Atlas, Centaur, Discovery, Challenger, Atlantis, Columbia, Luna, Aurora, Magellan, and Mercury. The dominant mythological figure, Apollo, names the successful series of craft that carried the first lunar explorers, Neil Armstrong and his crew. Preceding Apollo was Gemini, a ten-stage project named for the twins to reflect the craft's design for two human occupants, one to pilot and one to navigate. Designed in 1961 from an enlarged Mercury capsule, the original shape of the Gemini module was 5.6×3.1 meters and weighed 4,500 pounds. Protected from heat by a plastic shield and launched by a Titan rocket, successive stages practiced in-flight docking and orbital rendezvous techniques as well as two-man biomedical experiments on heart rate, blood pressure, balance, and the effects of weightlessness on digestion and sleep. Virgil Grissom and John Young, aboard *Gemini III*, became the first duo of astronauts to orbit the earth. Seven stages later, *Gemini X* was the first to complete in-space docking with a target vehicle.

STAR LORE

In world literature, star lore is likewise universal, a reflection of the integration of the zodiac with all phases of human life. On stone tables in cuneiform, Sumerian scribes wrote of a primitive astronaut, Nanna, the moon god, who paddled his *quffah*, a circular boat, among the stars and planets. The Babylonians absorbed Sumerian icons and reiterated their themes; for example, the episode in which Gilgamesh relates a puzzling dream to his mother:

I had a dream.
A star fell from the heavens, a meteorite,
And lay on the empty plain outside Uruk.
The men and women came and wondered at it.
I strove with it to lift it but could not.
I was drawn to it as if it was a woman. (*Gilgamesh* 1992, 10)

She replies that the fallen meteor represents a "strong companion, powerful as a star, the meteorite of the heavens, a gift of the gods." Out of their faith in the reliability of heavenly bodies in their orbits, the Babylonians evolved the god Marduk, the powerful deity who organized the universe and established the solar and lunar cycles, the basis for the Assyrian calendar. According to cuneiform verse, Babylonian priests who slew a black bull at the New Year festival whispered in its ear that it was the "Great Bull that treadest the celestial herbiage," the bull the Romans later named Taurus (Hooke 1963, 62).

A parallel to Babylonian cosmogony, the Hebrew story of the heavens precedes the creation of humankind, who depended on the regularity of the seasons and heavenly motions as an assurance that order predominated over chaos. In the first days, God separated sky from earth, light from dark, and land from water. The delineations of nature progress to the heavens, as explained in Genesis 1:14–17,

And God said; Let there be lights in the firmament of the heaven to divide the day from the night; and let them be for signs and for seasons and for days and years. And let them be for lights in the firmament of the heaven to give light upon the earth: and it was so. And God made two great lights; the greater light to rule the day, and the lesser light to rule the night: He made the stars also. And God set them in the firmament of the heavens to give light upon the earth, and to rule over the day and over the night, and to divide the light from the darkness: and God saw it was good.

The Genesis author indicates that the heavenly bodies have an assigned role in nature—as timekeepers, bringers of seasonal change, and givers of light by day and night. This pivotal verse in the Judaeo-Christian tradition expresses the normality of stars and planets within an ordered universe.

In later episodes, star study remains pertinent to human behaviors. In Genesis 15:5, God challenges Abraham to count the stars, which are as numerous as the coming generations of Hebrews. The verse suggests two factors about the stars: that they fill the heavens with ample examples of God's creation, and that they provide a sure, unfailing pattern of celestial light. An older Hebrew work, the book of Job, composed in 2150 B.C., speaks of the constellations, naming the Pleiades, Serpens, Cetus, Orion, and Arcturus, which in Job 38:33 become the "ordinances of heaven," another example of biblical references to the stars as regulatory agents of the almighty.

A later book, the Psalms of David, contends that God named the stars. As signs to the psalmist, they evoke a conclusion from the viewer:

> O Lord our Lord, how excellent is thy name in all the earth! who hast set thy glory above the heavens . . . When I consider thy heavens, the work of thy fingers, the moon and the stars, which thou hast ordained; what is man, that thou art mindful of him? and the son of man, that thou visitest him?

The psalmist replies to his own questions, "Thou madest him to have dominion over the works of thy hands; thou has put all things under his feet" (Psalm 8:1, 3–4, 6). The sonorous quality of the lines has served liturgists and composers of church anthems with a suitably majestic contemplation of the skies.

Egyptian lore, particularly the intricate myths of Ra, Osiris, Anubis, Horus, Seth, and Isis, interwove celestial elements to universalize mythic figures, whom the ancients assumed lived in the skies and looked down on earth dwellers. In a violent episode from Egyptian mythology, Horus, the sky god, lost an eye while fighting his rival, Seth, the earth deity. The vacant spot on Horus's face represents the dark of the moon, which the gods reclaimed. A hymn to Osiris describes the tussle:

> Thy son Horus struck [Seth], he saved his eye from his hand, and gave it to thee, thy soul is within, thy power is within. Horus has caused thee to grip thy enemies, so that they cannot escape from thee. Horus has gripped Seth, and placed him beneath thee, that he may bear thee and tremble under thee. O Osiris, Horus has avenged thee. (Hooke 1963, 69)

The dispensation of punishment and the restoration of justice resembles early yearnings for order in the universe, which astrology provided to the Egyptians as well as all ancient sky gazers.

The zodiac flourished in Greek mythology through applications of sun signs to numerology. The recurrence of the number twelve, in particular, the twelve Olympian gods, corresponds to the twelve sun signs. The ancients used zodiacal interpretations to typify the twelve labors of the strongman Herakles, whom the Romans popularized as Hercules. Multiple triumphs follow the zodiac: Taurus with the killing of the Cretan bull, Gemini with the pillars of Hercules, Cancer with the vanquishing of the Lernaean hydra and the birds on Lake Stymphalus, and Leo with the Nemean lion. Virgo represents Hercules's victory over the Amazons; Libra corresponds with a restoration of balance—the purging of the manure-clogged Augean stables. The last five episodes return to monsters: Scorpio with the Erymanthean boar, Sagittarius with centaurs and Diomedes's horses, Capricorn with the golden-horned stag, and Aquarius with the eagle that pecked the liver of the villain Prometheus, who angered the gods by stealing fire from heaven to warm humanity. Pisces, the sign that governs the completion of Hercules's labors, corresponds to his rescue of Hesione from the Trojan sea monster. To restore order and remove obstacles from his fellows, Hercules slew two giants, Geryon and Cacus. His victory corresponds with Aries's renewal of the zodiacal year. A demigod who symbolizes reclamation of self and striving for perfection, Hercules, along with Perseus, Ajax, Jason, and other Greek heroes, atones for character flaws through struggles against perverse anomalies, such as Cerberus, the three-headed dog of the underworld. To a culture familiar with ethical and moral interpretations of myth, such monsters easily correspond to the sins and vices that torment and entice humankind.

Greek lore emulates surrounding civilizations in honoring constellations as significant elements in everyday life. Orion, one of the most familiar and frequently mentioned, figures in a twilight scene from Apollonius's *Argonautica*, a poetic epic of Jason's voyage on the *Argo*:

The night was now drawing darkness across the earth. Sailors on the open sea looked from their ships toward Helike and the stars of Orion, the traveller and the gatekeeper were longing for sleep, and an exhausted slumber embraced a mother whose children had died; through the city no dogs barked, no noise resounded—the darkening gloom was gripped by silence. (Apollonius 1995, 83)

In a naturalistic commentary on the seasons, Apollonius identifies autumn with the setting of the Pleiades;

Near the entrance [of Aietes's palace] vines flourished in profusion, their green leaves forming a canopy high overhead. Beneath them flowed four permanent springs which Hephaistos had dug out; one gushed forth milk, another wine, a third flowed with fragrant unguent, and the last streamed water which was said to be hot when the Pleiades set, but in turn when they rose it bubbled up from the hollow rock as cold as ice. (Apollonius 1995, 71)

The integration of the constellations in the seasons demonstrates a unity of nature in Greek thought, which embraced almanacs and zodiacal projection as essential to planting, reaping, sailing, worship, healing, finance, marriage, death, and other commonalities of life.

Ovid, the Roman mythographer from the Golden Age of poetry, displays appropriate reverence to the heavens in his *Metamorphoses*, a series of stories derived from Greek sources. In Book II, the poet turns to the night skies to tell of Phaëton, the boy who longed to drive the sun god's chariot: "And though thou shouldst hold the way, and not go straying from the course, still shalt thou pass the horned Bull full in thy path, the Haemonian Archer, the maw of the raging Lion, the Scorpion, curving his savage arms in long sweeps, and the Crab, reaching out in the opposite direction" (Ovid 1984, 67).

In his coordination of the constellations of Taurus, Sagittarius, Leo, Scorpio, and Cancer as images of menace, Ovid connects the study of star motions with capricious or grim aspects of human character and fate. As Phaëton faces the consequences of his foolish ride on the sun's chariot, he endangers the Bears—Ursa Major and Ursa Minor—with excessive heat and enlivens the fierce Serpent, a distant constellation that is usually sluggish in the firmament's cold extremes. Boötes realizes that the boy is caroming haphazardly and flees to safety. The Scorpion stretches out tail and arms and threatens to sting Phaëton, whom Zeus's thunderbolt strikes dead and catapults to earth. Ovid concludes that the decision to sacrifice the boy was appropriate. Otherwise, all creation might have suffered.

The Romans perpetuated the notion that the stars play a significant role in crucial aspects of rural life, especially the harvest. In Book I of the *Georgics*, Virgil compiles agricultural star wisdom:

> Sow beans and clover in a rotten soil,
> And miller rising from your annual toil,
> When, with his golden horns, in full career,
> The Bull beats down the barriers of the year,
> And Argo and the Dog forsake the northern sphere.
> (Godolphin 1949, 143)

Virgil's lyric farmer's almanac unites the forces of nature, both astral and botanical, to enhance the crop. Subsequent advice refers to "Maia with her sisters," "the bright Gnossian diadem," "the Bears," "the spiry Dragon," "Red Vesper," and "the slow Waggoner" as familiar star clusters. In his conclusion to the farmer's annual toils, Virgil balances out the agricultural calendar with lucky days from the zodiac's "twelve bright signs."

In a subsequent canto, Virgil turns to zodiacal prediction. He mentions the use of "starry signs" to foretoken spring, heat, rain, wind, and abrupt weather fronts. Of the heavens, he affirms that the sun never lies. Its daily show "reveals the secrets of the sky," including the rise and fall of empires, wars, plots, and revolutions. A survivor of the anarchy that followed Julius Caesar's assassination, Virgil claims:

> He first the fate of Caesar did foretell,
> And pity'd Rome, when Rome in Caesar fell;
> In iron clouds conceal'd the public light,
> And impious mortals fear'd eternal night. (Godolphin 1949, 152)

Rome's epicist supports reliance on stars, smoke streams, flights of birds, weather, ghosts, animal behaviors, and other aspects of augury and astrology as predictors of the upheaval that precipitated the Republic's collapse and the rise of the Roman Empire.

Another star-based verse treatise, Marcus Manilius's *Astronomica*, opens with a statement of astrology's worth:

> Stars conscious of our fates and arts divine,
> The wondrous work of Heaven's first wise design,
> In numerous verse I boldly first inclose;
> Too high a subject, and too great for prose. (Godolphin 1949, 496)

Manilius proposes to reveal "celestial secrets" extracted from the heavens. He declares sacred the work of priests, who observe 10,000 revolutions of the earth to divine "fates hanging at each star." Reverently, he acknowledges zodiacal powers:

> [Priests] markt the influence, and observ'd the power
> Of every sign, and every fatal hour;
> What tempers they bestow'd, what fortunes gave,
> And who was doom'd a king, who born a slave;

How aspects vary, and their change creates,
Though little, great variety in fates. (Godolphin 1949, 498)

Manilius subscribes to natal horoscopy, which determines the rule of birth
stars over earthly destiny. To the poet, their control generates "fixt unalter-
able laws." He urges the wise to learn constellations by shape and name and
to honor heavenly courses as a sign of godly mastery over humankind.

Star lore also illuminates imperial Rome's humor and satire. In 60 A.D.,
Petronius Arbiter composed *The Satyricon*, a sixteen-book parody of man-
ners and epic lore. The satiric gem of the few extant lines is "Trimalchio's
Feast," a banquet punctuated by ebullience, posturing, ribaldry, and clever
entrees. At a high point of the feasting, a tray arranged with the twelve signs
of the zodiac spelled out in food awaits celebrants:

> On the Ram ram's-head pease, on the Bull a piece of beef, on the Twins
> fried testicles and kidneys, on the Crab simply a Crown, on the Lion
> African figs, on a Virgin a sow's [udder], on Libra a balance with a
> tart in one scale and a cheesecake in the other, on Scorpio a small
> seafish, on Sagittarius an eye-seeker, on Capricornus a lobster, on
> Aquarius a wild goose, on Pisces two mullets. (Petronius 1925, 43)

The diners applaud the cook's witty symbolism. Their host comments in an
off-the-cuff speech about zodiacal influences. He characterizes Virgoans as
effeminate perverts, Scorpios as poisoners, Librans as tradesmen, and
Sagittarians as cross-eyes. Petronius derides the self-important host, whose
humor complements the course, but whose glib interpretation evaluates sun
signs with idiotic correspondences. The poet orchestrates this scene to
remind followers of the zodiac that serious application of planetary convergence must include more factors than birth signs.

A stark contrast to Petronius's frivolity comes from the Koran, the
collected sacred wisdom of Islam composed about 615 A.D. A stirring
description of the world's end in Surah 81 calls for the sun's overthrow,
collapse of stars, and rending of the skies. The speaker, who is the prophet
Mohammed during a revelation at Mecca, looks upward and cries:

> Oh, but I call to witness the planets,
> The stars which rise and set,
> And the close of night,
> And the breath of morning
> That this is in truth the word of an honored messenger,

> Mighty, established in the presence of the Lord of the
>   throne,
> One to be obeyed and trustworthy. (Miller 1970, 237)

The speaker vows on the stars that his prediction is true. Speaking of his encounter with Allah, he continues, "Surely he beheld him on the clear horizon." Attesting to Allah's might, the speaker declares, "This is naught else than a reminder unto creation, unto whomsoever of you willeth to walk straight. And ye will not, unless it be that Allah willeth, the Lord of Creation." The following surah reiterates the image of heaven's disruption as an emblem of Judgment Day, when Allah's order will supercede the plan of the stars. Mohammed's choice of heavenly bodies as symbols of reliability suggests that Muslims, like Assyrians, Egyptians, Greeks, and Romans, reverenced the rotation of constellations and studied them as guides to Allah's will.

Around 750 A.D., Chinese poet Tu Fu filled his verse with less forbidding zodiacal elements. In "Night in the Watch-Tower," he describes a figure contemplating the sky:

> While winter daylight shortens in the elemental scale
> And snow and frost whiten the cold-circling night,
> Stark sounds the fifth-watch with a challenge of drum
>   and bugle.
> The stars and the River of Heaven pulse over the three
>   mountains . . .
> Sleeping-Dragon, Plunging-Horse, are no generals now,
>   they are dust—
> Hush for a moment, O tumult of the world. (Tu Fu 1991, 238)

Tu Fu's crystal moment captures a stargazer in the act of naming asterisms. Like the Egyptian seer or Assyrian astrologer, the figure in the tower delights in stilling earthly disquiet by studying constellations, which resemble a river, dragon, and horse. The universal fascination suggests a need to confer order over events by locating a celestial pantheon, a force greater than war.

In the early years of the Italian Renaissance, Dante Alighieri published his *Divine Comedy*, a literary epic that surveys creation by degrees from heaven to the pit of hell. Permeated with astrology, his verse, like the philosophies of Augustine and Aquinas, declares the orthodox church position that no heavenly motion can destroy free will. Dante comments in Canto XVI of the *Purgatorio*:

> Ye lie subject, in your freedom, to a greater power and to a better nature; and that creates in you a mind which the heavens have not in their charge. Therefore, if the world today goeth astray, in you is the cause, in you be it sought. (MacNiece 1964, 140)

As Dante and his guide stray down the declivity into Purgatory, they discern that fortune-tellers and astrologers occupy Hell's eighth circle. Here the damned share Malebolge, the evil ditch, with seducers, panderers, flatterers, cheats, squanderers of church property, hypocrites, counterfeiters, alchemists, and conspirers and plotters. Fortune-tellers suffer an appropriate punishment:

> Each of them was hideously distorted
>   between the top of the chest and the lines of the jaw;
> for the face was reversed on the neck, and they came on
>   backwards, staring backwards at their loins,
>   for to look before them was forbidden. Someone
> sometime in the grip of a palsy may have been
>   distorted so, but never to my knowledge;
>   nor do I believe the like was ever seen. . . .
> I saw the image of our humanity
>   distorted so that the tears that burst from their eyes
>   ran down the cleft of their buttocks. (Dante 1982, 175)

In a moment of black humor, the poet pictures twisted bodies weeping rivulets that course the clefts of their rumps. Although the image is laughable, the debasement of human sorrow overcomes Dante. He weeps, leaning his face on a crag. Virgil, who has no sympathy for diviners, chastises Dante for pitying arrogant fools.

Among the noted fortune-tellers are three from Greek literature. Amphiareus, one of the Seven against Thebes, foretold his own death and tried to escape it. An earthquake devoured him as he ran. The second, Teiresias, was a Theban seer who separated with his walking cane two copulating snakes. For impiety, the gods forced him to live seven years in a woman's body. The sentence enabled Teiresias to empathize with both men and women because he alone had lived both lives. Following him, the diviner Eurypylus suffered punishment for advising the Greeks on a propitious moment to sail from Troy. One of the dark scenes from the era, the departure of Agamemnon's ships required the sacrifice of his daughter, the princess Iphigenia, to assure favorable winds. From Dante's time come three modern sinners: astrologers Michael Scott, Guido Bonatti, and Asdente. Virgil points out their companions in sin, "the wretched hags who left their spinning and sewing for soothsaying and casting of spells with herbs, and dolls, and rags" (Dante 1982, 178). Despite the degradation of star gazers, Dante believes in the zodiac enough to praise Gemini, his natal sign, and thanks the twin stars for granting him poetic genius.

Like the Gilgamesh poet, Muhammed, Tu Fu, and Dante, prominent English poets relied on astrological data for imagery and subjects of verse. In the fourteenth century, Geoffrey Chaucer, a knowledgeable diplomat and courtier, studied astrology and incorporated dream interpretation into his writings, which he composed in Middle English. Comments on astrology appear in *The Complaint of Mars*, *Troilus and Criseyde*, *On the Astrolabe*, *Equatorie of the Planetis*, *Canterbury Tales,* and *House of Fame*. In the latter, he says:

> For when thou redest poetrie,
> How goddes gonne stellifye
> Brid, fissh, best, or him or here,
> As the Raven, or eyther Bere,
> Or Arionis harpe fyn
> Castor, Pollux, or Delphyn,
> Or Athalantes doughtres seven,
> How alle these arn set in hevene.
> (For when you read poetry,
> How God created as constellations
> Bird, fish, beast, or him or her,
> As Corvus, or either Bear,
> Or Arion's fine harp,
> Castor, Pollux, or Delphinus,
> Or Atalanta's seven daughters,
> How all these are set in heaven.) (Chaucer 1961, 291)

This statement focuses on Corvus, Ursa Major or Ursa Minor, Lyra, Gemini, Delphinus, and the Pleiades, all of which Chaucer's readers recognized.

No testimony proves that Chaucer believed in astrology, but he appears knowledgeable on predestination and respects the influence of the planets on human life, as demonstrated by the character flaw of Criseyde in *Troilus and Criseyde* and in *The Canterbury Tales* by the Doctor's use of astral healing:

> In al this world ne was ther noon hyn lik,
> To speke of phisik and of surgerye,
> For he was grounded in astronomye,
> He kepte his pacient a full greet deel
> In houres by his magyk natureel.
> Wel koude he fortunen the ascendent
> Of his ymages for his pacient.
> He knew the cause of everich maladye,
> Were it of hoot, or coold, or moyst, or drye,
> And where they engendred, and of what humour.
> (In all the world there was none like him,
> To speak of treatment and surgery,
> For he was grounded in astronomy.
> He kept watch over his patient
> By the hour by employing natural magic.
> He could easily calculate the ascendent
> Of the signs for his patient.
> He knew the causes of every disease,
> And where it were of a hot, cold, moist, or dry influence,
> And where they started, and what humor caused them.)
> (Chaucer 1961, 21)

By calculating the influential stars at the time when a fever began or eruptions appeared on a patient's body, this "verray, parfit praktisour" made a worthy diagnosis. His knowledge of astral-based healing derived from Hippocrates, Galen, Avicenna, Averroes, and other noted healers.

In the seventeenth century, even though post-Copernican scientists doubted zodiacal predictions, popular interest inclined readers to expect star lore, especially in revelations of character motivation. There is a wealth of astral detail in Shakespeare's verse and drama, including favorable and unfavorable planets, conjunctions, oppositions, eclipses, equinoxes, comets, crescent moons, and planetary aspects. This pattern of astral influence suggests two conclusions: that astrology was popular in Elizabethan England and that the poet himself believed that the zodiac influences human destiny. Possibly, both statements apply, but certainly the first holds true. In the tragedies, Romeo hopes that a dose of poison will break the hold of "inauspicious stars," although the prologue declares that his love for Juliet is "star-cross'd" and therefore doomed. In Julius Caesar's tragedy, the protagonist equates success with the rise of tides; his wife Calpurnia cowers in fear from the "exhalations" of a raw night and claims that "the heavens themselves blaze forth the death of princes" (Shakespeare 1959, II, ii, 31). Likewise, Othello blames the moon for men's lunacies; conversely, Cassius declares that people must fault themselves and not the stars for their frailties. In a lighter vein, Beatrice, female protagonist of *Much Ado About Nothing*, declares that she was born under a dancing star; but, Cleopatra rejects the governance of the inconstant moon.

Shakespeare commented on horoscopy in *King Lear*, a tragedy that focuses on the theme of free will and the psychology of the dysfunctional family. In Act I, Scene ii, Edmund, Gloucester's bastard son, challenges fatalism:

This is the excellent foppery of the world, that, when we are sick in fortune, often the surfeit of our own behaviour, we make guilty of our disasters the sun, the moon, and the stars; as if we were villains by necessity, fools by heavenly compulsion; knaves, thieves, and treachers by spherical predominance; drunkards, liars and adulterers by an enforc'd obedience of planetary influence; and all that we are evil in, by a divine thrusting on. An admirable evasion of whoremaster man, to lay his goatish disposition to the charge of a star! (Shakespeare 1957, I, ii, 44)

Edmund tempers his outburst by reckoning his own sun signs—Dragon's Tail and Ursa Major—which predispose him to crudity and lechery. He concludes with brazen self-assurance that he would have been the same even if "the maidenliest star in the firmament twinkled on my bastardizing."

A generation later, John Milton, England's Puritan apologist and epic poet, perpetuated the tradition of zodiacal themes and subjects. He comments on the Ptolemaic star system in *Paradise Lost*:

When they come to model Heav'n,
And calculate the Starr; how they will wield
The mightie frame; how build, unbuild, contrive
To save appearances; how gird the Sphear
With Centric and Eccentric scribl'd o'er,
Cycle and Epicycle, Orb in Orb. (Blitzer 1967, 98)

Milton's denunciation of the astrologer's scribblings echoes the scientism of the Baroque Age, when people were more likely to embrace the physical laws of Copernicus and Newton than the astral horoscopes of Egypt, Babylon, and Greece.

The modern era returns to the patterned stars with as much vigor as did poets of old. In Mary Stewart's *The Crystal Cave*, the first of a trilogy of historical fiction about Merlin, the Mage of Camelot, a defining moment pits the intellectual Merlin against his choleric, evil-tempered uncle, Uther Pendragon, a career soldier turned king who spurns religion and star gazers. On a cold morning beside the Giants Dance, a lyric name for Stonehenge, Merlin prepares Uther for a spectacular light show:

> In the east night slackened, drew back like a veil, and the sun came up. Straight as a thrown torch, or an arrow of fire, light pierced through the grey air and laid a line clear from the horizon to the king-stone at our feet. For perhaps twenty heartbeats the huge sentinel trilithon before us stood black and stark, framing the winter blaze. Then the sun lifted over the horizon so quickly that you could see the shadow of the linked circle move into its long ellipse, to blur and fade almost immediately in the wide light of a winter's dawn. (Stewart 1970, 325)

By building an architectural astrolabe, Merlin, faithful to Ambrosius, his dead father, carries out a promise: "I will deck his grave with nothing less than the light itself." The mathematical precision with which Merlin planned the annual astral display impresses even the cynical Uther.

CORRESPONDENCE

As demonstrated in the arts and medicine, astrology lends itself to patterns of correspondence or sympathy, which derive from the belief that all nature interlinks. Obeying Aristotle's division of matter into earth, air, fire, and water, medieval science groups the sun signs into triads: Aries, Leo, and Sagittarius representing fire; Taurus, Virgo, and Capricorn the earth; signs, Gemini, Libra, and Aquarius corresponding with air; and the last three, Cancer, Scorpio, and Pisces, comprising the three water signs. Natural correspondence or sympathy between the sun sign and its complementary colors, gems, flowers, and metals has produced a series of groupings:

Sign	Colors	Stones	Flowers	Tree	Metal
Aries	red	amethyst	sage	thorn	iron

Sign	Colors	Stones	Flowers	Tree	Metal
		diamond	milfoil		
		bloodstone	geranium		
		aquamarine	honeysuckle		
Taurus	indigo	emerald	vervain	apple	copper
	pink	moss-agate	clover		
		sapphire	rose		
		turquoise	poppy		
		diamond	foxglove		
Gemini	yellow	beryl	gladiolus	chestnut	quicksilver
		aquamarine	vervain		
		agate	lavender		
		emerald	lily-of-the-valley		
Cancer	violet	moss-agate	comfrey	rubber	silver
	ice blue	emerald	acanthus		
		moonstone	anemone		
		pearl			
Leo	orange	ruby	cyclamen	palm	gold
	yellow-gold	diamond	sunflower		
		topaz	marigold		
		tourmaline	peony		
		sardonyx			
Virgo	gray	hyacinth	calaminth	hazel	quicksilver
	navy blue	pink jasper	morning glory		
	brown	carnelian			
		jade			
		peridot			
Libra	blue	diamond	needleplant	ash	copper
	rose	opal	scorpion's-tail		
		lapis lazuli	lilac		
		sapphire			
Scorpio	deep red	topaz	artemisia	blackthorn	steel
		malachite	hound's tongue		iron
		carbuncle	carnation		
		beryl	chrysanthemum		
		opal			
Sagittarius	light blue	carbuncle	pimpernel	lime	tin
	purple	turquoise	mimosa	oak	
		topaz	pinks		
			dandelion		

Sign	Colors	Stones	Flowers	Tree	Metal
Capricorn	green	white onyx	sorrel	pine	lead
	deep blue	moonstone	stinking tuscan		
	black	jet	pansy		
		black onyx	hyacinth		
		turquoise	ivy		
		zircon			
Aquarius	electric blue	sapphire	buttercup	cherry	uranium
		opal	edderwort	peach	platinum
		garnet	fennel		
		zircon	orchid		
			daffodil		
Pisces	sea-green	chrysolite	birthwort	willow	tin
		moonstone	aristolochia		
		amethyst	waterlily		
			tulip		

This alliance of natural elements demonstrates the extension of star study to the manipulation of plants, minerals, and metals in the analysis and treatment of human behaviors and physical ills.

Astral patterns have also been applied to numerous other disciplines; for example, the mathematical correlation of months of the year and the spectrologist's use of the twelve major tones of the color scale. In medieval times, astrologers connected sun signs with planets, shapes, senses, flavors, smells, pathology, and precious and semiprecious stones (See Appendix IV). People who valued nature-based horoscopy often grouped significant stones in symbolic patterns on jewelry, tableware, crests, or coats of arms to duplicate a favorable prediction. An outgrowth of the use of stones to reflect a propitious heavenly reading is found in the Holy Grail, a priceless Christian relic that was described as bearing a recognizable pattern of precious stones to denote its sanctification at the Last Supper.

In other rituals and ceremonies, Judaism and Christianity have used the signs of the zodiac to represent sequences of twelve; for example, the twelve tribes of Israel. Crosses were set with symbolic gems and metals to represent Christ's apostles. The twelve signs fit neatly: Aries corresponded with Peter, Taurus with Andrew, Gemini with James the Elder, Cancer with John the Divine, Leo with Doubting Thomas, Virgo with James the Younger, Libra with Philip, Scorpio with Bartholomew, Sagittarius with Matthew, Capricorn with Simon, Aquarius with Judas, and Pisces with Matthias. Three ritual crosses share the zodiacal signs. The cardinal cross—featuring Aries, Cancer, Libra, and Capricorn—have been associated with four archangels—Uriel, Michael, Gabriel, and Raphael. The moveable cross is composed of Gemini, Virgo, Sagittarius, and Pisces. The fixed cross, encompassing Leo, Taurus, Scorpio, and Aquarius, symbolizes the four directions and four Christian evangelists: Luke, the bull; Mark, the lion of God; John, the eagle; and Matthew, the angel. These concrete symbols aid art lovers and historians in identifying human characters. For instance, on the statue of St. Mark in the piazza of Venice, Mark's lion tops a dramatic column and holds a book, symbolic of the New Testament gospel of Mark. The walls of the cathedral at Amiens, France, are studded with stone rosettes containing zodiacal symbols. Priests also allied the twelve planets with the twelve stars set in the crown of the symbolic "heavenly woman" in Revelation 12:1. By resituating these pre-Christian symbols to correspond with elements of church doctrine, prelates intended to strip astrology of its glamour. However, superstitious worshippers continued to associate stones with a talisman that could ward off evil or counter acts of the devil.

PSYCHOLOGY AND HEALING

The correspondence between the twelve signs of the zodiac and the four elements gives some useful leads to analyzing human behavior and healing disturbed minds. Taurus, Virgo, and Capricorn, as earth signs, have a strong feel for solidity, pragmatism, and stability. These constellations predispose the personality and temperament to impressions of the five physical senses—seeing, hearing, tasting, smelling, and touching. Earth-linked people are passionate, enduring, tight-pursed, and patient folk who delight in meeting the body's need for food and sleep. The air signs are Gemini, Libra, and Aquarius. A connection with gaseous elements injects an uncertain note and inclines the trio toward abstraction, harmony, formal courtesy, and contemplation. As thinkers, the three seek the ideal and generally greet the day with optimism. The fire signs—Aries, Leo, and Sagittarius—form a combustive, powerful trio radiant with magnanimity, intuition, and self-confidence. The last triad—Cancer, Scorpio, and Pisces—comprise the water signs, which distinguish themselves through empathy and sensuality. As persuaders and fun-lovers, the watery three easily motivate others and enjoy close personal relationships.

Matchups with aspects of the earth's topography reflect personal proclivities. Aries tends toward the desert, Taurus to the plains, and Gemini to pairs of crags or peaks. A lush, abundant series of correspondences appears in the next quartet: Cancer to rivers, trees, and parks; Leo to mountains; Libra with palaces and estates; and Virgo to home. The last five move into a gloomier domain: Scorpio over caves and prison cells, Sagittarius to fens and quicksand, Capricorn to fortresses, Aquarius to sewers and cesspools, and Pisces to tombs.

In Chaucer's *The House of Fame* and *The Canterbury Tales*, the subjects of health and astrology recur frequently as reflections of character analysis. Perhaps the best of Chaucer's psychological studies is Alice, the Wife of Bath, a jolly companion who rationalizes her five marriages:

> For certes, I am al Venerien
> In feelynge, and myn hert is Marcien.
> Venus me yaf my lust, my likerousnesse,
> And Mars yaf me my sturdy hardynesse;
> Myn ascendant was Taur and Mars thereinne.
> (Surely, I belong to Venus
> In feeling, and my heart belongs to Mars;
> Venus gave me my lust, my lechery,
> And Mars gave me sturdy hardihood;
> My ascendant was in Taurus and Mars.) (Chaucer 1961, 82)

By establishing a correspondence between behavior and sun signs, Alice easily shucks off blame for her gadabout ways and hearty sensuality. In her explanation, a natal conjunction of Mars in Taurus predisposed her at birth to a lively, unfettered love life.

In matters of health, the twelve sun signs correspond to sympathetic plants and herbs classified by the mystical Hermetic cult in Egypt late in the second century A.D., when a mysterious Egyptian mage known as Hermes Trismegistus or "Hermes Thrice-Great," allied Asculapian wisdom with the Egyptian gods. In the resulting holistic nature paradigm, Hermetic astrologers systematized the magic correspondence of the zodiacal houses with herbs and plants. According to Hermetica, signs link natural cures with physical tendencies; for example, the Ariean's need of potassium in the diet to offset migraine headache, mouth and skin disease, depression, and psychosomatic ills. For good or ill, Hermetic practitioners mixed appropriate plants into decoctions. They also incorporated them into incantations that strayed from astral lore into the murkier realms of magic. Because tables of correspondence give no reason for their alliance, modern analysts of Hermetica dismiss cult writings as gibberish.

Apart from herbal tonics and abracadabra, the first formal tie between zodiacal houses and parts of the body comes from the Hermetics. According to one of the brotherhood of writers identified only as Hermes:

> The macrocosm has animals, terrestrial and aquatic; in the same way man has fleas, lice and tapeworms. The macrocosm has rivers, springs and seas; man has intestines. The macrocosm contains breath—the winds—springing from its bosom; man has flatulence. The macrocosm has sun and moon; man has two eyes; the right related to the sun, the left to the moon. The macrocosm has twelve signs of the zodiac; man contains them too from his head, namely from the lion, to his feet, which correspond to the fish. (Shulman 1976, 41)

Current astrological healing has rotated the houses, replacing Leo with Aries, the head of the year, which is linked to the cranium. The remaining eleven signs descend down the body to the feet, which are governed by Pisces. Between these two extremes, Taurus controls the throat and neck; Gemini the arms, hands, shoulders, and lungs; Cancer the upper torso, including stomach and breast; and Leo the back, heart, and liver. Digestion and the lower gut are governed by Virgo. Libra rules the skeleton and marrow, and Scorpio, the kidneys and reproductive organs. The lower extremities fall to signs nine through eleven: Sagittarius rules the thighs and hips, Capricorn the knees, and Aquarius the calves and ankles.

The mysticism and indeterminate source of Hermetic lore continues to puzzle historians. It appears to have followed and extended the writings of Galen and Hippocrates concerning the stars and health. According to the verse of the poet Manilius, the Romans already followed correspondences of natal signs with anatomy:

> The Ram defends the Head, the Neck, the Bull,
> The Arms, bright Twins, are subject to your rule:
> I' th' Shoulders Leo, and the Crab's obeyed
> I' th' Breast, and in the Guts the modest Maid:
> I' th' Buttocks Libra, Scorpio warms Desire
> In Secret Parts, and spreads unruly Fire:
> The Thighs the Centaur, and the Goat commands
> The Knees, and binds them up with double bands.
> And Pisces gives Protection to the Feet. (Shulman 1976, 44)

By establishing which diseases and ailments related to which signs, practitioners could estimate the onset of disease and predict the abatement or cure of each ill. As explained in Pliny's *Natural History*, the healer Crinas of Marseilles carried healing to greater extremes: he grouped foods according to astral signs and limited patients to diets of favorable dishes.

Practitioners of astral healing have carried zodiacal correspondence to minute applications. Astrologers apply astral sympathy specifically to the head. When the face is divided according to birth sign influences, Sagittarius and Gemini rule the right and left eyes, Capricorn the chin, Aquarius and Leo the right and left eyebrows, Pisces and Virgo the right and left cheeks, Aries and Libra the right and left ears, Cancer the forehead, and Scorpio the nose. As keys to psychology, sun signs indicate how the subject perceives and faces the world and the segment of life each controls:

Sign	Mode of Perception	Motto	Key Word	Age
Aries	intuitive	I am.	aspiration	conception–6
Taurus	sensuous	I have.	integration	7–14
Gemini	cerebral	I communicate.	vivification	14–21
Cancer	emotional	I feel.	expansion	21–28
Leo	intuitive	I create.	assurance	28–35
Virgo	sensitive	I serve.	assimilation	35–42
Libra	deliberate	I weigh.	equilibrium	42–49
Scorpio	emotional	I control.	creativity	49–56
Sagittarius	expansive	I philosophize.	administration	56–63
Capricorn	perceptive	I master.	discrimination	63–70
Aquarius	thoughtful	I universalize.	loyalty	70–77
Pisces	spiritual	I believe.	appreciation	77–84

The overlap of qualities illustrates how certain signs share archetypal traits. For example, Scorpio and Capricorn tend to tyrannize; Libra and Sagittarius see the greater picture and form broad-based conclusions about life. This detailed application of heavenly powers over person and personality impacts every human aspect, a correlation found in the study of individual horoscopes and their archetypal tendencies and behaviors.

5

ARIES

ASTRONOMICAL FACT

A symbol of spring, birth, regeneration, and the creative force, Aries (a' reez), abbreviated Ari, is the initial sign of the zodiac because it heads the traditional astral year. The Latin for male sheep or ram, Aries, also known as the Northern Fly, is the thirty-ninth constellation in size. An identifiable, but dim cluster of sixty-six stars, it borders Cetus, Perseus, Pisces, Taurus, and Triangulum. Aries is prominent in the Northern Hemisphere in late autumn and winter. Of the twenty-eight members in the group, there are four major stars:

alpha star	Hamal, the ram
beta star	Alsharatan, the two signs
gamma star	Mesarthim, the fat ram
delta star	Albotein, the belly

The gamma star was one of the first identified double stars, which Robert Hooke discovered in 1664. The brightest star is Hamal, the star on the ram's forehead, which shines at the second magnitude with a yellowish glow. The Hindu preferred Alsharatan, a pearlescent star on the ram's northern horn, which they called Asvini, the horsemen. A lesser star they identified by the Hindu is Bharani, the bearer. The Chinese made their own constellation, Leu, the train of the garment, by blending Alshartan with Hamal and Mesarthim. They formed Oei, the belly, from four minor stars in Aries. In addition to separate stars, Aries features a daytime meteor shower in June and a nighttime shower in December.

ASTROLOGICAL HISTORY AND TRAITS

Governing the thirty days between March 21 and April 19, Aries has remained a zodiacal constant in the art, religion, and lore of the Babylonians, Greeks, Persians, Hindus, and Egyptians. Ancient Akkadians referred to the constellation as Baraziggar, the altar of righteousness. Syrians called it Amroo and Hebrews named it Taleh, both meaning the lamb. Arabs preferred Alhamal, the sheep. Egyptians saw it as the ram-headed figure of the sun god and named it Tamelouris Amon, the Reign of Amon. In honor of Aries's rise, they, like the Persians, held an annual spring festival, which blended religious worship with a cultural celebration of winter's end and the planting of fields. They intended the propitiation of Aries to bolster their harvests.

To the Greeks, the constellation of Aries is noteworthy for its alliance with fire and with Mars, the god of war. According to Greek mythology, Aries's importance derives from the acts of Dionysus, the god of wine. During an expedition about the Mediterranean, he led his followers to Egypt. Because they wandered the Libyan desert without food or drink, Dionysus summoned a ram, who appeared alongside a spring that saved them from death. Dionysus commemorated the gush of water by hurling the ram into the firmament as a sign of heavenly blessing. There, it borders Pisces, the celestial fish, which thrive in its waters.

Another possible origin of the Aries sign is the myth of Phrixus and Helle, the son and daughter of Athamas, King of Thessaly. Because the children's stepmother plotted to sacrifice them to the gods to salvage a threatened harvest, their mother Nephele had Hermes, messenger of the gods, send Zeus's own golden-fleeced ram to the rescue. Phrixus and his sister flew on the ram's back from Greece toward the Black Sea. While soaring over the Bosporus Strait, Helle disobeyed one stipulation—not to look down. She lost her balance, slipped off the ram's back, and tumbled head over heels into the water below. In her honor, the strait was named the Hellespont. Poseidon, the god of the sea, retrieved Helle and turned her into a sea sprite.

The story of the ram and the children relies on the stereotype of the weak female and the enduring male. Phrixus, saddened at his first separation from his sister Helle, hung on until the ram reached Colchis, a kingdom on the southeastern shore of the Black Sea. In a sacred orchard guarded by a wakeful dragon, he slaughtered the ram to honor Zeus and placed its fleece over a tree limb. The gods rewarded the ram by turning it into a heavenly constellation to browse the skies near Pegasus, the flying horse. The weak glow of the golden fleece accounted for the cluster's dimness.

In a subsequent myth, Jason mounted a nautical campaign to retrieve the treasured pelt. Apollonius, the Greek poet, composed the *Argonautica*, the most stirring account of Jason's voyage on the *Argo*. The author recounts in detail the rescue of Phrixus, a figure represented in the bordered cloak that Athena gave him when he started building his ship:

Upon it was Phrixos the Minyan, depicted as though really listening to the ram, and the ram seemed to be speaking. As you looked on the pair, you would be struck dumb with amazement and deceived, for you would expect to hear some wise utterance from them. With this you would gaze long upon them. (Apollonius 1995, 21)

Jason's itinerary took him and his bold sailors far from Greece through the Hellespont to an unfamiliar harbor where Greek ships seldom traded. Jason's reclamation of the fleece is one of the major voyage sagas of Greek literature.

According to astrological archetypes, the Ariean personality is similar to Jason. A front-row figure connected with initiative, enterprise, and drive, the ram is typically wiry and muscular. Easily flattered and greedy for honors, titles, and medals, the type may overplay aggression and become overbearing, testy, disappointed, or peevish, a failing zodiac-based analysis charges to Ariean writers Isak Dinesen and Maya Angelou. In spirited word play, the Ariean can develop into a militant, sharp-tongued martinet rather than a debater or diplomat. Such expenditures of energy prove wasteful, often frustrating the purpose. For these reasons, Arieans who control dogmatism and domination make appealing conversationalists, a quality shared by authors Hans Christian Andersen and Washington Irving.

In traditional psychology, Arieans are enthusiastic friends and ardent lovers, blending well with Leos and Sagittarians. But the compliant mate should have a care: spirited Arieans such as Renaissance genius Leonardo da Vinci, poet Robert Frost, and feminist Gloria Steinem don't domesticate easily and may require a docile, appeasing human doormat for a mate. As a parent, the ram is stereotyped as hard-handed and unyielding, but never possessive. The empty nest syndrome is seldom a problem for Arieans, who look forward to retirement and the opportunity to develop hobbies, an endearing quality of electronics wizard Charles Proteus Steinmetz, who kept a greenhouse, collected animals for a zoo, and learned magic tricks to delight his guests.

Tradition depicts the ram as a thinker, pioneer, and leader who dislikes inactivity, a trait that marks entrepreneur Sam Walton, musician Arturo Toscanini, singer Aretha Franklin, U.S. Supreme Court Justice Sandra Day O'Connor, and labor leader Cesar Chavez. The ram is typified as soldier, financier, engineer, architect, or doctor, also firefighter and law enforcer. Astrologers name Arieans such as child-care expert Clara Hale, Holocaust survivor Corrie ten Boom, and primatologist Jane Goodall as examples of single-mindedness and attention to rules. A tendency toward self-promotion colors the style of the Ariean, especially the professional athlete, actor, and rock star. Assertive, reckless, and uncompromising, an Ariean similar to the poorly directed, passionate Vincent van Gogh is thought to blame others for failure and to rage out of control in annoying, even tyrannic behavior until balanced by an equally strong temperament. At its worst, the archetype is described as childish, self-absorbed, and candid to the point of embarrassing the unwary, a character pattern of Mattie Ross, heroine of Charles Portis's *True Grit*. Readers may forgive her annoyingly bold, outspoken confrontations with adults as adolescent weaknesses to be overcome by maturity and experience.

Astrologers describe people influenced by the ram as small, vigorous, and lean with a toughened frame. Neither handsome nor ugly, they walk briskly and present a firm handshake. The face displays an expressive brow, irregular features, and dark complexion. Those born under Aries are linked with perfect health and thus are said to reject medical advice, refuse to take prescription drugs, and deny advancing age. They supposedly die from accidents arising from impulsive, headstrong behavior, or they collapse in old age. In astral healing charts, the rare disease in Arieans emanates from the head—acne and skin irritation, migraine headache, tooth and gum disease, epilepsy, fits of anger, melancholia, high blood pressure, and psychosomatic illness, such as delicate digestion. Healthful regimens in Aries require a diet of citrus fruit, celery and tomatoes, apples, dandelion salad, and parsnips. Beneficial additives include potassium supplements and herbal decoctions of broom and wild cherry.

SYMBOLISM IN ART AND RELIGION

In iconography, Aries presents a fiery dawn image allied with the rising sun, symbol of the Sumerian sky god Baal, the Hindu fire god Agni, and the Egyptian Jupiter Ammon, god of fertility and creativity. Judaism and Christianity echo their admiration for the ram by allying it with the abstract qualities of strength and leadership. The virile symbol decorates coins that honor Alexander the Great, conqueror of the world. A rampant winged ibex with outsized horns is among the treasure of the sacked city of Persepolis, now housed in the Louvre Museum in Paris. The upward cast of the horned figure anticipates victory and a bold thrust into the unknown. The horns also point to heaven and establish a connection with the celestial realm. The design implies that Alexander achieved heroic stature because he was the gods' elect and because he used inborn traits for worthy purposes.

The ram implies a similar divine approval of Odysseus, hero of Homer's *Odyssey*. When he finds himself immured in the cave of Polyphemus, a one-eyed giant, Odysseus weakens the giant without killing him. Twelve mariners heat a sharpened stake, plunge it into the Cyclops's one eye, then hide among his herds. The Cyclops devours six men, but Odysseus survives. When the sheep and goats depart the next morning to graze, the blinded Cyclops feels the furry shapes as they exit the cave to prevent Odysseus and his men from walking out among them. The hero and his six surviving crewmen cling to the undersides of a trio of rams and flee unharmed.

According to the Bible, the ram also saved Isaac, the only son of the patriarch Abraham and his wife Sarah. God tested Abraham by commanding him to sacrifice his child on the altar. At the last moment, God stays the father's hand:

> And he said, Lay not thine hand upon the lad, neither do thou any thing unto him: for now I know that thou fearest God, seeing thou hast not withheld thy son, thine only son from me. Abraham lifted up his eyes, and looked, and behold behind him a ram caught in a thicket by his horns: and Abraham went and took the ram, and offered him up for a burnt offering in the stead of his son. (Genesis 22:12–13)

The passage is crucial to Christians and Jews. It delineates the Hebraic concept of faith at the same time that it prefigures the sacrifice of Christ, God's son.

The ram has a similar beneficent meaning in Arab lore. In 1295, Ibn Bakhtishu, court physician of the Caliph of Baghdad, published a bestiary, the *Manafi al-Hayawan* (The Uses of Animals). Of the Ram, Bakhtishu advises, "If one half dram of the goat's bile is taken in the juice of wild lettuce by a person when the sun is in the sign of Aries, he will have no fear and apprehension for one year, until the sun again reaches the sign of Aries" (Stewart 1967, 138). This blend of astrology and herbal healing suggests a tie between folk healing and star lore.

The story of the ram is a common symbol in religious art, stained glass windows, oratorios, chrismons, and statuary. As an icon of faith, the ram inspires the psalmist David to string its ten sinews into a lyre. In Judaic tradition, the blast of the *shofar*, or ram's horn, welcomes Rosh Hashanah, the Jewish New Year. In Yoruban and Germanic lore, Aries connects with thunder, symbolized by a blast on the ram's horn. Thor, the Germanic hammerer and storm god, also values the ram as a symbol of physical and political might. The problematic nature of the ram's thrust derives from its nature and body shape. Jungian interpretation notes the strength of the butting ram, but acknowledges the animal's restriction to an awkward downturn of the head to impale an adversary. A thrall to nature, the ram is therefore limited in effectiveness and versatility.

In 1385, Geoffrey Chaucer made extensive use of zodiacal signs in *The Canterbury Tales*. In the prologue to a collection of stories told by a motley assemblage of travelers going to the shrine of St. Thomas à Becket, Chaucer describes signs of spring, which presages good traveling weather and passable roads:

> Whan that aprille with his showres soote
> The droughte of March hath perced to the roote,
> And bathed every veine in swich licour
> Of which vertu engendred is the flowr;
> Whan zephyrus eek with his sweete breeth
> Inspired hath in every holt and heeth
> The tendre croppes and the yonge sonne
> Hath in the ram his halve cours yronne,
> And smalle fowles maken melodye
> That sleepen al the night with open yë.
> (In April when showers are sweet,
> They pierce to the root the drought of March.
> When sweet zephyrs blow their breath,
> They enliven on every meadow and heath
> Tender crops and the sun in Aries
> Has run half its yearly course,
> And baby birds sleep all night with open eyes. (Chaucer 1961, 17)

Balmy weather relieves the tedium of winter and causes the pilgrims "to seeken straunge strondes." Departing "from every shires ende of Engelond," they trek to Canterbury to "the holy blisful martyr," who cures the sick. The immediacy of spring enlivens the introduction to Chaucer's sequence and energizes the storytellers to do their best as they jog toward Canterbury.

In the English Renaissance, William Shakespeare drew on "a capteine of high courage" from Holinshed's *Chronicles* to create a vibrant, lusty Aries personality for Henry Percy, familiarly known as Harry Hotspur, a volatile, headstrong scrapper in *Henry IV, Part I*. The dashing, ebullient son of the Earl of Northumberland, Hotspur represents the admirable, keen-witted qualities expected of a soldier, yet suffers inherently from an unbalanced personality. His courage and daring mark him as the natural rebel, but rashness and an uncurbed temper prove his undoing. A fierce, vain, excitable warrior who anticipates combat as rousing sport, Hotspur at age thirty-nine serves as a foil to the phlegmatic Prince Hal, a sixteen-year-old laggard who prefers vulgar barroom companions to the king's forces on the battlefield.

Hotspur, whom Shakespeare honors as "Mars in swathling clothes," acquaints Hal with the manly pursuit of chivalry and honor. With Hotspur in the lead, Prince Hal thrusts himself into battle and eventually kills his mentor in a duel at Shrewsbury, where rebel forces threaten the English monarchy. In typical form, the precipitate, ever-feisty Hotspur expires without completing his final sentence. Rueful at sight of his quicksilver opponent's mangled corpse, Hal speaks his eulogy:

> . . . Brave Percy: fare thee well, great heart!
> Ill-weaved ambition, how much art thou shrunk!
> When that this body did contain a spirit,
> A kingdom for it was too small a bound . . .
> I'll thank myself
> For doing these fair rites of tenderness.
> Adieu, and take thy praise with thee to heaven!
> Thy ignominy sleep with thee in the grave,
> But not remember'd in thy epitaph!
> (Shakespeare 1960, V, iv, 87–101)

As though parting with a compatriot, Hal acknowledges Hotspur's brimming vitality and gallantry and regrets his impulsiveness. An honest fighting man deserving of his medals, Hotspur merits soldierly honors.

Astrologers maintain that great nations, especially England, Germany, and ancient Rome, flourished under the sign of Aries. As prime players in the balance of power, the opinionated Ariean nation thrives on empire-making and domination of lesser countries. History has proved true the charge with England in the New World, India, Africa, and Australia; Germany during World War I and World War II; and Rome throughout most of its ancient past, especially the late Republic and early Empire. Aries is often confused with a homonym, Ares, Greek god of war, but was originally pronounced Roman style with three syllables (ah' ree · ays), which sets it apart from the Greek. In Roman times, a major assault weapon was the *aries*, or battering ram, which soldiers hauled over open ground to a walled city and swung on heavy ropes against a gate as they did during the assault on Masada. The hammer was a single tree trunk rounded at the end with a carved ram's head topped with curling horns—a stirring, fearsome figure not unlike the archetypal Ariean personality.

Memorable Arieans have established their place among orators, particularly Moses, Israel's lawgiver, and the prophet Mohammed, the redoubtable founder of Islam. Ariean leaders include Hitler, the militarist who tried to "purify" the Aryan race by exterminating the Jews; Lenin, the father of the Russian Communist state; and Thomas Jefferson, a failed soldier who proved an invaluable leader during the formulation of citizen rights and reponsibilities in the U.S. Constitution. On the American frontier, Ariean Wyatt Earp, marshal of Dodge City, Kansas, adapted his zeal for authority to law enforcement. His lack of control over inherent traits may have precipitated the shootout at the OK Corral, a recurrent event in frontier literature and film. In addition to outstanding political figures, Arieans include leaders in the arts and entertainment: Johann Strauss, the Austrian composer who introduced the waltz craze in Europe; Charlie Chaplin, pantomimist and creator of filmdom's Little Tramp; Harry Houdini, illusionist and escape artist; and Marlon Brando, the captivating actor who played Fletcher Christian in the film *Mutiny on the Bounty*.

6
TAURUS

ASTRONOMICAL FACTS

Taking its name for the Latin for bull, Taurus (taw' ruhs), the second sign of the zodiac, is abbreviated Tau and symbolized by a circle topped with curving horns, which mimics its configuration. The seventeenth constellation in size, Taurus is alternately known as the V, the Winter Octagon, the Winter Oval, and the Hyades. Bordered by Aries, Auriga, Cetus, Eridanus, Gemini, Orion, and Perseus, Taurus is visible on January nights in midnorthern latitudes high over the southern horizon. Of the ninety-eight heavenly bodies in the group there are seventeen major stars:

alpha star	Aldebaran, the follower of the Pleiades
beta star	Alnath, the butting horn
gamma star	Hyades I, the rain star
delta star	Hyades II, the rain star
epsilon star	Ain, the bull's eye
zeta star	Alhecka, the driver
eta-one star	Alcyone, the light
eta-two star	Althurayya, the many little ones
Taurus 16	Celaeno, the swarthy
Taurus 17	Electra, the fox
Taurus 19	Taygeta, the long-cheeked
Taurus 20	Maia, the great one
Taurus 21	Asterope, the sun-faced
Taurus 22	Sterope II, the stubborn-faced
Taurus 23	Merope, the mortal
Taurus 27	Atlas, the sufferer
Taurus 28	Pleione, the sailing queen

Most spectacular of Taurus's members is Aldebaran, a cool rosy-orange star that has teased the imaginations of viewers from early history. It reposes at the heart of the constellation and burns forty-five times brighter than the sun. Because the star marked the vernal equinox, about 3000 B.C., the Persians named it the Watcher of the East. They established a body of myth that connects the alpha star with activities leading the bold to fame and fortune.

Aldebaran joins Antares, Regulus, and Fomulhaut in forming Persia's four Royal Stars, the Watchers of Heaven. The sign of the summer solstice, Regulus, the Little King, is a triple star burning white and ultramarine. Lying on the lion's torso, it bears the Persian designation of Watcher of the North. Alnath, Taurus's beta star, is the twenty-fourth brightest star in the heavens. Residing on the bull's north horn, it was ascendant during two London disasters of the seventeenth century—the bubonic plague in 1664–1665 and the devastating city fire in September 1666. The Hindu called the alpha star Rohini, the Red Deer; the eta star they called Krittika, the General of the Celestial Armies. The Chinese also focused on these two: the alpha star they called Pi, the Handnet, or the Rabbit Net; the eta star they called Mao, the Constellation.

Taurus is unique in that it features a meteor shower in June and two in November. It also displays a notable cluster in which lies Hyades, a star on its upper limb favored in ancient times by farmers. Directly northeast appears the Pleiades or Seven Sisters, a diffuse nebula known to early stargazers and characterized by the poets Aratus and Virgil and the astronomers Eudoxus and Ptolemy. The Pleiades is the brightest and most prominent cluster in the sky. It derives from Greek mythology; its stars were named for Atlas's daughters—Electra, Maia, Taygete, Alcyone, Merope, Celaeno, Sterope—who ran from Orion, a handsome giant unlucky in love. Artemis, the celibate goddess of the hunt, tossed the girls into the sky to rescue them from the would-be ravisher. Only six stars are clearly visible; the seventh, Merope, the Lost One, requires some magnification to be visible on earth. Another account of the myth says Zeus assisted the maidens by arranging them into a pattern of stars. In the sky, Orion still pursues them. Because the stars are fixed in their celestial positions, they never elude him, but he moves no closer.

The Hyades cluster, the celestial rainmakers, features gamma Tauri as the chief star. The group derives its lore from the myth of the seven Nysaean nymphs, named by varying combinations of Adraste, Aesyle, Althaea, Ambrosia, Bacche, Brome, Cleia or Cleis, Coronis, Dione, Eidothea, Erato, Eudora, Macris, Nysa, Pedile, Phaeo, Phaesyle, Philia, Phyto, Polyxo, and

Thyene. The seven sisters were daughters of Aethra and Atlas, who is also the sire of the Pleiades and the Hesperides. Their name may reflect their love for a brother, Hyas, whom they mourned after beasts killed him in the wilds near Libya. As a reward for sheltering the infant Dionysus in a cave and feeding him milk, Zeus placed the sisters among the stars. At Medea's request, the god also made them perennially young. An alternate myth claims that the seven nymphs wept at the pitiable wreckage of their brother's body and were turned into celestial rain-bringers.

Other stars in Taurus draw viewers' admiration. The Babylonians called the eta-one star Temennu, the foundation stone; the Hindu thought of it as Amba, the mother or the hen. Taurus also contains the double star Alnath, composed of one white and one gray star at the tip of the bull's northern horn. Hebrew astrologers named it the shepherd. Alhecka, connected with harsh and fearful moods, sits on the bull's southern horn. Alcyone, the brightest of the Pleiades, whom the Greeks called the Pleiad, perches on the bull's shoulders. Misinformed astronomers thought the yellow-green star was the core or axle of the universe.

Important astronomic phenomena and discoveries have occurred in Taurus. The Crab Nebula, the ruins of the brightest supernova in the sky, was first sighted in 1054 A.D. and was named around 1850 by Lord William Parsons Rosse, an Irish astronomer. From the heart of Taurus beats the strongest of the heavenly pulsars. It was also the site of the discovery of the first asteroid, a small heavenly body shaped like a star. In 1801, Giuseppe Piazzi, a monk who taught mathematics in Palermo, Sicily, established an observatory, where, on New Year's Day, he discovered Ceres in Taurus. He made valuable observations about constellations and published a catalog of stars in 1814.

ASTROLOGICAL HISTORY AND TRAITS

Governing the thirty-one days between April 20 and May 20, Taurus, one of the original members of the zodiac, once heralded the sun on the first day of spring. Like Syrians, Sumerians, and Arabs, Babylonians valued the bull as a symbol of light and a sign of earth's rejuvenation. The Egyptians identified the constellation with Osiris, god of fertility; the Chinese saw it as a white tiger or huge bridge. Derived from one of Zeus's many amorous escapades in Greek mythology, Taurus was his incarnation when he spied on Europa, the Phoenician princess, while she played by the Tyrian sea-shore. After she agreed to climb on the back of the magnificent white bull, Zeus easily seduced her. Because he swam with her on his back from

Phoenicia to Crete, Zeus's constellation contains only the bull's head, upper torso, and front legs. This fanciful story is a favorite in ancient lore and art and appears in Homer's *Iliad* and *Odyssey*, the *Homeric Hymns*, Apollonius's *Argonautica*, Ovid's *Metamorphoses*, Hyginus's *Fables*, and Horace's *Olympic Odes*.

A second erotic myth connected with the bull is the story of the Minotaur, the monster of Crete. Zeus had the bull appear as a heavenly token to legitimize Minos's rule, which dates to 2500 B.C. At his splendid palace at Knossos, ritual bull leapers honored Minos and his court with graceful tumbles over the horns of prancing bulls. Because the king failed to follow orders to sacrifice the original bull to Poseidon, the sea god stirred an abnormal passion in Queen Pasiphaë to mate with the animal. The lurid bestial story involves the inventor Daedalus's creation of a device that would accommodate their perverse sex act. He also designed the subterranean labyrinth in which the royal family hid their shame—the Minotaur, Pasiphaë's half-human, half-taurian offspring. Each year, the Minotaur demanded seven maids and seven youths from Athens as a blood sacrifice. The hero Theseus volunteered for martyrdom with the next contingent of human offerings. On advice from the princess Ariadne, he used a ball of string to mark his way into the dark labyrinth, slew the bull with his sword, and followed the string back to daylight. Scenes from the myth highlight the ruins of Knossos, statues of bulls, and other Cretan artifacts.

According to standard astrology, Taurus is a fixed earth sign ruled by Venus. Under the influence of her love and appreciation of beauty, Taurians avoid ugliness and value art, luxury, physical comforts, and camaraderie. In astral healing, the bull's attention to health and frequent outdoor walks build stable physical constitutions. Strengths such as determination, persistence, modesty, tolerance, and common sense balance the negative traits of taciturnity, slow motion, and indolence. Emotionally, the archetype avoids hysteria or depression. As a friend, the Taurian is considered truthful, straightforward, and caring, and values a good joke.

The bull stereotype is a land lover. A natural farmer who respects the earth, the Taurian is said to keep all four feet solidly planted in reality. Lumbering at a stolid, unremarkable pace, the typical Taurian recognizes the rhythms of agriculture and remains in tune with the seasons. Gardens tended by a Taurian are said to flourish from proper cultivation, organization, and attention to soil building. The traditional Taurian establishes a satisfying flower bed and prolific vegetable garden as a natural part of the homestead.

Honored for integrity, the standard Taurus governs wealth and resources. In business and friendly relationships, Taurians are drawn to Capricorns, Virgoans, and Cancerians. Because bulls possess judgment and patience for managing investments and adapt well to shifts in the economy, Taurians achieve business and financial success, especially through sale of art, jewelry, fine china, and antiques. Just as Taurians know when to plow, plant, and sow, as investors they are described as conservative, but surefooted in purveying real estate, stocks, bonds, and securities. As workers, they supposedly hate new beginnings, changes in the chain of command, and moves to unfamiliar offices or work sites. They accept direction from authority figures and maintain scrupulous business ethics. Bulls are allegedly ambitious, yet conventional. They tend to work for the same company or in the same elected post or professional career over a long period without losing enthusiasm for a product, responsibility, or service.

Astrologers declare that, as a mate, the bull is deliberate and somewhat calculating, particularly where money is concerned. Marriage to a Taurian is said to produce a staid, loving relationship grounded on loyalty and trust, but a breach of faith unleashes torrents of anger, even violence. The Taurian demands good food, beautiful surroundings, and a tight family bond. Because Taurians are allegedly shy and backward, they are thought to make wooden, unromantic wooers, but to develop into loving, trustworthy, and faithful mates who remain married for life. The archetype needs no complicated love rituals to inflame ardor and shies away from glamour or allure. When their usual devotion and good nature give way to jealousy or anger, the bull is said to strike out without mercy or may nurse a grudge. This transformation from lover to hater explains the ambivalence that accrues to the bull symbol. Other detractions from the bull's good traits include self-indulgence, inertia, absurd rituals, and extremes of caution.

As parents, Taurians are characterized as excellent care-providers and character-builders in their young. Astrologers claim that children delight the bull parent, who is said to pressure offspring to attend the parent's alma mater, pursue the same clubs and profession, and rear the bull's grandchildren according to Taurian standards. Traditionally, family arguments erupt when independent offspring reject any aspect of the Taurian point of view, including religion, politics, deportment, and mores. Wise children do not court confrontations with the disgruntled bull.

According to astral healers, the Taurian's health is among the best of the twelve houses of the Zodiac. In youth, the archetype offsets a tendency toward awkward, squarish hands and unappealing hair with wide-spaced eyes, broad face, and generous lips. Although powerfully built, the Taurian is said to avoid fights until sufficient provocation turns a mild personality into a raging, snorting pugilist. In mid-life, the typical Taurian mellows. Gluttony and a mellow type B personality inclines the chubby archetype toward burliness and a well developed paunch. A marked thickening of the jowls exacerbates the bull sign's love of exaggerated facial expressions and a deep rumbling chuckle.

In astro-medical tradition, sickness will fell the mighty bull for a long period of time. Taurians are thought to make good patients because they scrupulously follow doctors' instructions and health care regimens. The most inert and leisure-loving extend recuperation until forced back into the daily routine, which uplifts and renews by its familiarity. The worst afflictions arise from overeating, imbibing in wine and rich foods, and excess weight. Sudden shock is said to force the predictable Taurian into collapse or even death. As demonstrated by astrological anatomy charts, weakness runs to joint and throat disease, congestion, tooth decay, and allergy; organ complaints center on the kidneys and liver.

Lack of attention to diet is said to dispose the Taurian to lethal stroke or heart failure. Owing to deficiencies in sodium and calcium, the Taurian should build meals around salads of celery, chard, radish, and spinach and eat plenty of apples and strawberries. A hearty appetite and slow, deliberate eating habits are thought to produce numerous Taurian gourmands as well as hearty, good-natured cooks and genial pubkeepers.

Critics suggest that Chaucer had the Taurian character in mind when he created Harry Bailly, owner of the Tabard Inn and guide for the Canterbury pilgrims. According to the Prologue to *The Canterbury Tales*:

> A semely man Oure Hooste was withalle
> For to han been a marchal in an halle.
> A large man he was with eyen stepe—
> A fairer burgeys is there noon in Chepe—
> Boold of his speche, and wys, and wel ytaught,
> And of manhod hym lakkede right naught.
> (Our host was a seemly man
> To have been manager of an inn.
> He was large with great eyes—
> No fairer burgess lived in Cheapside—
> He was bold of speech, wise, and well educated,
> And lacked no quality of manhood.) (Chaucer 1961, 24)

Chaucer speaks through Bailly, who organized the mirthful pilgrims with a formal arrangement of storytelling, two per person on the ride to the cathedral and two on the return ride. Because of his choice of so hearty a person, critics assume that Chaucer assigned some of his own personality traits to his spokesman.

In business and industry, standard Taurians are hard workers who value the salary they earn and frequently grow wealthy from shrewd saving and investment. Typically loners, Taurians are too self-absorbed to succeed at team sports and group efforts. However, like determined dray animals broken to the shaft or plow, Taurians are said to work until they drop to solve a puzzle or complete a task. Traditionally, they don't shun dirty jobs, yet prefer to remain clean and unstained. For this reason, the Taurian makes a worthy scholar, scientist, musician, singer, philosopher, or director of a project, but never a humble day laborer or research assistant. Taurian archetypes succeed as coaches, choir singers, priests, or clerics and bask in public glory, uniforms and robes of office, and badges of honor. They treasure trophies, busts, and statues to their accomplishments. As keepers of sacred rituals, they are pious, faithful, and dependable, but may condone unconventional worship styles.

SYMBOLISM IN ART AND RELIGION

Taurus is a prevalent form in art. The sign represents raw magnetism. Usually depicted in profile on murals and urn friezes, the bull displays prominent horns, which complement a hefty, sometimes oversized phallus, symbol of virility and regeneration. Characters riding bulls appear in Greek, Cretan, Sumerian, Semitic, and Hindu mythology and art. Bull sacrifice figures in Iranian, Minoan, and Roman art serve as emblems of renewal and physical vigor. Buddhists saw the bull as the incarnation of ego; Celts equated the bull with power and strength. Egyptians and early Greeks drew the gods Apis and Dionysus with bull heads as enhancements of manhood and authority.

In prehistoric European cave art, the bull is a creative, resurgent figure often connected with divine favor and success. From early times, anonymous artists, possibly shamans or priests, drew two-dimensional side views of horned bulls in charcoal on cave walls at Lascaux and Font-de-Gaume, France. A ceremonial bas-relief found in Babylonian war loot features the bull on which stands Teshub, the Hittite sky god. Cretan palace art and sculpture favors the full-chested bull deity, whose horns loom sharp and lethal. Egyptian and North African art shows the same figure with the disc or medallion of the sun god suspended between the horns as a sign of beneficence or blessing. Egyptians honored the bull in tomb art by having him bear the ruined body of Osiris. The bronze cult figure of Apis depicts Taurian strength and fertility. His appearance on sarcophagi links the bull with protection of the dead and with the heavens, where he reposed in glory alongside Osiris as cosmic water bearer and life-sustainer. On the slate palette of Narmer of Hierakonapolis, which dates to 3100 B.C., bas-relief depicts the king as a bull using his horns to batter the walls of enemy strongholds. Another view on the slate shows the bull goring a victim. His bold, forthright actions earn him the title of "Horus, the Strong Bull, Appearing in Right, Lord of the North and the South."

In the time of Sargon II, the Babylonians used the bull as a national emblem and carved it in marble as a tyrannic symbol on temple portals and palace entranceways. An imaginative beast, the heavy-hooved bull stands four meters high on parallel front legs. A side view displays three more legs to present the body in motion. Blended with the muscular legs and elongated tail are fantastic variations—graceful wings and the bearded head of a king. Rising above the forehead reposes the cylindrical crown, flanked by two stylized horns. The impact of the statue, which is housed in the Louvre Museum in Paris, represents Sargon's supremacy as administrator and builder of the palace at Khorsabad.

In Greek and Roman mosaic and mural art, the bull is a dramatic icon. Often, these works display the beasts that Jason yoked and hitched to a plow, bulls that accompanied the processions of Dionysus, or the Roman sacrificial bull wreathed in garlands and decked with herbs and wildflowers. A temple at Selinus, Sicily, dating to the sixth century B.C., features a bas-relief of Zeus as a lusty bull carrying Europa on his back. The artist expressed animal appeal in the inward curve of the elongated tail and in the girl's loving pat on his side and her grasp of his right horn. In the fifth century B.C., artists constructing the temple of Zeus at Olympia added to the metopes a scene in which Hercules challenges a rampant bull. The two figures occupy crossed diagonals, with the hero's uplifted arm forming the left leg and the rearing bull's head and shoulders forming the right. Now housed in the Louvre Museum in Paris, the badly scarred bas-relief still reflects the energy of human against beast.

The use of the snorting bull as a royal symbol presaged defeat in fifth-century B.C. Persia. Pairs of limestone bulls atop the one hundred densely packed columns supported the hypostyle Hall of Xerxes at Persepolis in what is now Iran. Exotic fringed tapestries linked the columns and repeated the motif in antimony, lead, and copper oxide pigment on cedar ceiling and pediments. The period reflects the over-confidence that accompanied the spread of Persian authority from the Indus River to the Aegean Sea. Xerxes's display of semi-divine grandeur and arrogance embodies two Taurian qualities that brought the king low after he sacked Athens. In 480 B.C., he capitulated to the Greek navy at Salamis and was assassinated by one of his officers in 465 B.C. At the urging of the courtesan Thaïs, Alexander the Great burned the hall, depriving Xerxes of his architectural bid for immortality.

In Rome stands a more modest, stately monument, the *Ara Pacis*, or Altar of Peace, erected in 9 B.C., an imposing rectangular building honoring Augustus's safe return from campaigns in Spain and Gaul. Across the scrolled capital in bas-relief marches an entourage of worshippers to a *suovetaurilia*, the traditional tripartite sacrifice of a pig, sheep, and bull. The bull stands in profile with attendants at his rump, flank, and head. The front figure appears to draw the animal forward to keep the procession moving. An eastern view of the building displays the earth mother between two adoring females. At her breasts she fondles twins. A bull and sheep repose at her feet alongside generous supplies of water, grain, and fish. The scene combines notable zodiac figures—Aquarius, Taurus, Gemini, and Pisces.

A bas-relief on the Arch of Marcus Aurelius dedicated in 178 A.D. characterizes the philosopher-emperor, who ruled from 161 to 180 A.D. He pulls his toga over his head in the standard Roman gesture of reverence as he presides over the sacrifice. The gravity of the four onlookers, young girl, flutist, axeman, and water bearer, harmonizes with the emperor at left of center and bull to the right. Behind the party of Jupiter-worshippers looms a magnificent temple decked in Corinthian splendor, featuring a carved pediment and a bas-relief of a bull charging a human adversary. The control of the complex work reflects Aurelius's goodness, piety, generosity, and wisdom. The Vatican Museum houses a simpler procession of Bacchantes flanking a bull. The dramatic drapings of linen on the two figures contrast the crescent horns, flared nostrils, and wrinkled hide of the bull, which lowers its head in a menacing stance.

An Anatolian figure from the same era displays a male worshipper in triumphant pose. Wearing a tunic and boots, he grasps the thyrsis, a ceremonial staff composed of a pine cone draped in myrtle, as a gesture of fealty to Bacchus. In his left arm he cradles a cornucopia, symbol of a plentiful harvest. His left foot appears to subdue a bull, which collapses on the lower right corner of the bas-relief. The inscription in Greek lettering indicates piety: "Agathapous of Kaouala Offers His Prayer to Humankind."

The combination of symbols syncretizes Dionysiac worship with the stringent military cult of Mithras, which entered Rome by way of Persia. Mithraism was a demanding, secretive belief system that pressed male followers to adhere to a staunch moral conduct, brotherhood, and underground veneration. For Roman soldiers, an unblemished bull was the sole sacrifice acceptable to Mithras. A recurrent theme in Mithran temple art is the human figure grasping the bull's head and plunging a dagger into its heart. The symbolism suggests a stalwart male quelling the bestial side of human nature, a motif common to the writings of St. Paul, who demanded soldierly valor and self-control among disciples of Christ.

In Indian art, the bull balances the cow as the active procreative force that fertilizes the placid ruminant. Christian symbolists abandoned the lusty bull in favor of the castrated plow animal, the epitome of chastity, sacrifice, self-denial, and patience. Hebrew symbolism reflects the biblical connection between the bull's horns and the sacred altar, which they adorned. Suppliants received asylum when they grasped the horns, thereby putting themselves under Yahweh's power. In primitive Christian art, the horns of the bull point upward as though directing the faithful to God. The transposition of authoritative horns onto Michelangelo's statue of Moses confers godly power and moral authority on the Hebrew spokesman for the almighty. The elevation of Moses seems appropriate for the patriarch who conferred directly with God and who presented the Ten Commandments to his followers.

Bull lore is also significant to classic literature. Dating to the ninth century B.C., Homer's *Odyssey* features cattle in one of Odysseus's escapades. On land owned by Helios, the sun god, Odysseus's mariners slaughter sacred cattle. Odysseus had received warning of their importance when he visited Teiresias in the underworld. The prophet promised:

If you do harm them, then I testify to the destruction of your ship and your companions, but if you yourself get clear, you will come home in bad case, with the loss of all your companions, in someone else's ship, and find troubles in your household, insolent men, who are eating away your livelihood and courting your godlike wife and offering gifts to win her. (Homer 1967, 171)

Homer links most of the ills that plague Odysseus to Helios's cattle. After butchering enough beef to last for a six-day feast, the men realize that they have committed sacrilege, for which they must suffer a penalty that inhibits their return to Ithaca from the Trojan War and denies Odysseus a grand and joyous reception when he arrives at his palace.

A sixth-century vase painting depicts Helios's sacred herd with hefty animals topped by lethal curved horns. To the left of the herd is an oversized daisy-shaped sun representing Helios's power. In the 1950s, Ernle Bradford, author of *Ulysses Found*, retraced the voyage and set the poetic episode on Taormina, a Sicilian beachhead on the island's eastern promontory overlooking a dangerous strait opposite the toe of Italy's boot. A valley named *Val del Bove* (Valley of the Cow) bears out Bradford's supposition that Odysseus's wanderings have a basis in fact.

Roman poetry reprises the Greek admiration for the massive bulk and strength of the bull. Virgil, the Roman epicist, opened his *Georgics* with a nod toward "the white bull that with his golden horns opens the year," the traditional New Year's figure (Cavendish 1970, 112). In the first century, the poet Marcus Manilius depicted Taurus as dull, honest, and strong. An unadorned, unassuming dray animal, he plods through the fields, dropping manure on the furrows and laboring to produce a good crop. According to the writings of Valens, the zodiacal Taurus produces quality artisans, laborers, farmers, and construction workers. In the French epic, *Chanson de Roland*, which is based on classic Roman themes, the bull is reduced to a single element, its horn. The hero's blast on the horn symbolizes refuge and safety.

Overall, the Taurian author is contemplative and cautious in developing a plot. The bull sign is said to dispose the writer to a fundamental humanism rooted in the commonalities of life, as reflected by John James Audubon, author and artist of *Birds of America*. The consummate example is William Shakespeare, whose solid, unembellished structure has become a touchstone of Western drama. His ability to blend comic and tragic elements displays the Taurian's rumination over all elements of human life. Examples of his most durable characters include Hamlet, Falstaff, and Portia. In the twentieth century, novelists Daphne du Maurier, author of *Rebecca*, and Harper Lee, author of *To Kill a Mockingbird*, display the bull sign's meticulous crafting of fiction. Similar qualities undergird the works of poet Randall Jarrell, dramatist J.M. Barrie, naturalist Farley Mowat, and L. Frank Baum and Gary Paulsen, successful authors respectively of *The Wizard of Oz* and *Hatchet*, both young adult classics.

7
GEMINI

ASTRONOMICAL FACTS

The Latin for twins, Gemini (jeh' mih • ny), abbreviated Gem, is the third sign of the zodiac. Formally known as Alpha and Beta Geminorum, the duo has been called Adam and Eve, the Kids, the Heavenly G, the Winter Octagon, and the Winter Oval. The heavenly twins are known jointly as the Dioscuri (dy' uh • skoo' ree), a Greek term for "sons of god." An uneven pair of lights visible in the Northern Hemisphere each spring, they resemble two stick figures holding hands. The constellation borders Auriga, Canis Minor, Lynx, Monoceros, and Orion and lies below the bowl of Ursa Major between Cancer and Taurus. Of the forty-seven components in the group there are fourteen major stars:

alpha star	Castor, the beaver
beta star	Pollux, much wine
gamma-one star	Alhena, the brand
gamma-two star	Almeisan, the proud marcher
delta star	Wasat, the middle of the sky
epsilon star	Mebsuta, the outstretched (paw)
zeta star	Mekbuda, the retracted (paw)
eta star	Propus I, the (first) forward foot
iota star	Propus I, the (second) forward foot
mu-one star	Tejat Posterior, the hind foot
mu-two star	Tejat Prior, the (forward) back foot
mu-three star	Dirah
xi star	Alzirr, the button
Gemini-one star	Propus III, (adjunct to) the forward foot

The thirtieth in size, this constellation showcases its beta star (Pollux or Polydeuces), an orange star on the southern twin's head. The Chinese called the beta star Tsing, the well or pit. Arab astrologers named it Aldhira, the forearm, and the Hindu identified it as Punarvarsu, the two good again.

Like earthly siblings, the brothers are uneven in brightness. Pollux is a giant light of the first magnitude; Castor, one of the hottest and most complex astral clusters in the sky, is a six-part mass on the head of the northern twin. Castor contains three sets of blue-white binary stars that produce light of the second magnitude. Because of its instability, this six-way combination may betoken a future separation. Another bright star, Alhena, a showy spot in the southern twin's left foot, was called the bright foot in antiquity and connects to the story of Achilles's wounded tendon, caused by his mother's attempt to singe away her infant son's human elements. Diagonal from Alhena is Wasat, a double star glowing purple and pale white in the northern twin's right forearm. Dirah, the mu star, is also a doublet formed of a blue and a yellow star that repose on the northern twin's left foot. Dirah is sometimes identified as the abused one. Iota Geminum, another minor star, stands guard between the twins' shoulders.

Gemini's two claims to momentary notoriety took place 240 years apart. In 1781, Sir Frederick William Herschel of Bath, England, found Uranus in Gemini's boundaries. Herschel, an organist who became royal astronomer for George III, named the planet Georgium Sidus (the Georges' Star). In 1930, Clyde William Tombaugh from Streator, Illinois, a self-taught astronomer at the Lowell Observatory of Arizona State College in Flagstaff, Arizona, discovered the planet Pluto in Gemini. The constellation contains the summer solstice, the year's longest day, which occurs on June 22. In October and early December, Gemini rekindles in meteor showers, brief displays that mimic the summer's celestial brightness. In similar fashion, the duality of Ursa Major and Ursa Minor reflects an uneven sharing of the heavens, with one constellation outdistancing the other in size and light.

ASTROLOGICAL HISTORY AND TRAITS

Governing the thirty-one days between May 21 and June 20, Gemini lies between Taurus and Cancer. A feminine symbol, the dual sun sign was represented in earlier zodiacs by notable pairs, beginning with a man and woman in Egyptian lore and two strongmen, Apollo and Hercules, in early Greek nomenclature. In their current identification, Homer casts them as complements: Castor the horse-tamer and Polydeuces the boxer. In Roman sea lore, the twins were carved on prows of merchant ships because it was thought that they helped clear Mediterranean shipping lanes of pirates. The brothers became images of light. They sent meteors to illuminate the skies and to highlight ships by dancing across masts in fiery blue sparkles. The designation is a poetic description of St. Elmo's fire, a collection of positively charged ions that collect on spires and ship's rigging when storm clouds import a concentration of negative ions. An auspicious sign, these appearances supposedly preceded fine weather.

The constellation of Gemini answers to the planet Mercury, the god of Roman mythology who carried the caduceus, a godly baton. He was powered by winged hat and sandals and delivered divine messages from Mount Olympus to mortals. Associated with loquacious, playful, expressive people, the sun sign traditionally bears a duality or ambiguity suggesting a two-faced, unpredictable personality. According to zodiacal stereotypes, dualism is so firmly ingrained that the Gemini clothes-buyer is said to prefer two-piece bathing suits and dresses, two-toned shoes and spectator pumps, polka dots, checks, and stripes.

Astrologers picture the Geminian archetype as a perennial scoffer at danger who performs shenanigans and foolhardy feats of daring, but makes a poor career soldier. Allegedly, Geminians avoid a fray by being logical debaters or ombudsmen who remain calm and disinterested while examining both sides of a dispute for a sane, nonviolent solution. Positive and effervescent with the possibilities of compromise, the typical Geminian personality eludes the battlefield by working for peace and by applying vigorous intellectual energy to the complexities of diplomacy. At social functions, Geminians are said to be garrulous, exuberant, and sporting. Although capable of feigning merriment, they genuinely love life. On the negative side, their skill at repartee marks them as indecisive, frivolous, and tedious.

The two-sidedness of the Gemini personality is easily identifiable in behavior patterns. The youthful, popular Geminian is thought to maintain a keen zest for life and to pursue a wide array of hobbies and interests, yet, like a flitting Peter Pan, the personality annoys others by childishly denying age and avoiding maturity. Geminian bipolarity intrigues the curious, who may enjoy the vicarious thrill of associating with unstable personalities. To escape ennui, Geminians are said to revert to infantilism, pranks, practical jokes, and a silly argot. Acquisitive and self-gratifying, Geminians who follow the astrological pattern overspend out of a need for the latest bauble or newest car. Erratic and inconstant, they are quick to discard belongings, even heirlooms and titles, as they search for the next treasure or distraction. A sweet-natured, but theatrical gush fails to convince others of their sincere friendship.

As described in astrological handbooks, Geminians are consummate business leaders and pour themselves into meticulous studies that require skill with numbers and calculation, such as accounting and tax preparation. Easily bored and incapable of such drudgery as assembly lines, farm work, gardening, or carpentry, they follow an erratic course to stardom, often startling the unwary with bursts of brilliance. The twins supposedly enjoy teaching, inn management, music, mathematics, laboratory research, and astronomy. They typically switch from one task to another and, like bartenders, pastry chefs, or restauranteurs, take pleasure in displaying their skills.

According to tradition, Geminians are devoted, but fickle friends who tire easily of others' woes. As lovers and mates, the Twins are said to demand attentive wooing, but move cautiously toward matrimony. In marriage, they harmonize with Librans and Aquarians, but drain marriage of joy by perpetually seeking their own good at all costs. Despite their failure as companions and mates, Geminians redeem their childhood reputation for dalliance by becoming devoted, long-suffering parents. Once established in a home, Geminians weary of tedious yard chores and a regular routine. They expect regular visits from friends, constant celebrations of holidays and personal milestones, and frequent vacations. Children thrive under the archetypal Gemini parent, who becomes a companion rather than a mentor to older offspring.

Physically tall, light, well-shaped, agile, dark-haired, and fine-featured, stereotypical Geminians easily attract others with their intent gaze. They require regular rest, sleep, and outdoor recreation to stem persistent infection and delicate respiratory systems. In astral medicine, bipolarity predisposes Geminians to flu, bronchitis, tuberculosis, eczema, and dependence on tobacco, alcohol, and drugs. During difficult times, they are said to weary friends with exaggerated tales of woe and displays of hardship and desolation. On the other hand, those born under the sign of the Twins have themselves to blame for self-medication, rejection of medical advice, and the inability to rest in bed. They are thought to blame a faulty sense of logic for rationalizing their choices of bad diet, alcohol, and late hours. The wily Gemini is reputed to circumvent a sensible bedtime with lengthy telephone conversations, reading, and writing notes and personal letters. As designated in handbooks of astral healing, for maximum well being, the archetype should eat watercress and sprouts, green beans, and pineapple. Gemini's health is projected to improve by supplementing the diet with potassium chloride and by drinking goat's milk and consuming compounds of licorice, tansy, vervain, yarrow, and marigold.

In nature as in myth, the Gemini assume two opposing roles, an uneven duality that forever teeters to and fro. Weather prognostication, like horoscopy, depends on a commitment to understand, predict, and prepare for cosmic imbalance. The physical struggle between earth and sea during storms and rip tides permeates the lives of fishers, sailors, and coastal dwellers, reminding them of the fragility of life, which must have both air and water to live. A standard figure in mythology is the drowning victim, who loses the struggle of the elements, either through imprudence or ill fate. Like Gemini, survivors cope with their loss and accept the unyielding human situation that leaves the living to mourn the dead, one of life's most poignant, dismaying dualities.

The twins' archetype represents a universal strand of iconography that, from ancient times, has absorbed thinkers, philosophers, and astrologers. The traditional complements of the sun and moon, earth and sea, and air and water reflect the concept of twinning in the universe. Like Pollux, the sun is a constant, dominant power, upon which the inconstant moon depends for its 28–day cycle of reflected light. Together, as described in the first chapter of Genesis, the two heavenly orbs rule over day and night, establishing for themselves separate idiosyncratic patterns of ascendence. Both the lunar and solar calendars coordinate the motions of the moon and sun and challenge scientists and astrologers to balance their influences on nature, particularly on human life.

In sociological terms, human pairs share the give and take of Gemini's duality. Identical twins possess identical elements, the mirror-images or stereo-opposites that pair up like the palms of the hands laid together. A diverse pairing exists in same-sex fraternal twins, who may share a birth hour, but, like Castor and Pollux, bear no resemblance to each other in thought, attitude, posture, or temperament. The extreme of this model is the pairing of opposite-sex twins. In early China and West Africa, the birth of such pairs was considered a perversion of nature, a kind of *in utero* incest. The solution to this family quandary was infanticide, often of the twin born second.

SYMBOLISM IN ART AND RELIGION

In Christian parlance, the two elements of the Gemini sign symbolize prototypical partners. Biblical examples include mismatched siblings like Cain and Abel, Mary and Martha, Rachel and Leah, and Jacob and Esau. More pointed than sibling rivalry is the patriarchal power of the husband over the wife in marriage, a microcosm mirroring the position of God over the Church. Irrevocably linked in an intense relationship at the altar, each bride and groom vows to accept the one-sided power structure that dates to early desert nomads. Locked into an uneven dichotomy of the ruler and the ruled, the two shoulder rigidly sexist allotments of familial duties: who will procure food and shelter, who will train children, and who will make crucial decisions. To feminists, a lifestyle ordained by uncompromising patriarchy and precept allows no room for individual talents, preferences, or personal growth for either partner and dooms itself needlessly to tensions and misery.

Gemini furnishes art with an intriguingly mutable subject. The pairing of twin boys produces two separate beings, each of whom possesses distinct characteristics. To express dualism in nature and human life, early artisans depicted uneven duos. Babylonians paired two trees in heaven—the Tree of Life and the Tree of Truth, a parallel to the physical and emotional domains. In Islamic lore, Persians paired peacocks on opposite sides of the tree of life. When portraying twins in the stars, the tenth-century Persian artist Al Sufi depicted the two as rival males, one shoving the other out of the way. In Indian lore the Vedic horsemen known as the Asvins or Ashwins epitomized complementary twinning, as did the duality of Atma and Buddhi. The Egyptians paired brother/husband Osiris with his sister/mate, Isis, just as the Greeks joined Zeus and Hera, called Jupiter and Juno in Latin. The Hebrews likened the stars to Moses and Aaron, the brothers who grew up in separate homes, Aaron with his birth parents and Moses as a foundling reared in a palace. The two, like Castor and Pollux, coordinated individual talents of leadership and oratory. Together, they led the Children of Israel out of bondage in Egypt.

In religion and philosophy, Gemini epitomizes the evolving deification of heaven. Before the emergence of Christianity, priests stressed the darkness of the night sky illuminated by bright stars, a contrast of the mortal soul with the light of the divine. As the Roman world internalized these implications, they evolved the concept of *aeternitas* (eternity), a forerunner of the Christian heaven. Centuries before the Vatican was established in Rome, Cicero characterized the godhood of the sky as *summus ipse deus arcens et continens ceteros* (itself the highest god enclosing and containing the other [spheres]) (Cumont 1960, 64). Within this new perception of the universe, Roman paganism gave way to a new spirituality based on faith in an afterlife, the counterpart of earthly existence.

Just as the priestly view of heaven reminded Romans that life on earth bore little resemblance to the reward of an afterlife, the concept of duality juxtaposed wild with tame, life with death, and sin with salvation in cosmologies of many cultures. Amerindian, Hebrew, Teutonic, and Egyptian lore pictures the paired star shapes as emblems of the struggle between good and evil. Color schemes emphasize the contrast between the twins. For example, the black and white of morality tales depicts the extremes of ethical decisions; the Chinese antithesis of yin and yang usually pictures paired opposites as interlinking forms nested in stark red and black within the confines of a circle. Persian sketches of the twins link their arms and eyes in a mutual gaze. A crude fresco of a Gallic matron from Toulon sur Allier in the second century A.D. enhances her breasts to serve twin babes. In a martial example, Prussian military insignia display the duality of warfare in the double-headed eagle. In the statue of the Hermaphrodite, housed in Rome's Villa Borghese, bisexuality, another type of duality, takes shape in the anomaly of male and female genitals on a decidedly feminine body.

Common to the Mediterranean world was the depiction of twinning in mosaics, talismen, frieze art, pottery, and jewelry. Egyptian artists modeled twins in wall sketches that compare the younger and older Horus. The Greeks identified the twins specifically as Castor and Polydeuces in sixth-century vase art, which groups major participants in the Calydonian boar hunt as they score a kill. From the same era, the artist Psiax posed the celestial twins as cavalrymen in a classic red and black vase motif. The piece, now housed in the Museo Civico Romano in Brescia, Italy, provides a realistic study of equestrian dress and links the figures with upper-class riders. Another pair of twins forms the projecting adornment on the ends of a pediment topping an Ionic temple at Locri, Italy. Caught in the act of dismounting, the twin horsemen step onto the backs of twin Tritons.

In art that reflects Roman mythology, Gemini may foster cooperation and unity or represent a contradiction or blood feud. The Romans allied these concepts by relating the first motif to Janus, their doorkeeper, and the second to Romulus and Remus. The concept of unity appears in the back-to-back faces of Janus, the two-faced deity who presided over the end of the old year and the beginning of the new. Armlets, coins, and medallions feature the duplicated faces as a sober, bearded god in alert pose marked by distinct features, serious eyes, and fleshy lips. The harmonious juncture of the two profiles stresses the virtue of unity through tolerance and compromise.

In the obverse of Janus, the principle of duality undergirds the myth of Romulus and Remus. Born to a virgin royal princess, they were sired by Mars. Because the human world rejected them, they found nurturing in primal nature. In a fifth-century B.C. statue of Romulus and Remus, which once adorned the Temple of Jupiter Capitolinus in Rome (the nation's symbol), the pose allies hungry twin toddlers. They stretch their mouths upward to suckle the generous paps of *Lupa*, the grinning wolf who saved them from starvation after their mother abandoned them. In an ornate full bas-relief housed in the Vatican Museum, Mars and Rhea Silvia precede angels who reiterate the rounded baby limbs of Romulus and Remus. The processional is a vivid gesture of respect to Rome's godly beginning. In adulthood, the warring brothers came to blows over the establishment of Rome's foundations. Because Romulus slew Remus, their murderous sibling rivalry negated the bucolic warmth of their rearing in the wild and christened Rome with fratricidal blood.

According to Livy, Rome's lyric historian, the cult of the Dioscuri had an identifiable beginning. In 499 B.C., the god-sized sky twins rode winged horses down to the Forum to proclaim that the Romans had beaten the Tarquini and Latini at Lake Regillus. While local folk rejoiced, the heavenly duo watered their steeds at Lake Juturna. Fifteen years later, city fathers made good the vow of Aulus Postumius and erected a temple in Parian marble to honor the divine appearance of Romulus and Remus. Today, the ruins soar above the Sacred Way and contain three Corinthian columns, a detailed marble lintel, and a stone well, all of which Augustus reconstructed in 6 A.D. The temple attests to the inclusion of Castor and Pollux among the gods that the Romans actively worshipped: Aesculapius, Quirinus, Liber, Fides Publica, Roma, and Virtus. More realistic artistry divorced from duality comes from Apollonius of Athens, who sculpted "The Boxer," a first-century marble displayed in Rome's National Museum. Modeled on Pollux the boxer, the athlete's smooth beard, curled hair, and smooth musculature epitomizes Hellenism, but his uplifted eyes and complex questioning expression are typically Roman.

Christian art perpetuated the motif of twins, but moved away from mythological interpretation to Biblical symbolism. A fifth-century temple atop a hill in Agrigento, Sicily, honored the Dioscuri. After the area was Christianized, a natural substitution replaced Castor and Polydeuces with saintly evangelists Peter and Paul. In the Medieval period, artists contrast twins such as the biblical Cain and Abel and Jacob and Esau with varied gesture, facial expression, or implied temperament. In the *Book of Hours*, a medieval anthology, the boys turn toward each other; one informally clasps an arm on his brother's shoulder. The artist accentuates their differences by arming one with a scythe, the other with a lyre. A graceful blue sash links the two in felicity and harmony.

Renaissance art reprises the pose of the classic duo with wings, a post-pagan additive. Common to the frescoes and oil paintings of Michelangelo, Giotto, and Raphael are pairs of male cherubs, often in mischievous pose turning laughing mouths upward. Raphael's enhancement of the paired boys is captured in "La Belle Jardinière," a winsome oil painting of the Virgin Mary caressing the toddler Christ while his cousin and forerunner, John the Baptist, kneels in fealty and awe. The similarity of the harmonized male figures echoes the Biblical account of their tandem ministries.

In advertising and trademarks, Gemini represents synthesis or imagination through shared risks or inversion, often symbolized by the double-edged axe of ironworks and foundries, an emblem associated with the myth of the Minotaur in the Cretan labyrinth. The dual sign finds counterparts in writing, arithmetic, and physics in the letter H, the number 8, and the 90° rotation of the 8 into the symbol for infinity, a two-sided loop or double oval that has no beginning or end. The three symbols, like the Chinese yin and yang, share a balance of bilateral symmetry.

In Greek literature, an extensive duality motif underlies the myth of Castor and Polydeuces. The children of Leda, Queen of Aetolia, the twins were sired by Zeus, who took the shape of a swan to seduce her. Leda bore two periwinkle-blue eggs: one producing the two males and the other, two females, Clytemnestra and Helen of Troy. Because Leda's husband Tyndareus shared paternity with Zeus, Castor and Polydeuces shared immortality. In the ninth century B.C., Homer lauded the twins in "Hymn to the Dioskouri," which names them "Tyndaridai [sons of Tyndareus], riders of swift horses" and designates Mount Taygetos as their birthplace (Homer 1995, 152). A second verse in the *Homeric Hymns* allies the twins with sailors, who sacrifice white lambs to them in hopes of rescue from capsize or falling overboard. True to their character, the heavenly saviors appear, "darting through the air on steady-beating wings, and at once they check the blasts of harsh winds, and smooth the waves on white-capped seas." Homer comments gracefully, "For sailors they are fair signs, and seeing them they rejoice and stop their painful toil" (Homer 1995, 166).

According to Eratosthenes's *Catasterisms*, written around 225 B.C., the twin deities calm emotional turmoil as well as turbulent seas:

> [Castor and Polydeuces] exceeded all men in brotherly love, for they never quarreled about power or about anything else. So Zeus, wishing to make a memorial of their unanimity, called them "the Twins" and placed them together among the stars. (Morford and Lenardon 1977, 465)

In addition to their equanimity, ancient literature also stresses the twins' athleticism. In Apollonius's *Argonautica*, the two young men were among Jason's handpicked crew and took an active part in the *Argo*'s voyage east over the Black Sea to Colchis to reclaim the golden fleece. On the ship's departure, the poet Orpheus summoned tongues of flame to crown the twins with grace.

The duo were also among the Spartans who welcomed Paris to Menelaus's court. In a minor myth, the twins rescued ten-year-old Helen, whom Theseus and his pal Pirithous abducted and put under house arrest at Aphidna while they plundered the underworld. On the way home, the tender brothers procured Aethra, an aged servant who served as Helen's nursemaid. A second abduction myth placed the twins in the role of captors of young maidens. Suitors of the two victims pursued the twins and killed Castor. Polydeuces was so grief-stricken that he implored Zeus to allow him to share immortality with his fallen brother. The arrangement forever separated Polydeuces from Castor, who lived on earth while his brother took a turn in the underworld.

Post-Hellenic literature perpetuates the image of strength in the twins. In an obscure episode, Castor taught the infant Hercules to fence. In more recent Greek history, the myth of the Gemini takes on an auspicious role after Helen and her twin brothers became the patrons of Sparta, the strong Greek city they protected from treachery. Horace's odes laud the Roman version of the twins, who headed legions at the battle of Lake Regillus, where Romulus's Rome established its primacy over the Latin League. According to the poet, the brothers distinguished themselves at the Calydonian boar hunt and shone as "illustrious twins" at foot races and wrestling matches.

The classic canon draws on similar myths based on the duality of strong males. A favorite of Homer, the epic struggle of Greece and Troy contains similar literary foils, such as Hector and Achilles, two warriors of opposing attitudes and nationalities, and Menelaus and Agamemnon, brothers whose roles in the Trojan War cast them as opposites in both behavior and temperament. Aeschylus returns to the twin theme in *Agamemnon*, a tragedy in which the brothers are "twin-throned, twin-sceptered, in twofold power of kinds from God" (Snodgrass 1994, 656). Roman mythology recast them as the benevolent deities who watched over sailors and cavalry. In honor of their patrons, horsemen swore by the Gemini or "by jiminy."

In Hebrew lore, the protracted struggle of twins Jacob and Esau began at birth, when Esau emerged from Rebecca's womb with Jacob clinging to his brother's foot. In adulthood, the sibling rivalry continued with Jacob's theft of Esau's birthright. The story adds a second pair, Laban's daughters, Leah and Rachel. After Jacob fled his angry brother and worked for Laban, he found himself tricked just as he had deceived Esau. Laban followed the tradition of betrothing daughters by birth order, with the elder preceding the younger girl. On Jacob's wedding night, he embraced a silent form whom he assumed was his beloved Rachel. The next day, the deflowered maiden turned out to be Leah. Angered by his father-in-law's switch, Jacob threatened to humiliate the family by abandoning his wife. Laban relented and gave Jacob his intended, but exacted fourteen years of work from Jacob— seven for Leah and seven for Rachel. Thus the Gemini motif epitomizes struggle and persistence, a psychological pattern that reflects the warring of clans, as Shakespeare describes in *Romeo and Juliet*; a misalliance of nations, as in Charles Dickens's *A Tale of Two Cities*; as well as the power struggle between segments of an imperfectly allied personality, which is the focus of Robert Louis Stevenson's *Dr. Jekyll and Mr. Hyde*.

Writers displaying the fractured Geminian style include St. Paul, Dante, Sir Arthur Conan Doyle, Anne Frank, Ralph Waldo Emerson, and Walt Whitman. Paul's letters exemplify a soulful subject matter frequently interrupted with digressions and interpolations; Whitman vacillates between the spiritual and physical realms. More philosophical is Emerson, the American romantic whose essays counter his regard for the intellect or genius with his adulation of the spirit's oneness with the oversoul. Anne Frank, the budding diarist of World War II jewry, displays duality in adolescent sparring with her parents and a soulful longing for an end to Nazism and the return of peace in Europe. Perhaps more than the other examples, Sir Arthur Conan Doyle exemplifies a type of *sui generis* logic, applicable to his unique style of reasoning. His appealing Geminian character, Sherlock Holmes, displays an intriguing combination of nervous energy and self-renewal. Because detective work enervates him with pacing and rumination, he relieves the strain by coaxing gentle cadences from his violin.

Nations, too, display the Janus temperament. Off-setting an initial rush of energy in combat, settlement, or development, the surge of history may lapse into malaise, complacency, or economic depression. A blend of complementary aims—spiritual renewal with materialism—characterizes North America, which has lured European adventurers and fortune-hunters since the time of Christopher Columbus and the Spanish *conquistadores*. Like Gemini personalities, which are said to tire easily, alternating periods of boom and bust typify the Oregon Trail, California Gold Rush, Prohibition, and the high-strung flappers of the 1920s, which preceded Black Monday and the stock market crash, a disaster for financial, domestic, and governmental stability. In modern times, the glitter and throb of such neon-lit cities as Atlantic City, Las Vegas, Miami, New Orleans, and New York perpetuates the pattern by alternately teasing and wearying gamblers, entrepreneurs, and tourists.

8
CANCER

ASTRONOMICAL FACTS

The fourth house of the zodiac, Cancer (abbreviated Cnc), answers to both the element of water and to the moon. Among constellations, Cancer is thirty-first in size. In the Northern Hemisphere, the hazy three-pronged star grouping, which borders Canis Minor, Gemini, Hydra, Leo, and Lynx, is barely visible in the spring. Of its twenty-three visible stars there are six that stand out:

alpha star	Acubens, the claw
beta star	Altarf, the tip
gamma star	Asellus Borealis, the northern donkey
delta star	Asellus Australis, the southern donkey
zeta star	Tegmen, the cover
Cancri 44	Praesepe, the manger or the beehive

The gamma and delta stars, known jointly as the Aselli, represent the donkeys that Dionysus and Hephaestus rode during the war between the Titan and Olympian gods. The rough, cloudy star cluster called Praesepe resembles an amorphous pile of hay that fed the asses. Arabs and Greeks first called it the Asses' crib, then Karkinos, the Encircler; the Chinese called it Tseih She Ke, an exhalation of heaped corpses. The Hebrews adapted the animal imagery and called the gamma star Balaam's ass after the biblical talking beast. Praesepe has been known from ancient times, but was not fully understood until the invention of the telescope. Galileo first identified its stars in his *Sidereus Nuncius* (Star Messenger). Traditionally, the obscurity of Praesepe has been a reliable rain predictor because water vapor dims it.

The constellation stands out from its fellows in several ways. It contains two astral spectacles: zeta Cancri, a revolving quintet of stars, and Acubens, a doublet formed of white and red stars in the southern claw. The Chinese regrouped Cancer's phi and eta stars to locate Kwei, the spectre. The Hindu called Asellus Australis, the delta star, Pushya, the flower. Cancer is also marked by the summer solstice, the longest day of the year, which occurs on June 22 and links the sun sign with the change of seasons, high temperatures, and high spirits.

ASTROLOGICAL HISTORY AND TRAITS

Governing the thirty-two days between June 21 and July 22, Cancer lies between Leo and Gemini. Hindu and Chinese zodiacs pictured Cancer as a crab. Arabs knew it as Alsartan and the Syrians as Sartano, both meaning the Holder. Tibetans called it the frog. Identified as the scarab by Egyptians, who venerated the scarabaeus beetle, the figure appears to take the shape of the crab or an arm uplifting a sword, both emblems of struggle. When describing Cancer as a she-crab, astrologers saw the figure grasping a ball of fertilized eggs in a protective claw.

The sign may take its name from a crab-like motion. This sidestep occurs during the change in the sun in midsummer, when it appears to shift direction. In similar fashion, the crab is able to creep in more than one direction. In ancient times, the crab's perverse movements suggested duplicity. For these reasons, the Cancer sun sign produces the most nebulous of archetypes. In 421 B.C., comic playwright Aristophanes noted, "You cannot teach a crab to walk straight" (Bartlett 1992, 73). His words capture the exasperation of friends of Cancerians. Those born under the crab are said to perplex all who hold them dear.

A feminine symbol, Cancer governs gestation, baptism, and rebirth; in psychology, it relates to sympathy and the awakening of the conscious mind. Astrologers describe the crab as a tough, carapaced opponent who sports a resilient shell that encloses a vulnerable interior and an impressionable, sensitive spirit. In the height of a relationship, the type is fiercely loyal and sympathetic and combats the foes of a friend as though they were personal enemies. Because of an inability to confront personal differences, the Cancerian allegedly presents a crusty exterior epitomized by emotional withdrawal, seclusion, and self-exile. When troubled or thwarted, the Cancerian is said to vegetate and brood over a secret agenda of hurts and betrayals. Following these predictive patterns, Cancerians are said to make excellent parents, but intolerant or inaccessible friends. Often lucky and prosperous, they are said to suffer unforeseen reversals of fortune and health.

The Cancer archetype allies with Pisceans, Scorpios, and Taurians and is thought to enjoy limited periods of imaginative work and pleasant group activity. In childhood, traditional Cancerians display a love of fancy and imagination. They relish heroic tales of chivalry and daring and retreat from reality to fantasies of knights, warriors, magic, and the occult. The resulting inconsistent self-evaluations and moodiness produce a convoluted person- ality, which dismays family and teachers. Hampered by a wishy-washy character and poor judgment in selecting associates, Cancerians are said to slip into corrupt lifestyles and shift their opinions and loyalties to suit their needs. Teenage Cancerians may devote themselves to morbid self-castiga- tion and fear family and social gatherings. Self-conscious and desperate for love, they force themselves into renewed efforts at friend-making. As an antidote to foiled relationships, they are said to adopt outrageous poses— suicidal, psychotic, rebellious, or swaggering and delinquent. When swamped by unmanageable emotions, the retreating crab sinks into re- morse, bitter reflection, gloom, and psychosomatic ills. If this pattern persists, astral healers claim that the sufferer may trigger a life-threatening disease and premature death.

Traditionally, the crab is a conscientious laborer, sailor, hotelier, and shopkeeper, also, a sensitive teacher, nanny, or nurse. As a manager or department head, the typical Cancerian is reliable and faithful to a task, but tends to be bossy, emotional, and difficult to please. For obvious reasons, the type makes an unreliable business partner, a suspect politician, and an unstable or unfaithful mate. A longing for sentiment and romance is said to disrupt stable relationships that display too little elan and too much realism. As parents, archetypal Cancerians adore babies and take pride in thriving young, whom they tend with extra caution toward health, vitamins, and diet. On holidays, Cancerian parents are said to spend generously and insist that family and guests gather around the table for ceremonial meals.

Typified by novelists Aldous Huxley and Ernest Hemingway and play- wright George Bernard Shaw, Cancerians usually do well in writing and journalism because they are fueled by a desire for gossip, melodrama, and public opinion. Whether plunged into bizarre occultism like Huxley, sur- rounded by raffish hangers-on like Hemingway, or seated atop a self-made throne like the opinionated, self-adulating Shaw, they are thought to cherish fame, influence, power, and independence. Another aspect of Cancerian curiosity and drive are a passion for data and a desire for mystical truths, two qualities shared by cultist Mary Baker Eddy, founder of Christian Scientism; mystic Madame Helena Blavatsky, leader of the theosophy movement; and French philosopher Henri Bergson, a Nobel prize winner in literature, who believed in the *élan vital* or creative impulse.

Physically, the crab's stereotyped endowments are striking, even hand- some. Astrologers describe the typical Cancerian as long-limbed with prominent jaw and forehead and small eyes, a physiognomy found in Hemingway and Shaw. The archetype draws admirers to a generous mouth and graceful, expressive hands. As teachers or actors, Cancerians are thought to flourish in the spotlight. Their powers of concentration, memory, and absorption in history and genealogy put them at the center of attention. As orators, they perform well through dramatic gesture, compelling style, and winning enthusiasm, a quality that enabled Mary Baker Eddy to draw disciples to her quasi-religious cause.

According to astral medicine, Cancerians prefer vitamins and drugs to sensible lifestyles or to preventive maintenance of a weak stomach, breast, or uterus or an overall sickly constitution. Nonthreatening ailments such as heartburn, sluggish digestion, irregular menstrual periods, and biliousness are said to develop into life-threatening illness, especially in the mid-years. However sick they appear, Cancerians are credited with miraculous powers of recovery. However, to circumvent problems and extend periods of well-being, astral physicians advise Cancerians to observe moderation in scheduling appointments, to relax from work, and to sleep at regular hours. The best diet for the restless, fretful Cancerian includes decoctions of wintergreen, plantain, and honeysuckle along with hearty servings of cabbage, watercress, kale, and parsley to accompany a core diet consisting of rye bread, onions, eggs, milk, and cottage cheese.

SYMBOLISM IN ART AND RELIGION

Underplayed in art, the crab is often an unassuming addendum linked with deception and negative powers. To Buddhists, the icon equates with an ominous sleep of death; the Inca share the sign's foreboding, which enshrouds the waning moon and earth in darkness. A coin from Acragas, Sicily, in the late fifth century B.C. pairs the monster Scylla—a fishtailed woman— with a crab, representing the sea or perhaps suggesting the city's reputation for devious dealings. The medieval anthology *Book of Hours* features Cancer as a chubby circlet topped by three bright stars and featuring eight legs tipped with smaller stars. Two sets of stars line up parallel on the body. Associated with the gate through which humanity enters the world, the constellation bears a Roman title—the *janua inferni* (gate of hell), which opens from the Milky Way to earth.

Sometimes interpreted as a lobster or crayfish, Cancer is a minor character in a segment of the twelve labors of Hercules in Greek myth. In the story, Hera sent the crab to nip Hercules on the heel as he wrestled with the Lernaean hydra, a nine-headed serpentine monster. Seemingly insignificant during the bout, both combatants trampled the crab as they grappled for mastery. Because Hera disliked the boastful Greek demigod, she rewarded the small crab by transforming it into a constellation to symbolize tenacity and courage in the face of certain death. However, the crab keeps a safe distance from the strongman, whose constellation lies far from Cancer.

In iconography, Cancer, like Gemini, was born to duality. Because it sheds its shell, Christian apologists used the figure to represent repentance and rebirth. Both of these New Testament concepts are significant aspects of Christ's injunction to the quibbling pharisee Nicodemus, who asked how he could be saved. In the third chapter of the book of John, Christ explained salvation to him:

> Verily, verily, I say unto thee, except a man be born again, he cannot see the kingdom of God.
>
> Nicodemus saith unto him, How can a man be born when he is old? can he enter the second time into his mother's womb, and be born?
>
> Jesus answered, Verily, verily, I say unto thee, Except a man be born of water and of the spirit, he cannot enter into the kingdom of God. That which is born of the spirit is spirit. Marvel not that I said unto thee, Ye must be born again. (John 3: 3, 5–7)

Further explanation of baptism and the regeneration of the spirit reassure Nicodemus that he can avoid going to hell for his sins. This segment of the gospels launches a pivotal passage, John 3:16, which expresses why Christ was martyred and how humankind profited from his earthly death.

In classic literature, Emma Bovary, protagonist of Gustave Flaubert's *Madame Bovary*, displays the stereotypical Cancerian behaviors. Given to daydreams and sentimentality in girlhood, when she lived at a convent school, she replaced reality with the mysticism and longings of standard pre-teen escapism. However, these mental coping mechanisms remain her bulwark against adversity in adulthood. Unable to focus on mundane matters, she forces reality into her ethereal mental images. In the role of wife and mother, Emma vacillates between creative efforts, charity work, and women's magazines to relieve her yearning for the exotic. Yoked to a complacent, unexciting country physician, she resorts to adultery with Rodolphe and then Leon to provide passion and ecstasy to neutralize the tedium of home.

Emma combats the collapse of her nebulous dream world by committing suicide. Shamed by enormous debts she owes to an unscrupulous loan shark, she flits crab-fashion over the miasma in which she has enveloped herself:

Disappointment at her lack of success intensified her indignation about her outraged honor. She felt that Providence was determined to hound her, and the thought strengthened her pride. Never had she had so much respect for herself or so much scorn for others. A kind of warlike emotion was transporting her. She wanted to fight all men, spit in their faces, crush them all; and she continued to walk rapidly, pale, trembling, and furious, scanning the empty horizon with tear-filled eyes and almost relishing the hatred that was stirring her. (Flaubert 1964, 284)

As though recreating the archetype of Cancer, Flaubert follows Emma Bovary through her rationalizing into the grotesquely protracted scenes of her death from swallowing arsenic. At the end, black vomit spouts from her mouth, a suggestion of the vileness that poisoned her mind.

In government, the crab sign is said to have marked the personalities of significant leaders and rulers. Notable Cancerians include Henry VIII and politician Nelson Rockefeller. According to astral historians, Henry VIII's personal and political turmoil denied him the joys of a stable family by propelling him through six rocky marriages fraught with childlessness, betrayal, executions, and loss. His headstrong confrontation with the Catholic hierarchy ended medieval ecclesiastical power. Henry established autonomy and financial control over his own state church, but he failed in the quest for a fulfilling, companionable marriage. In bitter self-defeat, he died without realizing the consequences of his monarchy or the strength of his daughter Elizabeth, perhaps Europe's ablest queen.

Similarly wracked by events beyond his control, Cancerian Nelson Rockefeller endured a difficult childhood marred by his grandfather's severe religious fundamentalism and his father's insistence that he stop favoring his left hand and become righthanded. A lackluster pupil and athlete, Rockefeller overcame dyslexia and ran successfully for the vice presidency of the United States. His bonhomie concealed misgivings about himself and his aims. Detractors ridiculed his "edifice complex," a penchant for building large, imposing buildings, such as the World Trade Center. When his public life ended, he withdrew crab-fashion into cultural and philanthropic interests, substituting facades and money for more genuine, personal pleasures.

In science, two medical terms derive from the ancient words for the crab. In Greek, *carcinus* is the root for carcinogen and carcinogenic, the name and adjective for any substance that precipitates cancer. Hippocrates, the father of modern medicine, was the first to use the metaphor of the crab for cancer, a dread wasting disease. The Latin word *cancer* entered English in its pure form as the designation of a malignant tumor. The sun sign Cancer shares with human tumors the grasping tentacles that victimize organs by shutting off their life forces. For this reason, Cancer is one of the least popular sun signs in iconography, art, literature, and language.

LEO

ASTRONOMICAL FACTS

The fifth sign of the zodiac and the twelfth constellation in size, leo (lee' oh) is the Latin word for lion. The star pattern has also been called the Diamond of Virgo, the Scythe, and the Spring Triangle. Located between Virgo and Cancer, the constellation touches on Cancer, Coma Berenices, Crater, Hydra, Leo Minor, Sextans, Ursa Major, and Virgo. A sickle-shaped cluster with a triangular tail, Leo is one of the most clearly defined shapes in the heavens. Star-gazers find it by looking in the opposite direction from the two stars of Ursa Major that align with Polaris. The constellation is best viewed in spring in the Northern Hemisphere. Of the fifty-two stars in the group there are fifteen that deserve recognition:

alpha star	Regulus, the prince, little king, or lion's heart
beta star	Denebola, the lion's tail
gamma-one star	Algieba, the forehead
gamma-two star	Alsarfah, the (weather) changer
delta star	Zosma, the loincloth or girdle
epsilon-one star	Ras Elased Australis, the lion's head
epsilon-two star	Algenubi
zeta star	Adhafera, the curl
eta star	Aljabhah, the forehead
theta-one star	Chort, the rib
theta-two star	Coxa, the hip
kappa star	Al Minliar al Asad, the lion's nose
lambda star	Alterf, the glance
mu star	Ras Elased Borealis, the lion's head
omicron star	Alzubra, the mane

The site of this constellation is also the beginning of three Leonid meteors, which appear in February, April, and November. The last meteor shower, which reaches peak activity every thirty-three years, was spectacular in 1799, 1833, 1866, and 1966 and will return in 1999.

Ancient stargazers admired Leo. The Hindu called the beta star Uttara Phalguni (the latter bad one) and the delta star Purva Phalguni (the former bad one). Regulus, which shines bluish-white, is Leo's brightest, hottest star, which the Hindu named Mahga, the mighty. First identified by Ptolemy around 150 A.D., Regulus marks the figure's heart and augments its natural glow with light from two companion stars. The ancient Persians placed Regulus among the four Royal Stars, which included Aldebaran, Antares, and Fomalhaut.

More than the famous Regulus catches the star-gazer's eye. The second most powerful star is Denebola, a blue star dotting the lion's tail. In Hebrew tradition, it is an ominous figure—the judge or the lord who cometh. Adhafera, also called Alserpha or the funeral pyre, is a double star. The epsilon-two star, Algenubi, glows yellow at the lion's mouth. The delta star, Zosma, highlights the lion's back with a blend of violet, blue, and yellow. A second constellation, Leo Minor, was discovered in the 1600s by Johannes Hevelius, who named it the lion cub. In the Northern Hemisphere, Leo Minor emerges in April at 9:00 P.M. and is accentuated by Praecipua, its principal star.

ASTROLOGICAL HISTORY AND TRAITS

Governing the thirty-one days between July 23 and August 22, Leo is a hot, summery sign, ruled by the sun and fire and emblematic of the sultry weather that follows the summer solstice on June 22. The Chaldeans honored Leo at the height of warm weather activities. Egyptians called the constellation Knem and worshipped it because it coincided with the flooding of the Nile River, the earth's gift of another year of fertile fields and rich harvests. Tutankhamen's lavish coronation throne displays medallions in the shape of lion heads at the juncture of the seat and front legs. All four legs end in clawed feet, suggesting firm contact with the earth and suitable preparations for self-defense or attack.

In Greek mythology, the lion plays a prominent role, including pulling the chariot of Cybele, consort of Saturn, and facing off against the he-man Hercules. Because the lion attacked Cybele's horses, she hurled it to earth near Nemea. Hercules came to the city's aid and tracked the lion into its lair. As a part of twelve labors that King Eurystheus required him to perform,

Hercules strangled the beast and skinned it in one mighty pull on its pelt. Hercules adopted the lion's skin as a symbol of courage and invincibility. He wore it either over one shoulder or flowing from both shoulders. In the sky, Hercules resides far from Leo. The lion appears to steer clear of his old adversary.

Astrology allies Leo with royalty, perhaps because the lion is the king of beasts. Regardless of social station, the archetypal Leo is likely to demand respect. Leadership, pride, and self-confidence are significant aspects of the stereotyped personality, but the negative aspects include pomposity, attention seeking, and victimization of the vulnerable. A proud, lordly figure, Leo is allied with preening, worldliness, and ostentatious dress and hairstyles. In religion, the lion is said to prefer splendor and a "Te Deum" or praise anthem over quiet faith and concealed stewardship. These self-aggrandizing qualities allegedly predispose Leo to the arts, haute couture, high-church religion and evangelism, and theater.

Astrologers charge the Leo personality with indolence and insensitivity to weaklings or followers. Among flatterers, the lion is thought to glow with self-importance and to shower sycophants with favors. In conflicts with an adversary, the invincible Leo is said to become complacent while noncombatants fight the wars. When pressed into military service, the traditional lion strides to the front in a show of might. At the moment of conquest, Leo typically shows no mercy and considers captivity or execution the losing warrior's rightful penalty.

Except in company with the truly great or venerated, Leos are said to put themselves first and to expect to head every project. They seem unaware of their intimidating presence and arrogance and insist on being called by honorifics and titles. An advantage to the archetype's awe at greatness is true piety, self-denial, and respect for the Almighty. The lion allegedly makes a worthy community leader, attentive host, and stalwart conservative. Astrologers insist that, in times of political upheaval, the typical lion will follow the status quo and oppose rebels. The type's conviction and noble posture influence followers to take heart and to raise expectations of victory.

The stereotypical leonine personality has no skill in cunning or subterfuge and prefers to conduct business honorably and face-to-face. As a captain of industry, the lion is said to set the example for punctuality, resourcefulness, and pragmatism and to delegate authority by sizing up staff and assigning each to a suitable position. To avoid work and tedium, the lion manager passes hard tasks on to underlings. Staff members are said to adore the sunny, ebullient lion manager or CEO and to stroke his ego as payment for good treatment and reliable leadership. In zodiacal tradition,

Leos are outgoing, altruistic, lively, and willful and consider themselves the most important of the twelve star children. Their inclination toward sincerity and dependability makes them prime political candidates. On the down side, boldness in Leo is an illusion: the lion roars at danger in a vain show of courage.

In human relationships, the leonine personality is thought to harmonize with Sagittarius and Aries, with whom the lion establishes a reciprocal companionship. As friends, Leos gather a pack of acquaintances, but few bosom pals. When picking a mate, Leos are said to pass through numerous affairs and live-in attachments before selecting lifetime companions. Misguided affection may result in faulty mate selection, but the lion heals rapidly from a broken heart by asserting a strong trust in the future. In moments of despondency, the lion is said to quell doubt by renewing faith in self.

In astrological handbooks, Leo is stereotyped as a swift-moving target who avoids a chummy domestic scene and keeps the mate slightly off-base by demanding scrupulous cleaning and order. Often haughty and peevish to adults, the lion caves in to children's demands and fosters fun and play. To guests, the Leo parent is said to show off handiwork, report cards, and trophies and to summon the family to perform. Content among young children, Leo enjoys being looked up to; however, parent-child conflict in the teen years lessens the lion's contentment.

In astral medicine, Leo, like Taurus, enjoys excellent health and exercises to the limits of endurance, especially in bright, sunny climates. Physically, the lion frame is generalized as sturdy with a regal posture and imposing expression. A full-bodied shape with a commanding cranium, wide trunk, and narrow flanks, the archetype tends toward silken hair, rosy complexion, and prominent eyes. Dark, dank rooms and oppressive climates are anathema to the lion, who restores energy and well-being in sunlight. Apart from consistent robustness, in rare instances of lameness or disease, the lion moves to the other extreme into collapse. Catastrophic illness, particularly in old age, is said to derive from impaired circulation or heart disease. To stave off leg cramps, high blood pressure, seizures, back pain, palpitations, and lung infection, astral healers advise the health-conscious Leo to take supplements of magnesium phosphate and to consume bran, oats, and peas; salads of lettuce, sorrel, dill, and fennel; and citrus fruit, cocoa, and mint-flavored snacks.

As an example of the stereotypical Leo at his best, Joseph Merrick, England's freakish "Elephant Man," suffered scrofula, a disease that bent his frame, contorted his skull and right hand, and covered his body in warty, globular mounds of skin. When he grew too awkward to roll cigars at a local factory, he took to the streets as a glove peddler. While recuperating from surgery that removed pendulous flesh from his head, he learned to read and memorized passages of the Bible and the Book of Common Prayer.

Depicted in a 1980 black-and-white film, *The Elephant Man*, Merrick survived capture by a cruel barker, who displayed his find to gawkers for a penny admission. After Sir Frederick Treves rescued Merrick from the sideshow, he thrived under the sympathetic staff of the Medical School of London Hospital. Publicity generated by curious newsmen brought him high-ranking friends, including royalty, nobles, and actresses. On rare outings, Merrick dressed with care to attend a play and accepted an invitation to the country home of Lady Knightley. Until his death, Merrick maintained dignity and decorum, expressing himself courteously and generously to his many admirers and supporters, some of whom he received at his hospital room.

SYMBOLISM IN ART AND RELIGION

Like Joseph Merrick in the film, Leo in art tends to symbolize strength, creativity, magnanimity, and vigor, but other possibilities crop up across world cultures. Sumerian, Roman, and Japanese iconography characterizes the lion as a kingly beast. Conversely, in Taoism, the lion represents emptiness. In Mycenaean, Phrygian, Spartan, and Lycian art, the lion was paired with the virgin as a balance of weak with strong. The Christian alliance of the lion and lamb creates the same complements, which replicate the duality of Gemini and of the Chinese figures of yin and yang. In Buddhism, the lion represents zeal, courage, and spirituality; to the Hindu, the lion is the power of the word. Early Hebraic art characterized the lion as cruelty. In contrast, Muslims saw the beast as protective. In medieval jewelry, seal rings, shields, door plaques, entrance figurines, and heraldry, the figure represents splendor, warmth, majesty, and might.

The lion appears in Egyptian symbolism as Sekhmet, a lion-headed female deity representing the scirocco, the hot, murderous desert wind that quickly depletes the body of moisture. Armed with fire-tipped arrows, she shot her victims through the heart. The male equivalent of Sekhmet was Re, the sun god, the giver of strength to desert nomads and antidote to the death-dealing goddess. Because the Nile River was crucial to Egypt's agricultural autonomy, Leo symbolized the part of the year in which the waters overflowed their banks and bestowed rich sediment on the loose, sandy soil. For this benefit, Egyptians were willing to welcome the season, despite its liabilities.

In art, Leo is often pictured rampant with claws extended and teeth exposed in a snarl. A notable example is still visible in the Lion Gate at Mycenae, where paired lions stand atop the lintel. In Sarnath, India, a third-century B.C. monolith features three composed lions sitting on the finial. Following a Hittite political alliance of 1300 B.C., sculptors carved suppliant lions stretched out submissively beneath the feet of the winged gods of the sun and moon. The allegorical pose stresses the subservience of earthly strength to cosmic power. King Ashurbanipal of Babylonia commissioned two unusual poses: a male lion transfixed with an arrow to the heart and vomiting blood and the lion's mate, riddled with darts that sever her spinal cord, leaving her to drag stiff hind legs.

In a typical stylized pose, the Greek lion stands open-mouthed with tongue extended. Its elongated tail curls up and out to a shaggy tip that matches the sun-rayed circular mane in splendor and panache. Golden-brown or reddish-gold, the beast displays the notable characteristics of the sun. As king of beasts, a lion fantasy figure in crown and a rudimentary cape dominates tapestries and mosaics. A tyrannic ruler, the male lion raises a scepter over lesser animals, which grovel at his throne.

A departure from the lion as head of the animal kingdom recurs in depictions of Hercules, who usually bears a club in one hand and stands glowering with the fierce lion skin draped over torso and shoulder. Commodus, son and successor of Marcus Aurelius, commissioned a statue of himself in a similar pose. In one hand he raises a club; about his neck are tied the forepaws of the lion skin, which drapes down his back. In the rock-relief in Commagene near the Euphrates river, Antiochus I, a minor Persian king, shakes hands with Mithras. The two wear stylized dress: Antiochus on the left in star-sprinkled tunic and mitre, Mithras on the right dressed in Herculean lion skin. Both men reflect strength in their set expressions, burly arms, rippling pectoral muscles, and stocky, trunklike legs. A mosaic from Hippo Regius in the third century A.D., now housed in Bone, Algeria, departs from mythology and depicts the lion realistically as one of the fierce beasts being herded into a circle. Warriors, who conceal the net, intend to capture a male and female lion and three leopards. The shrinking open field suggests the uncivilized environs, which were gradually falling to Roman imperialism.

In 1295, Ibn Bakhtishu, court physician of the Caliph of Baghdad, produced an ornate bestiary, the *Manafi al-Hayawan* (The Uses of Animals). Among real and imaginary beasts, he featured a lion and lioness seated among native grasses, flowers, and birds. The pose contrasts the curling mane of the male with his mate's feathered mane. Both flaunt red tongues and spiked teeth, but the commentary assures the reader, "He is quieted by hearing a sweet musical voice; when he bathes himself he becomes so gentle that a child might sit on him and lead him everywhere" (Stewart 1967, 133).

In literature, Leo appears in numerous fables. Aesop featured the animal in female form in "The Lioness." She ridiculed claimants of the most whelps per birth by claiming that she bore only three sons, but each was a thoroughbred. In "The Fox and the Lion," Leo tolerates a fox, which grows careless in the presence of the stronger beast. In "The Lion, the Mouse, and the Fox," Leo emotes before a fox claiming that the mouse has taken liberties in running over his mane and ears and in disturbing his nap. The moral declares, "Little liberties are great offenses" (Aesop 1986, n. p.). The most opportunistic of Aesop's literary lions stars in "The Lion and the Three Bulls," in which he conquers a trio of attackers by separating them and overpowering them one by one.

In singular examples, Aesop exhibits a change of heart in the redoubtable Leo. While battling a boar in "The Lion and the Boar," the lion joins the boar in a temporary halt to catch their breath. Panting in unison, they discover that vultures await the loser of the battle. United against predators, the lion and boar agree that it's better to patch up their quarrel than to make dinner for vultures. A greater humbling of a lion occurs in "The Lion and the Mouse." In the beginning of the fable, the lion scoffs at the mouse for offering to save his life if danger threatens. When hunters snare the lion and tie him down, the mouse proves true to his word by gnawing the ropes and releasing him. The small animal exults, "You ridiculed the idea of my ever being able to help you, not expecting to receive from me any repayment of your favor; but now you know that it is possible for even a mouse to confer benefits on a lion" (Aesop 1986, n. p.).

A perversion of romance occurred in Greek myths to form the chimera and sphinx, two monsters that evolved from the amalgamation of a lion with other beasts. The former was a tripartite monster joining a goat's head and serpent's tail to a lion's body and limbs. A bronze figure of the beast, housed in the Archeological Museum in Florence, Italy, dates to the fourth century B.C. The statue poses a stylized lion with mouth open in a roar and its body seated on thin haunches that ripple powerfully. Additions of the goat's head and serpentine tail add little to the natural fierceness of the supple, muscular lion.

The second compound monster, the sphinx, derived its body from the lioness, its head from a human female, and wings from the eagle. The union of these unlikely parts symbolizes the complexity and allure of woman. In a similar visual conundrum, the griffin (or gryphon) joined the lion with an eagle, a blend of intelligence and strength. The resulting fierce flying beast bore Apollo, the sun god, on its back. The synergy of rider and mount is forecast in the derivation of *Apollo*, which means "from the bowels of the lion." In the legend of Alexander the Great's attempt to mount the griffin and fly away from earth, the monster symbolizes the Greek concept of *hubris* or overweening arrogance, the deadliest of sins.

Reinterpreted in Christian lore, in Revelation 4:7, the lion joined the calf, eagle, and man in guarding God's throne. In church symbolism drawn from *Physiologus*, an early illustrative text produced in Alexandria in the second century, the allegorical lion possessed the strength required of the Christian in defying temptation. Endowed with unusual idiosyncrasies, the Christianized lion is capable of sweeping its tracks with its tail and sleeping with eyes open, always alert for evil. A bizarre trait is its failure to breathe at birth. Christian apologists concocted this story to parallel Christ's resurrection: after three days of lying supine beside the lioness, the cub responds to its father's breath, which calls it to life as God called Christ from the tomb.

During the Middle Ages, a paradox entered lion lore. In the meeting of the lion and the maiden, she easily pacified the beast. Christian mythographers declared that Virgo, the unsullied maiden, could overpower Leo by the strength of her virtue. Thus, the Medieval myth asserts the civilizing force of purity over brutality. In the English Renaissance, a secular love plot that serves William Shakespeare's *A Midsummer Night's Dream* is the tale of Pyramus and Thisbe. The villain of the piece is a lion, which attacks Thisbe, but runs away, leaving behind her blood-stained scarf. Pyramus is so grief-stricken by the upheaval and blood that he assumes that Thisbe is dead and commits suicide. His love returns and, mourning Pyramus, pierces her breast with his sword. Like Romeo grieving for Juliet, the lion's haste and aggression precipitates a double tragedy.

A born achiever among lion sun signs, Julia Child demonstrates the bold, unself-conscious display of talent and bravura onstage cooking. After studying French cookery and mastering the art of sauces, pastry, and grand entrees, she widened her following through television demonstrations, popular cook books, and two television series, "The French Chef" and "Dinner at Julia's." A wholesome, upbeat speaker, she faced the camera with the same confidence she imparted to budding gourmet cooks. Her step-by-step preparations won audiences nationwide and gave her the confidence to instruct First Lady Rosalyn Carter on methods of updating the White House menu. Ever the energetic optimist in the kitchen, she has influenced the American palate for four decades.

10

VIRGO

ASTRONOMICAL FACTS

Often mistakenly translated as a strict biological term for virgin, Virgo is the Latin word for maiden or unmarried woman. Abbreviated Vir, it is a complex sidereal pattern sometimes called the Diamond, the Spring Triangle, and the Y. The second largest constellation, Virgo is composed of a cluster of hundreds of galaxies. In the mid-latitudes of the Northern Hemisphere, it lies east of Leo and borders Boötes, Coma Berenices, Corvus, Crater, Hydra, Leo, Libra, and Serpens. Of the fifty-eight stars in the group there are sixteen featured heavenly bodies:

alpha-one star	Spica, the spike (of wheat)
alpha-two star	Azimech, the branch
beta-one star	Alaraph
beta-two star	Zavijah, the corner
gamma-one star	Arich
gamma-two star	Porrima, the Roman goddess of childbirth
gamma-three star	Kaphir, the suppliant
delta-one star	Alawwa, the barker
delta-two star	Minelauva
epsilon star	Almureddin, the ruler, or Vindemiatrix, the vine-harvester
zeta star	Heze
eta star	Zaniah
iota star	Syrma, the train
kappa star	Alghafr, the covering
lambda star	Khambalia
mu star	Rijl al Awwa

An embodiment of justice, Virgo stands west of Libra, the balance beam on which judgment is weighed.

In the evening late in May, Virgo is barely visible above the southern horizon. Much of the constellation is too dim to be seen without a telescope. Also called Arista or the grain harvest, Spica is a hot blue-white binary star, which the Hindu named Citra, or the bright one. The Chinese grouped Spica with Heze to complete Kio, a constellation known as the horn or spike. They also regrouped the kappa and iota stars to make Kang, the neck. Mentioned by Eratosthenes around 850 B.C., Spica, stands out from the 160 smaller visible stars, including seven elliptical and four spiral galaxies. From ancient times, Spica has served as a significant navigational aid. An offshoot, the Virgo Cluster, appears east of Vindemiatrix near Coma Berenices, an area called the Realm of the Nebulae, which contains the Sombrero Galaxy.

Observers have been fascinated with Virgo's spectacular makeup, particularly the double star, Porrima. At the base of the head glows a lemony star, Zavijah, the beta-two star, which confirmed one of Albert Einstein's theories during a solar eclipse on September 21, 1922. Vindemiatrix, the epsilon star, was originally masculine—Vindemiator, an eponym of the grape-gatherer Ampelus, whom Dionysus honored as a bright maize star on Virgo's northern wing after the boy tripped and broke his neck. The eta star, Zaniah, is a variable star located on the maiden's southern wing. Kaphir, the gamma star, is a white binary variable star on the maiden's left forearm; Kaphir's complement, Khambalia, is a minor star that identifies the maiden's left foot.

Virgo hosts three spring meteor showers, one in late March and two in April. Also, the fall equinox occurs in Virgo. The constellation contains eleven Messier objects or small heavenly bodies too indistinct to be described (second only to Sagittarius, with fourteen), which French astronomer Charles Messier numbered in 1784. At Virgo's center is the strongest astral radio signal, which is thought to be a high-energy gas stream emanating from a huge black hole. Northwest of gamma Virginis beams the brightest quasi-stellar star, commonly known as a quasar. Dutch-born American astronomer Maarten Schmidt studied the quasar from the California Institute of Technology in 1963 to determine variances in wavelengths. He concluded that the changes in intensity indicate great distance and give credence to the Big Bang theory of creation.

ASTROLOGICAL HISTORY AND TRAITS

Governing the thirty-one days between August 23 and September 22, Virgo is the sixth sign of the zodiac and one of the oldest. An earth sign, it is the only astrological entity symbolized entirely by a passive, unadorned human figure. The companion sign, Aquarius, pours from a water ewer, but Virgo has no assigned task. Ptolemy associated the constellation's outstretched hand with a sheaf of wheat. Babylonians and Assyrians pictured Virgo as the goddess Ishtar, a love deity who, like the Egyptian Isis, sought her mate Tammuz beyond the seven gates of the underworld. While she navigated the dark path, the earth was shrouded in thick night. When Ishtar returned to earth with her husband, she restored the planet to light and warmth. Hebrews, Arabs, and Greeks called Virgo by the same designation, which is Bethulah in Hebrew, Adarah in Arabic, and Parthenos in Greek. The poet Aratus declared that Virgo was Dike, daughter of Zeus and Themis, an abstract figure who dispensed justice. Virgo may also represent the Greek goddess Demeter and the Roman Ceres, goddesses of grain and bounteous harvests.

For good reason, Christian symbolists exalted this constellation. They pictured Virgo with wings, thus merging the maiden with Mercury, the Roman messenger of the gods and ruler of the constellation. Later interpretation altered the figure to the Virgin Mary holding the Christ Child. According to the *Zend Avesta* of the prophet Zoroaster, Hebrews were awaiting a new star to signify the birth of the messiah whom the Old Testament prophet Isaiah had foretold. The sidereal phenomenon coincided with the birth of Jesus of Nazareth, whom the Persian member of the magi sought as the Desired of All Nations. The star, which outshone the morning star, was sanctified as the Star of Bethlehem.

Grounded in the common sphere, the astrological archetype of Virgo is a practical, sensible personality who gets along well with the elderly and thrives in useful jobs in libraries, newsrooms, printshops, garages, surgical wards, or pharmacies. Wise and prudent, the type is said to work diligently and is rarely found wanting, but tends toward a shrewdness that looks out for self before others. Allegedly, Virgoans are excellent artisans who tolerate meticulous chores such as clerical tasks, library maintenance, lower-level management, and minor medical jobs. Negative aspects of Virgoans include a picayune insistence on details, fault-finding, and trivia. Orderly and steady, they are thought to make excellent soldiers, researchers, anthropologists, and factory workers, but are incapable of leadership or of deviating from narrow rules, regimens, and expectations.

According to astrologers, a penchant for snappish criticism, discrimination, good taste, and exactitude makes Virgoans excellent museum curators, book editors and proofreaders, and theater critics, but difficult friends and mates. Because of the personality's alleged jealousy, irritability, and impatience, Virgo is often depicted as an old maid. Love comes rarely to Virgoans, usually with a Taurus or Capricorn. Traditionally, the Virgo marriage is grounded in money, prestige, and family ties. A stable relationship with Virgo requires a generous mate because Virgoans withhold personal funds while spending from a mate's purse for selfish luxuries. Although parenthood is well ordered and productive, marriage often founders or proves disappointing because of the type's rigid demands and expectations. On the rebound from a failed relationship, true Virgoans seek soul-numbing work, often jeopardizing health. They are said to be charitable to strangers and philanthropic foundations, but disdain playful affection, sexual entanglements, and public displays of love or praise. Likewise, they avoid children and family get-togethers and stick to themselves.

In matters of religion, Virgoans are said to temper their responses and labor to follow precise sectarian ritual or to attain sainthood. A tendency toward self-righteousness makes them puritanic, unpleasant, often overbearing. Other detractions from the archetype are pride and insensitivity. As keepers of the purse, they excel at accounting and insurance, purchase wisely, and provide for their own retirement to prevent reliance on others. The most rigid Virgoans supposedly pattern their declining years after religious hermits and live celibate in a chaste dormitory with little adornment and only a housecat for company.

Traditionally, a Virgo is strikingly handsome and usually neatly dressed but avoids haute couture in favor of unassuming attire. In place of ostentation, the fussy Virgo typically stocks up on clothing that will last a lifetime. Facial expression and gestures tend toward the grave and sober. Smiles often look pasted on as a show of social conformity rather than genuine welcome. Handshakes may be cold and perfunctory. The voice tends to be shrill, but the words witty and well-chosen.

According to astral medicine, the Virgoan is muscular, resilient, and over-cautious about taking vitamins, exercising, and scheduling immunization and annual checkups. The maiden's day-to-day health leans toward the robust, a trait that reduces Virgo's compassion for invalids. For this reason, the Virgo nurse or physical therapist is likely to be pinch-lipped and disapproving of frail patients or malingerers. The Virgoan typically weakens in the lungs and breathing passages with diseases ranging from rhinitis to pneumonia and pleurisy. A precautionary measure is a supplement of potassium sulphate and herbal cures compounded from valerian and motherwort. According to tradition, the Virgoan profits from a diet of tomato and dandelion salad, dressings featuring celery and rosemary, parsnips or beets, citrus fruits, and apples. As a food handler, the type is said to demand absolute cleanliness and quality, yet shows little concern for elegance and presentation. On the positive side, Virgoans arise early and greet the day with energy and enthusiasm. However, rather than spend the best hours of the day with others, they feel secure in rutted routines, whether repetitive jobs or absorption in housework.

SYMBOLISM IN ART AND RELIGION

Virgo supplied classic Mediterranean art with one of its most enduring feminine figures. The maiden is often pursued by lovers Ares, Adonis, and Hephaestus and by her human admirer, the sculptor Pygmalion, who prayed that Aphrodite would transform his statue of Galatea into a real maiden. The Greeks honored the virgin for eight centuries. A decoration painted in an Aeginan temple around 480 B.C. pictured a stylized smiling maiden dressed in fluted, calf-length dress and stole. The artist armed her with a round shield, spear, and crested helmet; on her breast was a bronze or gold medallion shaped like the head of Medusa, the snaky-haired gorgon killed by Theseus.

In the goddess's own city, Athenians exalted Athena Parthenos (the Maiden) in the design and ornamentation of the Parthenon, the focal temple that Pericles built in 480 B.C. He placed the monument on the Acropolis, Athens's citadel, to commemorate the overthrow of Persian invaders, who burned his first hill monument. In glory, the goddess, carved from gold and ivory, towered over the temple's interior. Her lustrous gray eyes, made of precious stones, drew visitors to an embodiment of godly wisdom. To the original complex Pericles added a huge bronze statue of Athena in a martial pose—the maiden's alter ego, who wears a tall crested helmet and grasps a spear. Her presence turned the hill into the sacred heart of Athens, which demure caryatids (columns shaped like women) guarded along the Maiden's Porch. Suppliants hailed Athena as *Pallas Athene Parthenos Gorgo Epekoos* (Maiden Athena, Virgin, Terrible, Hearkening-to-Prayer). A nurturer of divine wisdom and skill, in her incarnation as *athene ergane* (Athena the worker), she sheltered smithies, weavers, cobblers, seamstresses, potters, carpenters, cooks, masons, and millers. In addition to craftsmen, she answered to *athene promachos* (front-line Athena) and guided military strategists, professors, philosophers, and statesmen.

The Parthenon embellishes the myth of Athena by positioning her among honored deities. The eastern gable grouped the Olympian gods so that Athena stood alongside Zeus and Hera, the king and queen of heaven. Side walls expressed Athena's birth as a full-grown maiden springing from

Zeus's brain. The frieze that capped the Parthenon contained the Pan-athenaic Procession, a quadrennial event honoring the goddess. The original resides in the British Museum among the much contested Elgin Marbles, which Greece has unsuccessfully tried to reclaim for over a century.

Although the Parthenon's Athena did not survive, miniatures preserve its stately pose and magnanimous gesture. The work of Pheidias, the renowned sculptor who lived from 490 to 430 B.C., the statue blends the magnificence of Greek engineering with elegant craftsmanship. An emblem of state and imperial power, the majestic female torso and graceful limbs served as models to Mediterranean artisans. In a fifth-century relief in Tarentum, Italy, she stands among the other eleven Olympian deities. The artist charac-terized her tie to intelligence with a common symbol, the owl, which appears on the Athenian tetradrachma, worth four drachmas. Her head and shoulders adorned coins of Alexander's farflung empire and on monies in Macedonia, Thrace, Pergamum, Cappadocia, Syria, Egypt, Syracusa, and India.

A multiple pose of maidens was common in the depiction of a trio of goddesses—sisters Aglaia or splendor, Thalia or abundance, and Euphro-syne or jollity, known as the Three Graces. Nubile and demure, the curly-haired trio is usually pictured nude, the center female facing the background with two flanking sisters looking ahead. Their rounded arms with extended hands and fingers intertwine in perpetual unity and felicity. The sheen of their bodies and the understated rosiness of their complexions suggest health and the promise of passion.

Athena also prefigured the Roman images of Roma, Britannia, Colum-bia, and Minerva. In an early Roman sculpture, Minerva stood in classic drapery ringed about the shoulders with Medusa's snakes. To the Byzantine world, she was Saint Sophia or *Hagia Sophia*, the jewel of a shrine in Constantinople. The cult of the virgin permeates Roman religion. Romans honored Rhea Silvia, the undefiled mother of Romulus and Remus, by appointing thirty Vestal Virgins to tend the sacred flame of their national hearth. In rotation, ten beginners studied the rituals, ten performed them, and the oldest ten taught the next generation of Vestals then retired from service. Virginity was so rigorously enforced that any Vestal caught touch-ing or consorting with a man was buried alive. The Vestal's power was absolute; her glance toward a condemned prisoner could set him free. Vestals advised Roman authorities, often writing letters and interceding with the imperial court.

The Christianization of the Parthenon posed little problem to Church dogmatists: they transformed Athena into the Virgin Mary and honored her in Greek as *Mater Theou Parthenos Athenaia Gorgo Epekoos* (Mother of God, Virgin Athenian One, Terrible, Hearkening-to-Prayer). When pictured with scallops, oysters, and other bivalves in Pompeian frescoes and in Sandro Botticelli's *The Birth of Venus*, one of the treasures of Florence's Uffizi Gallery, the virginal quality of the maiden is reflected by the two-part shell, a vulvar image. The pearl hidden inside the clasped shells represents both the untried virginity of the maiden and the infant Christ, described in Matthew 13:46 as the "pearl of great price." On balance, water imagery emphasizes sexuality and fecundity, perhaps an allusion to scientific beliefs that all life sprang spontaneously and asexually from the sea.

Recast as the mother of Christ, in early Christian art, the figure of the unstained maiden took on a central significance in statuary, murals, paintings, and iconography. A union of the divine with the earthly, she is the untouchable, untouched female chosen to mother and suckle the son of God. Symbolized by the white rose, which offsets its passion-rich fragrance by the absence of color, Mary equates with the queen of flowers, elevated in liturgy to the thornless rose or spotless rose. The conventions of mariology feature her in a shapeless white or red tunic or stola, which may be loosely belted, but generally gives no definite outline of breasts or hips. Over her head and shoulders descends the palla, usually a deep blue as a sign of faithfulness, loyalty, spirituality, and celestial leanings. When augmented with ears of grain, the garment ties Mary to Demeter and Ceres, the ancient goddess of fertility. An accompanying unicorn symbolizes the uniqueness of the virgin. Its horn takes on the mystical quality of a godly phallus.

The virgin's girlish pose calls for downcast eyes and hands folded in her lap or clasping a lily, symbol of purity, abstinence, and virginity. When Mary holds the infant Christ, she concentrates on him to the exclusion of all other distractions and seems to anchor him between her arms to protect him from the secular world. In song, chant, and prayer, worshippers honor her constancy and maternity by referring to her as "Mary, ever virgin," a paradox that singles out the only human female worthy to produce a deity.

In Greek mythology, virginity is a defining quality in commentary on three female figures—the huntress Artemis, Persephone before her abduction into the underworld, and Themis, mother of Justice. In Apollonius's *Argonautica*, he characterizes Hera as the long-suffering wife of Zeus, the philandering Olympian whose taste runs to nubile maidens. In a lengthy speech to Thetis, Achilles's mother, Hera carps about Zeus's pursuit of Themis:

I have brought you up and cherished you beyond all other goddesses who dwell in the sea, because you were not wanton enough to lie in

> Zeus' bed though he desired you—his mind is always on such things,
> whether it be immortals or mortals he wants to sleep with! . . . [T]he
> revered Themis told him in detail how you were fated to bear a son
> greater than his father; though he was still keen, he left you alone out
> of fear that some rival would rule over the immortals and so that he
> could preserve his power for ever. (Apollonius 1995, 117)

Apollonius's verse preserves a centuries-old pattern of power and lust, the
motivating factors that caused the Trojan War and, in general, typified
male-female relationships until the advent of democracy and women's
suffrage.

The chastity motif also dominates accounts of the Amazons and their
bellicose leader, Penthesilea. Their matriarchy stood aloof from the hetero-
sexual world and used men briefly as procreators. An aggressive anomaly
in a male-centered culture that devalued women and denied them autonomy
and citizenship, the Amazons rose above patriarchy and lived like men, even
sending troops to fight during the Trojan War. Diodorus Siculus, a Greek
historian, describes their conquests in Egypt and the eastern end of the
Mediterranean. Counter to the Amazons was the disdainful Daphne, an
anti-male nymph whose ability to love Cupid froze with a single lead-tipped
arrow loosed from his bow. To elude the embrace of Apollo, she fled through
the forest. Gaea, the earth mother, heard her cry and transformed her into a
laurel tree. Forever afterward, the lovesick Apollo wreathed his head with
one of her boughs.

A wistful strand of virgin lore comes from the story of Orpheus, the singer
and poet. Upon his marriage to the chaste Eurydice, he walked with her in
the fields, where a serpent struck her heel and instantly killed her. Overcome
by mourning, Orpheus wandered the wild calling her name and weeping.
He journeyed to the underworld and sang so plaintively before Pluto that
the god allowed Eurydice to return to earth. The only stipulation was a
command that Orpheus not look back on his bride's shade until she was
restored to flesh. On the return trip, he breathed fresh air at the entrance to
Hades and turned to embrace his wife. With her foot still on the infernal
path, she slipped from his grasp and evaporated in his embrace. The myth
appealed to composers Christoph Gluck, Josef Haydn, and Claudio Mon-
teverdi, who wrote operas about it, and to Pieter Brueghel, Peter Paul
Rubens, Giovanni Tiepolo, and Jacopo Tintoretto, who painted it.

According to the zodiacal archetype, the literary Virgo echoes Orpheus's
frenzy for work, particularly while recovering from loss or failed love.
Charles Dickens exemplified the driven Virgoan writer by publishing at a

killing pace and by creating a mirror image of his Virgoan nature in David Copperfield, who lives with his aunt and works as a clerk to finance both his aunt's failed household and his own doomed marriage. His cameos of Victorians provide a glimpse of his age and its virtues and shortcomings. Dickens's failure to create normal, realistic characters is typical of a Virgoan. His most striking personae are figures drawn to excess, for example, Ebenezer Scrooge's miserliness, Dora's inability to keep house, Miss Havisham's consuming hatred of men, Uriah Heep's oily subservience, and Mr. Micawber's unfailing generosity in spite of penury. Although a skilled social critic himself, Dickens resented literary criticism, which frequently offered useful tips on improving his novels. His marriage failed from his intense faultfinding against his wife, who resembled his mother in lifestyle and weaknesses.

A worthy Virgoan from American art, Anna Mary Robertson Moses inadvertently created a niche for herself in the field of abstract painting while adapting to physical signs of age. A model of the sun sign's traits of perseverance, hard work, and attention to detail, Moses turned hardship to good advantage after her hands became too gnarled with arthritis to hold an embroidery needle. She continued creating primitive scenes from her girlhood in the country by painting them on glass, canvas, and Masonite board at the rate of one or two a day. Best known of her 1,000 canvases are "Applebutter Making," "Taking in Laundry," "The Quilting Bee," "The Night Before Christmas," "Williamstown in Winter," "Over the River to Grandma's House," "The First Skating," and "Bringing in the Maple Sugar." The sobriquet "Grandma Moses" fit her engaging personality and memorable recreations of a simpler time in American history when responsibilities, tasks, and homemade pastimes occupied rural folk. A workaholic farm wife turned creative genius, she advanced New England folk craft into the art world's treasure.

LIBRA

ASTRONOMICAL FACTS

Named in Latin for the scales used for weighing dry or solid substances, Libra (abbreviated Lib), is the seventh sign and the only inanimate object in the zodiac. Bordering Hydra, Lupus, Opiuchus, Scorpius, Serpens, and Virgo, Libra is an unassuming constellation composed of frail lights scarcely visible to the unaided eye. Its shape begins with an irregular triangle at the top and trails two uneven lines below. Of the thirty-five stars in the group, there are eight that stand out:

alpha-one star	Kiffa Australis, the scale's southern tray
alpha-two star	Zuben Elgenubi, the southern claw
beta-one star	Kiffa Borealis, the scale's northern tray
beta-two star	Zuben Elschemali, the northern claw
gamma star	Zuben Elakrab, the war price
delta star	Zuben Elakribi
lambda star	Zuben Hakrabi
sigma star	Brachium, the arm

The twenty-ninth constellation in size, Libra hosts a meteor shower in early June. It sports two stars that the Arabs called Aljubana, the claws. The Chinese named them Ti or the bottom; the Hindu saw them as Visakha or branched. The only celestial cluster containing a green star, Libra features a faint duo in its alpha star, a greenish duo in its beta star, and a third binary in the delta star. A pale emerald star on the northern pan, the beta-two star, is also known as the full price. Its balance, Zuben Elgenubi, is a double star blending light gray with pale yellow, the colors visible in the southern pan. This pairing was once called the insufficient price.

ASTROLOGICAL HISTORY AND TRAITS

Governing the thirty-one days from September 23 to October 23, Libra is modeled on a mundane market measuring device, but serves as a mystic symbol of equity. The Hebrews called it Mozanaim or the weighing scales. The Arabs knew it as Alzubena, the purchase, a figure lifting scales in one hand and a lamb in the other. Coptic lore referred to Libra as Lambadia, the gracious branch. Unlike these beneficent images, the Greek designation pictured the constellation as Chelae, the Claws.

In Roman times, Libra took its current name from the balance beam scale, a bilateral device that suspends two pans from a central pivot. The amount to be measured sat on one pan while the user added weights to the opposite pan until the two sides hung equidistant from the base. By counting up the weights required to achieve a balance, the user computed the weight of the other substance. The English abbreviation for pound, *lb.*, evolved from *libra* but applied to a unit of weight rather than the device itself. The English word *pound* springs from *pondus*, the name of the weight piled into the empty pan.

Overall, the concept of balance refers to the separation of daylight and darkness at the autumnal equinox, which in ancient times passed through Libra. Because Libra is adjacent to Virgo, the designation may allude to the powers of Astraea, goddess of justice. Mythology connects her to the myth of the ages of man. After the demise of the blissful gold and silver ages, she removed justice from the earth, leaving humankind to bestial, violent humanity.

The zodiacal sign is ruled by the air and by Venus, Roman divinity of love and beauty. Lacking the strength of the Sun in its domain, Libra, the consummate diplomat and statesman, is said to avoid taking the initiative and to opt for harmony rather than confrontation. According to astrologers, Librans follow rules and statutes and have an inborn distaste for quarreling or fighting. The key to the sign's appeal is an inherent trustworthiness and an absence of prejudice or bias. An affable, sociable group, Librans abhor unfairness and encourage broad-mindedness, forgiveness, and logical settlements of disputes. Traditionally, they make excellent harbor tenders, postal and customs officials, and minor government assistants.

Gracious, charming, and hospitable, the archetype has become a favored sun sign. The typical Libran is said to adore homey touches and to invest in art for art's sake. Safe and companionable, Librans are stereotyped as fuddy-duddies who lack Leo's drama, Virgo's grace, and Aries's verve. Because Librans are incapable of hard-heartedness and dogmatism, they earn scorn for being pliant or malleable. In the military, their fluidity allows them to negotiate for the sake of the common good. Many outstanding Librans are poets, fiction writers, composers, couturiers, art collectors and appraisers, agents, buyers, and portrait artists.

As lovers, Librans bear a reputation for naivete and sincerity. Bereft when alone, they demand a mate, even a so-so lover of questionable fidelity and suspect character. Strong Libran marriages are typically long-lived and their relationships tender. According to zodiacal tradition, they combine well with Gemini or Aquarius personalities and go out of their way to please mates, both domestically and sexually. The Libran housekeeper allegedly pursues a sensible schedule and oversees even the smallest task. It is rare that the Libran rips out a stitch or retypes a letter, for "do it right the first time" is ingrained in the Libran personality.

The typical Libran prospers as householder and parent, even though some incline toward self-sacrifice in serving the needs and wishes of children, or, in the extreme, toward martyrdom. The Libran parent is said to adore an attractive child and tends to parade bright or talented offspring like prize show animals. In family discussions, the archetype squelches sharp retorts and muffles complaints to keep a modicum of peace, but yields to any who have a comment, no matter how out of place or ill-founded.

In the arts and sciences, the stereotype is said to yearn for music and beauty and fares well in research. In the classroom or in the workplace, the Libran impresses teachers and co-workers with flashes of brilliance, while rejecting a regular schedule of studies or a steady output of work. In worship, the Libran allegedly chooses humility, restraint, and serenity over sectarian wrangling, schisms, or cults. As priests, missionaries, or rabbis, the type serves a congregation well by refraining from hurtful criticisms and by stressing the value of all lifestyles. As speakers, they choose stout, dependable maxims over picky doctrine, lengthy tirades, or arcane philosophies, such as Zen or orthodox Judaism.

The down side of Libra comes from stern Saturn, the self-righteous planet it obeys. Under Saturn's gloomy rule, the archetype becomes stodgy, dull, and bureaucratic. Libra is said to depend on consensus and to forestall a hasty judgment, investment, or decision. As the hallmark of successful attorneys, orators, and entrepreneurs, astral symbolism points to Libra's gift for fairness and compromise in politics and administration. A predictable quality in Libra is colorlessness, which comes from taking refuge on the safe side out of harm's way. Never a risk taker, Libra tempers progressivism with conventionality and humdrum bourgeois aims.

According to astral medicine, the Libran is wholesome, merry, and appealing in appearance and deportment. The standardized body type is generous and rounded, the voice mellifluous and memorable, and the eyes entrancing. Except for a tendency toward bladder and back problems, health is secure in balanced Libra, who instinctively eats well, refrains from wearisome worries, and cultivates a rational attitude. Drawn to numerous pastimes, the archetype samples varied hobbies without developing any beyond the rudiments.

Because the typical Libran prefers the present over the past or future, aging is not a burden, nor is loss of youthful grace and suppleness. When troubled with a faulty renal system, especially in old age, the archetype is resigned to illness and demands attention. For this reason, Librans make devout invalids and relish constant nursing and a monitored diet. Astral healers advise that the best diet for this sign consists of cereal grains, peas, citrus fruits, and plums. Salads of lettuce, sorrel, dill, and fennel plus supplements of sodium phosphate offset minor ills.

SYMBOLISM IN ART AND RELIGION

In ancient art, Libra simulated such symmetric icons as the Tree of Life, Pisces's paired fishes, and Gemini, the twins. The symbol evolved from a concept of reciprocity or equity: for every crime a corresponding punishment, for every virtue, a reward. As a balance, Libra holds in equal measure body and soul, humanity and bestiality, truth and order. A coin from the reign of Titus around 80 A.D. displays Annona, a harvest deity standing before the prow of an Egyptian ship and alongside a grain basket topped with lotus, a gift from Egypt, the country from which Rome bought grain. The cornucopia in her left hand dominates the pose. In her right hand is the figure of justice holding a scale, an emblem of even distribution of produce.

The *Book of Hours*, a medieval anthology, reveals Libra as a delicate female holding a balanced scale in her fingertips. The pose derives from Libra's conjunction with Virgo, the maiden, the only female associated with the traditional twelve zodiac signs. Mythology allies her with the Greek concept of Nemesis or comeuppance, a dispenser of retribution and righteous anger symbolized by scales, yardstick, and sword. As Astraea or Fortuna, she is the decisive judge who doles out penalties and rewards without regard to prestige, wealth, or power. The statue that stands before the U.S. halls of justice to embody constitutional jurisprudence duplicates the Roman version, adding a blindfold to assure that justice plays no favorites. Her rather prissy, goody-goody pose is a standard figure in political cartoons, especially those lampooning public figures who suffer less prison time than common working-class thugs. In the aftermath of O. J. Simpson's criminal trial for the murder of his ex-wife, Nicole Simpson, and her friend, Ronald Goldman, the statue appeared on editorial pages holding her nose.

In heraldry, the concept of balance attests to a type of justice that is neither too harsh to felons nor too light to court favorites. The symbol simulates the Caduceus, the twin-snaked icon of the medical profession. The symmetry of Mercury's raised sword with serpents entwined establishes an equilibrium between self-governance and strength, which carries over to health and well being. Tarot cards picture justice as a symmetrical female face and form dressed in red and blue, a balance of hot and cool colors. The maiden's hands clutch the characteristic emblems—a balance-beam scale to weigh right against wrong and a sword to dispense justice.

In Roman verse, Libra receives beneficent treatment. In Book I of the *Georgics*, Virgil states the importance of heavenly star clusters as adjuncts to the farmer's calendar. In a passage of advice on plowing and sowing, the poet urges:

> Nor must the ploughman less observe the skies,
> When the Kids, Dragon, and Arcturus rise,
> Than sailors homeward bent, who cut their way
> Through Helle's stormy straits, and oyster-breeding sea.
> But, when Astraea's balance, hung on high,
> Betwixt the nights and days divides the sky,
> Then yoke your oxen, sow your winter grain,
> Till cold December comes with driving rain.
> (Godolphin 1949, 143)

The tempering of the farmer's life with the calendar attests to Virgil's belief that Roman city life required a corresponding number of days in the country, where bucolic simplicity eased the spirit and neutralized the ravages brought on by metropolitan hurry.

Historically, stereotypical Librans have served as models of high-mindedness and grace. One of the beloved Librans from American history, Eleanor Roosevelt, displayed most of the archetype's admirable qualities. She idolized her husband, President Franklin Roosevelt, and attempted to earn his affection by performing home chores punctiliously and by seeing to their children's needs. Because of her husband's paralysis, Mrs. Roosevelt served as his legs by visiting slums, meeting with mining authorities, making speeches to labor unions, and setting an example of tact to contentious groups, especially racist agitators. Genuinely at home among strangers, she ennobled the title of First Lady by promoting gentility, civil rights, and humanitarianism. An ungainly woman who looked awkward in formal dress, she ignored political cartoons that skewered her shortcomings as a public figure and White House hostess. In private, she brooded over the cruelty of these public jests, especially when they implied that her husband had reason for being unfaithful.

After the president's death in 1945, following valiant service as a wartime president, Mrs. Roosevelt accepted a significant post among world peacekeepers. The only woman among the first delegates to the United Nations, she chaired the initial human rights commission, functioning effectively in both French and English. After two years of debate on issues concerning the wounded, refugees, orphans, prisoners of war, and displaced persons, she held out for every statute and saw them codified in the United Nations Charter. The opening lines of its preamble convey her regard for human rights:

We the peoples of the United Nations determined to save succeeding generations from the scourge of war which twice in our lifetime has brought untold sorrow to mankind, and to reaffirm faith in fundamental human rights, in the dignity and worth of the human person, in the equal rights of men and women and of nations large and small. (United Nations, XXVII, 456)

Until her death, Mrs. Roosevelt crusaded for a peaceful world where the weak and the strong, the conqueror and the conquered, behaved amenably and civilly by avoiding rancor, vengeance, and brutality.

In similar Libran mode, both Elie Wiesel and Esther Hautzig represent humanitarian interests. Wiesel, the author of *Night* and *All Rivers Run to the Sea*, survived a Nazi death camp and educated himself in philosophy at the Sorbonne. He has built an impressive career as a professor of the humanities at Boston University and as a multilingual journalist and humanitarian. Like Eleanor Roosevelt, he made peace his life's work and earned a Nobel Peace Prize for involving himself in international issues in which human misery and blatant victimization of the weak or vulnerable were focal issues. A survivor of the same war, Esther Hautzig returned from years of hard labor on the Russian Steppes and published *The Endless Steppe*, an autobiographical account of her youth and education in wretched work camps. Eleanor Roosevelt, Elie Wiesel, and Esther Hautzig have become icons of diplomacy to school children who read their words and profit from their selflessness.

12
SCORPIO

ASTRONOMICAL FACTS

A bright, sprawling summer constellation visible in the Northern Hemisphere, Scorpio, the eighth sign of the zodiac, derives from the Latin word for the scorpion. The term also names a lethal dart catapulted by Roman siege engineers during assaults on walled cities. Abbreviated Sco and called Scorpius or the Fish Hook by astronomers, the constellation ranks thirty-third in size. Situated west of Sagittarius near Centaurus, the group borders Ara, Corona Australis, Libra, Lupus, Norma, and Opiuchus. Of the sixty-two stars in the cluster, thirteen stand out:

alpha-one star	Antares, the anti-Aries
alpha-two star	Vespertilio, the bat
beta-one star	Graffias, the crab
beta-two star	Acrab, the heart
delta-one star	Dschubba, the forehead
delta-two star	Isidis, the oppressor
theta star	Sargas, the seizer or smiter
lambda star	Alshaula, the raised tail
xi star	Grafias, the crab
sigma star	Alniyat, the (heart's) support
tau star	Alniyat, the (heart's) support
upsilon-one star	Iklil Jabbah, the forehead's crown
upsilon-two star	Allas'ah or Lesath, the stinger

Scorpio makes a spectacular show. The Hindu rated Dschubba a lucky sign and named it Anuradha (propitious); Alshaula, the gamma star, they named Mula (the root). The Chinese combined the pi, beta, delta, and rho stars and named the cluster Fang (the chamber or house). They also grouped alpha, tau, and sigma and named the cluster Sin (the heart). A stream of stars—mu, epsilon, zeta, eta, theta, iota, kappa, and lambda—they saw as Wei (the tail).

Scorpio draws attention for several unusual members. Two meteor showers highlight Scorpio in early May and early June. The constellation also features the Butterfly cluster, Ptolemy's cluster, Acumen and Aculeus, and two globular clusters. An ominous star, Isidis, lies in the scorpion's right claw. The tip of the stinger is Lesath, the upsilon-two star, a minor heavenly body ennobled by its position in a significant spot. Beside one of Libra's pans, Scorpio and its menace balance the promise of Virgo, which flanks the opposite pan.

Appearing in mid-July, Scorpio lies south and low on the horizon. Its shape includes a long, sinuous trail of stars that concludes in a jutting tip. The constellation contains the strongest X-ray in the sky, which looks like a twinkly blue star from the emission of synchrotron radiation. Another attraction, Graffias, which the Romans identified as Frons Scorpii (the scorpion's forehead), is a triple star shining lilac and pale white. The head branches into a pair of projected arms that curve inward. Other clusters, nebulae, star systems, and individual companion stars are observable without a telescope.

In the Coal Sack, the densest part of the Milky Way, lies Scorpio's Antares—the heart of the Scorpion. A red supergiant of the first magnitude, it fascinated Ptolemy around 150 A.D. The Arabs called the star Alkalb (heart) and the Hindu named it Jyestha (oldest). Other names are Shiloh, the biblical town in which the Ark of the Covenant was stored, and *cor scorpionis*, Latin for the scorpion's heart. Antares is a binary that burns red, the color of the coolest stars. Its lambda star, a part of the raised tail, is the twenty-first brightest star in the sky. Its diameter is over 450 times the width of the sun. Antares was also called Alpha Scorpii, or Anti-Mars, because of its nearness to the planet Mars, which it rivals. A tiny green companion star flanks Antares and serves as the scorpion's body. Antares joins Aldebaran, Regulus, and Fomulhaut to form the four Royal Stars, the watchers of the heavens. In 3000 B.C., the Persians named Antares the watcher of the west, a sign of the autumnal equinox.

ASTROLOGICAL HISTORY AND TRAITS

Governing the thirty days between October 23 and November 21, Scorpio is an ancient star shape that once included Libra. As a sun sign ruled by water, Scorpio is a dark unknown, a menacing factor that astrologers consider both devious and deadly. From early times, watchers have associated the constellation with evil. Arab astronomers called the figure Elakrab, the scorpion or war. Copts named it Isidis, the oppressor; Sumerians referred to it as the outlaw. Hebrews knew it as Lesath, the equivalent of Lesha, the perverse. Mayas also sensed danger in the constellation, which they called the death god's sign.

In Egypt, star gazers associated Scorpio with Selek or Selket, the patron of herbal healing. As keeper of burial vaults and canopic jars, Selek received frequent mention in *The Book of the Dead*, a ritual manual in ancient Egypt. In Greek mythology, the goddess Artemis sent Scorpius, a giant scorpion, to sting Orion's foot to halt his joy in killing. To honor the great hunter, the gods set Orion in the sky along with his hounds. Artemis rewarded Scorpio with a separate constellation on the opposite side of the heavens from Orion. According to Pherecydes of Athens, a fifth century B.C. folklorist, the myth accounts for the setting of Orion's familiar shape as Scorpio rises. Roman astrologers altered the story by parting the two clusters at the claws, thus forming the separate constellation of Libra.

Like Aries, Scorpio answers to Mars, the despotic war god and maker of disasters. According to astral handbooks, their alliance incites forceful, violent moods in Scorpios and predisposes them to conflict and treachery. Mercurial and unpredictable, Scorpios resemble serpents in their ability to rechannel ominous brooding from ire to a poised calm. Traditionally, they are capable of courtesy and pleasant deportment, but strike out in unexpected bouts of rudeness, sardonic retort, and confrontation. The influence of Pluto injects a note of secrecy into this complex archetype. The blend allegedly produces a fascinating, charismatic analyst or a leader who maintains control by keeping followers slightly off-balance, never knowing from moment to moment what to expect. Bursts of optimism, wit, and humor may conceal the lurking passions that drive the Scorpio. For these reasons, Scorpio is said to make a superb detective, artisan, or artist.

Scorpios allegedly perform well in most arenas, particularly engineering and business. In finance, Scorpio is the consummate investor who manages money more effectively for others than for self. In the military, Scorpio the powermonger volunteers for dirty work or dangerous missions if it enhances ego or elevates rank. In the professions, the Scorpio type is thorough and uncompromising, frequently completing a task just to savor the satisfaction of closure. Unsympathetic and impatient with weakness or timidity, the archetype tramples on underlings if they stand in the way. A popular Scorpio stereotype is the prima donna surgeon, who makes an incisive diagnosis, then dispatches the operating room team with sharp, authoritative barks. The doctor claims glory from a notable success, but blames failure or mediocre performance on the patient's weakness or an assistant's ineptitude.

In body, the Scorpio is said to display an enviable physique and to discount the importance of health until exhaustion or illness precedes collapse. In treatment, the type is apt to agree to extremes of regimen rather than to accept relaxation and adequate sleep as suitable remedies. The morbid Scorpio quickly begins obsessing on his illness and nursing secret fears that medical people are bunglers because they reject the patient's self-diagnosis. As age withers the body, the Scorpio type denies the accompanying compromise to former strengths and tends not to survive long after losing sense perception and mobility.

Although tough in frame and mind, Scorpio traditionally suffers ailments of the genitals, bladder, and rectum. In tight control of excreta, the type engulfs the body with toxins. In place of professional health care, Scorpio may self-medicate with painkillers, laxatives, and other palliatives or may choose harsh alternative treatments over sugar-coated nostrums. Only the worst ills force the stereotypical Scorpio to seek traditional medical advice. To stave off liver, genital, and kidney problems and the annoyance of ulcers, boils, and abscesses, astral healers advise Scorpios to eat cabbage, kale, and watercress and to center the diet on rye bread, onions, cottage cheese, eggs, and prunes. In addition, supplements of calcium sulphate protect Scorpio from a tendency toward genital and anal distress.

In zodiacal lore, the emotive Scorpio harmonizes with Cancer and Pisces to create lasting friendships or passionate love matches. It is not out of character for the ardent Scorpio to declare an intention to marry on a first meeting. In wooing, the Scorpio writes a memorable letter spiced with wit, details, and bold declarations of love. As mates, however, the typical Scorpio discloses little of feelings or misgivings. Day-to-day relations are said to require frequent realignment and allowance for Scorpio's obduracy, tantrums, and tactlessness. Tyranny cankers at Scorpio's domestic contentment. Forgiveness and understanding are doled out in pinches and dabs, for compassion in Scorpio's heart is limited. As a parent, the Scorpio archetype takes pride in family but fails to discipline children or to heal family rifts.

In matters of faith, the Scorpio typically clings to tenets adopted in youth and may develop a satisfying profession in church hierarchy. Neither pious nor irreligious, the type maintains conservatism in doctrine and prefers sensible statements of philosophy with no saccharine overlayer. The archetype rejects liberal precepts and refuses to evangelize nonbelievers. The most comforting ritual to Scorpio is predictable, all-encompassing, and easy to follow.

SYMBOLISM IN ART AND RELIGION

In art, the scorpion appears among the most lethal of beings and may represent an imminent and painful death such as poisoning. As a representation of regeneration, the sign shares the symbolism of the eagle, snake, and phoenix. Emblematic of female treachery, the scorpion was sometimes depicted on sarcophagi or murals with a woman's face contorted into a sarcastic leer or enticing smile. A Babylonian field stone marking a property line about 1120 B.C. displays a clear inscription in cuneiform. Currently on display at the British Museum in London, the stone links the crescent moon with stars, a turtle, and the scorpion. Nearly twelve centuries later, a vivid bath mosaic from Pompeii pictures a pair of fish facing in opposite directions and tops the circular seascape with a tentacled scorpion.

The archetype colors the Greek myth of Phaëton, Apollo's young son who insisted on driving the chariot of the sun. On the boy's first arc into the heavens, the scorpion stung one of the horses, causing them to bolt. Phaëton was too inexperienced to manage the rampaging beasts and plunged from the car to his death. An interpretation of Scorpio's influence is the piercing sting of truth. For Phaëton, the vaunting *hubris* that encouraged him to supplant his father led to the reality of a quick, violent death. To incredulous humans below, his demise was an appropriate end to a wayward, willful youth.

In biblical literature, Scorpio's cruelty places the creature among the other inhabitants of hell named in Revelation. In II Kings 12:11, the profligate Rehoboam merits punishment with whips and scorpions. A reprise of the wording appears in II Chronicles 10:11. When Ezekiel is commissioned as a prophet, the Lord places a fearful charge on him:

> And thou, son of man, be not afraid of them, neither be afraid of their words, though briers and thorns be with thee, and thou dost dwell among scorpions: be not afraid of their words, nor be dismayed at their looks though they be a rebellious house. (Ezekiel 2:6)

In the New Testament, Luke quotes Christ in a charge to seventy appointees: "Behold, I give unto you power to tread on serpents and scorpions and over all the power of the enemy: and nothing shall by any means hurt you" (Luke 10:19). In acts of torture, application of the scorpion refers to whipping or flogging with a scourge tipped with nails, spikes, or raw metal. This punishment, which Christ endured before his crucifixion, was erratic, often ripping out an eye or lacerating enough flesh to cause the victim to bleed to death. In sea history, the same punitive device was known as a cat-o'-nine-tails.

In literature, Scorpio authors, such as Robert Louis Stevenson, Victor Hugo, and Martin Luther, are known for vigor. Both Stevenson and Hugo wrote of turbulent times when their principled heroes must specify personal beliefs and hold to them. Examples are abundant in Stevenson's *Treasure Island*, where pirates lure the young protagonist, Jim Hawkins. He maintains his honor in match-ups against Long John Silver, the notorious bender of morals. In a telling face-off between Jim and the pirates, he states his faith in right:

> I've seen too many die since I fell in with you. But there's a thing or two I have to tell you. . . . [H]ere you are, in a bad way: ship lost, treasure lost, men lost; your whole business gone to wreck; and if you want to know who did it—it was I! (Stevenson 1962, 184)

Certain of his values, Jim returns home aboard the *Hispaniola*, a mature sailor who has profited from his brush with the sea's dark underside.

Just as Stevenson exalts his hero, Victor Hugo celebrates Jean Valjean, the burly convict of *Les Miserables*, who resides in the depths of the *Orion*, a prison galley, almost completely abandoned. In the somber, punitive atmosphere, he develops into a humanistic mayor and industrialist known as Monsieur Madeleine. A shadowy idealist, he later abandons his mask when an innocent man is accused of the notorious Valjean's crimes. Before a disbelieving prosecuting attorney, Valjean admits the reprehensible side of his past life: "The galley changed me. I was stupid, I became wicked; I was a log, I became a firebrand. Later, I was saved by indulgence and kindness, as I had been lost by severity" (Hugo 1961, 80). At the end of Valjean's long and eventful life, Hugo bestows on him a well-deserved sainthood, yet resigns him to a scorpion's lair—Potters' field, far from the elegant Père Lachaise cemetery, beneath a yew choked with bindweed. He lies eternally under an unmarked tombstone, blackened by the elements.

SCORPIO AND NATURE

In nature, Scorpio lurks in a similarly dismaying atmosphere. The sun sign closely identifies with a stinging arachnid of the same name. The scorpion flourishes in warm climates, both dry and wet. Resembling the crab, crayfish, and lobster with its carapaced thorax, two front pincers, eight jointed legs, and caudal sting, the scorpion bears a reputation for aggression.

Although small and lightweight, it wields an elongated, curved tail to inject a harmful, sometimes fatal neurotoxin from the parallel glands that flank the appendage.

Reproduction showcases the scorpion in its most stylized ritual. Potential mates hoist their tails and dance around each other, alternately twining and releasing their holds. When fertilization is complete, the female may devour the male. She bears living young, which cling to her segmented back for a week after birth. The scorpion thrives on meals of insects and spiders, its nocturnal prey. The scorpion eats like a vampire: after paralyzing a victim, it grasps the body in prehensile claws, rips it apart, and sucks out fluids. Numerous misconceptions attach to the scorpion's aggression, such as the suicidal dance of death which concludes in self-stinging. Also false is the belief that the young feed on the mother's flesh. However, the claim that the scorpion grows frantic when intimidated is true. In a frenzy to elude a captor, it may sting at random, sometimes striking its own body.

According to Pliny's *Natural History*, the scorpion bears an antidote in its body. Treatment of a bite involves binding the scorpion to the wound or feeding the victim a roasted scorpion, either unsauced or blended in a cup of wine. In the sixteenth century, medical lore named basil as an antidote. The standard recipe calls for a handful of basil leaves ground or beaten with ten sea crabs, an outgrowth of the belief that the sea crab resembles the scorpion and may counter its poison, like with like. This recipe also yields bait to rid the premises of scorpions. Tattoos of the scorpion supposedly deflected the insect's stinger.

13

SAGITTARIUS

ASTRONOMICAL FACTS

Sagittarius [saj' ih • ta' ree • uhs], the Latin term for bowman, is the ninth sign of the zodiac. The fifteenth in size, the constellation is 75 percent larger than its neighbor, Scorpius. Sagittarius appears at the center of earth's galaxy and borders Aquila, Capricornus, Corona Australis, Microscopium, Ophiuchus, Serpens, Telescopium, and Scutum, the bowman's shield. The archer's arrow, Sagitta, lies some distance away as though it has gone astray.

Sagittarius is a complex shape posed in the midst of heavy gas, dust, and stars in the brightest sector of the Milky Way. The bowman is observable in mid-August from the mid-northern latitudes in the southern portion of the sky. A showy cluster of the second and third magnitudes, it contains sixty-five stars. There are two minor members, Spiculum and Facies, and nineteen standouts:

alpha-one star	Alrami
alpha-two star	Rukbat, the knee
beta-one star	Arkab Prior, the front hamstring
beta-two star	Arkab Posterior, the back hamstring
gamma-one star	Nash
gamma-two star	Al Nasl, the arrowhead
gamma-three star	Nushaba
delta star	Kaus Meridionalis, the middle bow
epsilon star	Kaus Australis, the southern bow
zeta star	Ascella, the armpit
lambda star	Kaus Borealis, the northern bow
mu star	Polis, the foal
nu star	Ain al Rami
omicron star	Manubrium, the handle
pi star	Albaldah, the bright one

sigma-one star	Nunki, or Enki, a Sumerian water deity
sigma-two star	Pelagus, the open sea
omega star	Terebellum
Sagittarii 42	Facies, the face

The sign also features star masses—the Lagoon Nebula, Omega (Swan or Horseshoe) Nebula, Trifid Nebula, the Milky Way patch, dense star clouds, and eleven spherical clusters that include Kaus Australis and Nunki. A fortuitous star, Ascella, is a binary in the bowman's underarm. Ptolemy identified the omega star, Terebellum, as the chief star of the four-sided asterism in the tail. Sagittarius hosts a meteor shower in early June.

The constellation of the archer has a long history. The Arabs called the convergence of the zeta, sigma, tau, and phi stars Alna'am, the ostriches. The Hindu aligned the stars in another configuration: Ascella, the zeta star, they identified as Purva Ashadha (the former unconquered); Kaus Merio-donalis, the delta star, they called Uttara Ashadha (the latter unconquered). The alignment of gamma, delta, and epsilon they named Ki (the sieve); in a similar configuration of phi, lambda, and mu they saw Tow (the ladle or measure).

Sagittarius is unusual in several ways. It contains fifteen Messier objects, the largest number that French astronomer Charles Messier, called Louis XV's "comet ferret," identified in his *New General Catalogue*, the first nebula compendium, published in 1784. Facies, numbered 42 M (its Messier number), twinkles in the archer's face; the omicron star is part of a facial cluster. The combination of 8 M, 20 M, and 21 M produces Spiculum, the dart, which adorns the bowman's arrowhead. A minor star, Pelagus, sits on the feathered butt of the bowman's arrow; Polis, the tripartite mu star, lies on the arrow's upper shaft.

Overall, Sagittarius features more variable stars than the total number of stars visible in the entire sky. The cluster's complex shape resembles a ladle, called the milk dipper. Past astronomers called another portion the teapot, which is topped by steam and flanked by a sugar spoon and slice of lemon. A welcoming constellation, the region hosts the sun at the winter solstice on December 22.

ASTROLOGICAL HISTORY AND TRAITS

Ruled by the planet Jupiter and the element of fire, Sagittarius governs the thirty-day period between November 22 and December 21. The glyph that symbolizes Sagittarius is a double-fletched arrow. One of the oldest identified astral shapes, it dates to the Babylonian zodiac of the eleventh century B.C., which depicted the constellation as a mounted bowman. The ancient Akkadians called the shape Nunki, Prince of the Earth. The Egyptians knew it as Knem, the conqueror. Arabs labeled it Alkaus, the arrow; Hebrews named it Kesith, the archer. To the Greeks, the figure represented the centaur Chiron, an erudite herbalist and teacher who trained Jason, Actaëon, and Hercules and treated Achilles's burned foot by grafting flesh from a corpse onto his instep. In the stars, Chiron violates his peaceful myth by adopting the pose of the archer with bow flexed and arrow aimed toward Scorpius to protect his student Hercules from the scorpion's sting.

The arrow, Sagitta, connects the archer with Apollo in a revenge myth that begins with the deflowering of Coronis, a Thessalian princess. Because Coronis committed sacrilege by coupling with her lover Ischys while she was carrying Apollo's child, the goddess Artemis killed her with an arrow. As the sweetly feminine body of Coronis reposed on a funeral pyre, Apollo extracted her unborn fetus and gave him to Chiron, the centaur who taught young boys. The child was named Asclepius, the Greek doctor who studied under Chiron and mirrored Apollo's divine gift for healing. Because Asclepius violated the law against *hubris* by bringing a corpse to life, Zeus struck him with a thunderbolt. The cult of Asclepius elevated him to a god late in the fifth century B.C. To wreak vengeance on Zeus, Apollo killed Zeus' sons, the Cyclopes, with arrows, which were immortalized in the sky as Sagitta.

In zodiacal tradition, Sagittarians, like Chiron the centaur, are warm, idealistic, impulsive people fond of spending extravagantly and of sharing ideas. They are said to squander their earnings rather than to invest them in real estate or stocks. At home in any climate, the archetype loves air travel, new activities, and sporting competition. The domesticated archer prefers frequent changes in dwelling. A thoughtful, forward-looking type, Sagittarius accomplishes difficult tasks by envisioning the whole picture and applying vigorous thought to problem-solving. The type's enthusiasm draws others into projects and restricts a group to its focus. For these reasons, Sagittarius traditionally thrives in exploration, teaching, medicine, theater, and team sports.

As students in traditional educational systems, Sagittarians are said to seek attention inappropriately. In an open classroom, the type is free to satisfy intellectual questions about nature and history. In the lab or at the workbench, the archer quickly deduces cause and effect and understands laws that govern motion and speed. In language classes, the type excels at discussion and debate concerning literature, religion, and philosophy. Sagittarius is a successful student mentor to younger brothers and sisters. After hours, the type readily makes friends and welcomes activities requiring skill, energy, and steady aim.

In adulthood, the typical Sagittarian rejects desk jobs in favor of work in the open air. As soldier, pilot, geologist, or animal trainer, Sagittarius allegedly rises to a position of authority. The archetype possesses a pragmatic field knowledge that undergirds thorough book training. Examples of strong Sagittarian leadership abound in the political acumen of Abraham Lincoln and Winston Churchill, both of whom led their nations during threatening days by relying on practicality and an intuitive feel for the right action at the right moment. An example of Lincoln's even-handed vision occurs in his commentary on the lives of slaves and masters: "As I would not be a slave, so I would not be a master. This expresses my idea of democracy. Whatever differs from this, to the extent of the difference is no democracy" (Bartlett 1992, 448). Churchill, in a poetic comment on tyranny, wrote in *While England Slept*: "Dictators ride to and fro upon tigers which they dare not dismount. And the tigers are getting hungry" (Bartlett 1992, 619). In both instances, the aphorists reflect on threats to freedom, which they helped their nations to quell by applying wisdom to thorny issues.

Typical Sagittarians change jobs frequently, impulsively seeking greener pastures in a new field or a work community more sympathetic to the type's willful, zealous, creative rhythms. In explanation of their short-term career loyalties, astrologers cite the Sagittarian's resolute, unshakeable self-direction. The archetype chafes under petty rules and supervision and dislikes tedium and details. Overall, the archer chooses amusement over intense work sessions or staff meetings and trusts instinct and luck over grueling labor. In matters of morality and ethics, the type tends toward fanaticism; in business, the archer bucks the status quo and presses for excellence. At the extreme of the sign's influence, the untempered Sagittarian is characterized as a gambler, workaholic, or miser.

Astrologers claim that Sagittarians harmonize with Aries, Leo, and other Sagittarians. If they maintain independence, Sagittarians thrive and profit; if constrained by overprotective parents or tyrannic bosses, they rebel in ingenious ways. At family gatherings, Sagittarians may or may not enjoy relatives. They typically foster doomed love matches. Once soured on romance, they become cynical flirts, transparent bounders, or self-deprecating curmudgeons. Late into adulthood, Sagittarians are said to avoid matrimony or to forge a lasting life partnership with a friend. The Sagittarian's inability to express affection robs these brother-sister alliances of affection;

only steadfast mates survive shell marriages to the archer. Even then, the warmth of homefires eludes the archetype, which prefers a loose schedule free of boring commitments.

Physically, Sagittarius is stereotyped with a broad countenance, blunted nose, and riveting eyes incapable of hiding opinions and attitudes. Restless and undisciplined, the archer destroys the grace of winsome features by gesturing frantically to make a point. Generally stocky in childhood, the type thickens in middle age. The sign runs to weakness in the liver and pelvis. Dismal and negative, the Sagittarian rejects bed rest and confinement and becomes a bitter, complaining invalid. A literary example of the archer's skill at manipulative whining is found in Edith Wharton's *Ethan Frome*. Zenobia Frome, the ailing wife of Ethan, thwarts a budding affair between her cousin and her husband. Like the self-centered Zenobia Frome, the standard Sagittarian is described as a poor patient, but an enthusiastic healer or visitor to the sick who uplifts others by disseminating good will.

SYMBOLISM IN ART AND RELIGION

In art, the archer, a symbol of wholeness, power, control, and spiritual balance, makes a strong, militant appearance in ancient temple and palace architecture. On balance, the act of shooting an arrow also symbolizes an irrevocable act, which may enhance or harm human fate. At Susa, the winter palace of Darius, a Persian King, showcases bearded bowmen in profile. Steady of eye and posed in readiness, they grasp tall spears and carry bows slung on their left shoulders. Against the ornate fabric of their tunics, tall quivers bristle with ceremonial arrows. Glazed in enamel on tile, this procession of archers is one of the few specimens of Elamite art. A segment of the wall stands in the Louvre Museum in Paris.

Both music and history owe much to the exuberant, demanding Sagittarius, as demonstrated by the intense arias sung by Maria Callas or the fervent canvases painted by Swiss symbolist Paul Klee. At the end of the classical era, Sagittarian Ludwig von Beethoven refused to rein in his emotional symphonies. Into old age and progressive deafness, he demanded that the world listen and be moved by his compelling "Eroica" and "Appassionata." Similarly, historian Thomas Carlyle imitated on paper the vortex of emotion that produced the French Revolution. Freighting his chronicle with the precipitate torrent of feeling that forced the French aristocracy to the guillotine, he imbued his text with a candid recreation of passion gone awry.

The bowman is an equally striking figure in myth. A symbol of duality and strife, the centaur appears in Greek mythology as a male torso attached to the lower body of the ox. In the *Argonautica*, Apollonius accounts for the unusual juxtaposition of features in a reflection on the myth:

> [The Argonauts] sailed past the island of Philyra, where Philyra slept with Kronos, the son of Ouranos, when he ruled over the Titans on Olympos. . . . Kronos thus deceived Rheia, but the goddess came upon them in the midst of their love-making, and Kronos sprang up from the bed and rushed off in the form of a long-maned horse. In shame the Oceanid Philyra left that place and territory behind and went to the sweeping Pelasgian mountains, where she bore the mighty Cheiron, part of whom resembles a horse and part a god, because Kronos was transformed as he left her bed. (Apollonius 1995, 64)

Unlike the more violent, lecherous centaurs, Chiron earned fame for his wisdom and compassion. In the mode of martyr, he gave up immortality to benefit Prometheus. For this selfless act, the gods placed Chiron in the heavens as the constellation Sagittarius.

In a minor episode, Hercules became the bowman by shooting a deadly arrow into Nessus, the centaur who abducted Dejanira, the Aetolian princess. The story ends tragically for Hercules. After hearing Nessus's prediction that Hercules would eventually stray to another mate, Dejanira followed his advice and reserved some of the centaur's poisoned blood. She later daubed it on her mate's shirt, which clung to his torso and burned him lethally. The gods took pity and transformed Hercules into a constellation.

The centaur, a perverse being, is a frequent theme in folklore, scripture, and myth. Duality extends the figure to include heroic warriors who achieved greatness by subduing animals and monsters or anomalies, for example, Hercules and numerous beasts, Perseus and Medusa, Theseus and the Minotaur, St. George and Siegfried and their respective dragons, Beowulf and Grendel, David and Goliath, and Samson and the lion. A comic version of man against monster enlivens Lewis Carroll's witty "Jabberwocky," which pits the two figures in mortal combat:

> And, as in uffish thought he stood,
>   The Jabberwock, with eyes of flame,
> Came whiffling through the tulgey wood,
>   And burbled as it came!
>
> One, two! One, two! And through and through
>   The vorpal blade went snicker-snack!

>   He left it dead, and with its head
>   He went galumphing back. (Carroll 1958, 192)

Carroll extols his jabberwock hunter with delight: "Come to my arms, my beamish boy! O frabjous day! Callooh, Callay!" Such homage to gallant figures acknowledges the human preference for civility over animalism and the baser instincts, a central theme of myth and psychology.

For Homer, the archer dispensed suffering and death and served as Zeus's wake-up call to the unwary. It was Odysseus's offer of a bow and arrows that unmasked Achilles, whose mother had hid him among women and renamed him Pyrrha to save him from induction into Agamemnon's army. A necessary item in the Greek destruction of Troy was the bow of Philoctetes. Ironically, Paris's poor shooting of a bow killed Achilles. The arrow went awry, striking the Greek superhero in the heel, the only vulnerable part of his body. Virgil perpetuated the harmful role of the archer with Eros's dart, which penetrated the breast of Queen Dido, forcing her to pursue a doomed passion for Aeneas, founder of Rome.

To the harsher side of the Sagittarius personality stands the English epicist John Milton. An austere, unwavering Puritan, he battled his dismay at progressive blindness while mastering his misgivings about the handicap. Through a secretary, Andrew Marvell, Milton dictated lines and edited aloud from repeated readings. He redirected his talents from frivolous, worldly subjects to a pious contemplation of Eden and the fall of Adam and Eve. In *Paradise Lost*, Milton presented the Old Testament precepts with sobriety and sonorous grace. Unyielding to sympathy or compromise, he followed the exiled couple to the edge of Eden, where they took their solitary way into an ungentle world. As a husband and father, Milton was no more pliant than he was as poet and pamphleteer. His stringent expectations for his daughters riled the Milton household, costing him all but one child who could approach his high standards of conduct and scholarship.

On the positive side, astrologers list Mark Twain, whose exuberant writings display the Sagittarian at its peak of intellectual curiosity. He wrote humor, autobiography, epigram, historical fiction, allegory, travelogue, and after-dinner speeches. From the laidback insouciance of *Life on the Mississippi* to the dark satire of "The Man Who Corrupted Hadleyburg," Twain wrote in the style and form that suited his thoughts. Concerning his stagecoach journey across the plains, he produced *Roughing It*, an optimistic, tongue-in-cheek study of the American frontier. In an expansive mood, he put his personable tinker, Hank Morgan, back eight centuries into the Middle Ages and installed him at Camelot in *A Connecticut Yankee in King*

Arthur's Court. By the end of an eventful career, Twain had earned the title of most original American novelist and had achieved a high place among the world's most quotable aphorists.

In history, England is said to reflect the influence of Sagittarius, particularly the type's penchant for "cockeyed optimism," as demonstrated by the island nation's hope and persistence during the Blitz of World War II. Spain is also Sagittarian in nature: buoyant and self-seeking among nations and proud and vain at the negotiating table. In sports, both the Spanish and English excel at vigorous sport, including cricket, soccer, rugby, horseback riding, auto and bicycle racing, and bullfighting.

According to astral psychology, the arrow, an emblem of phallic sadism, expresses Sagittarian aggression and enhances images of assertiveness and impulse. On a nobler plane, the arrow can also reflect the sun god's beneficence in pouring rays on the earth. As such, the archer's projectile takes on the positive qualities of intuition, focus, dispatch, and determination. A whimsical example of the resolute arrow appears each February 14 in the stylized valentine, a modern version of the *billet doux* launched by St. Valentine, a third-century prelate martyred in Rome and buried north of the city beside the Via Flaminia. Commercialized in the 1840s, the valentine has become the message-of-the-day for the ardent wooer and a stock sales item for American greeting card manufacturers, candy sellers, and florists.

Sigmund Freud interpreted Sagittarius as the synergy epitomized by the ego's pacification of a warring id and superego. In his paradigm, when the id unleashes its energy by demanding sexual gratification or aggression, the superego blunts the id's ardor with a reminder of social, religious, and ethical principles forbidding excess. The ego, the psychic arbitrator, steps between the two, forcing the id to lessen its shrill insistence and the superego to stifle its self-righteous prating and moralizing. By directing energies toward a nonthreatening activity, the ego, like Sagittarius, soothes the combined drives and avoids frustration, inner turmoil, hysteria, or psychosomatic ills. For example, the ego may halt a rampant sexual urge and stifle the superego's flood of guilt and shame by allowing an ardent lover to partner in an energetic dance. The energy finds a worthy, satisfying physical outlet and engages in a socially acceptable prelude to mating.

14
CAPRICORN

ASTRONOMICAL FACTS

The tenth house of the zodiac, Capricorn, abbreviated Cap, is called Capricornus in astronomy. Capricorn's name derives from the Latin *capricornus* or goat's horn. It takes as its emblem the horned, fish-tailed goat or sea goat climbing a peak. Easily spotted in autumn from the Northern Hemisphere, Capricorn lies between Sagittarius and Aquarius and borders Aquila, Microscopium, and Piscis Austrinus. Of the thirty-one stars in the group there are twelve major stars:

alpha-one star	Prima Gieda, the first goat
alpha-two star	Secunda Gieda, the second goat
alpha-three star	Gredi
beta star	Dabih, the slaughterer
gamma star	Nashira, the fortunate one
delta star	Deneb Algeti, the goat's tail
epsilon star	Castra, the camp
eta star	Armus, the shoulder blade
theta star	Dorsum, the back
nu star	Alshat, the sheep
pi star	Oculus, the eye
rho star	Bos, the cow

This modest constellation, which is fortieth in size, is the smallest in the zodiac, but one of the oldest. It dates to 2449 B.C., when Chinese astronomers first observed it.

Capricorn makes no spectacular display but has been called the smile in the sky. The Arabs identified as the goat's southern horn the alpha star, Gieda, a multiple star colored lilac, ash, and yellow. Hebrews named it the slain kid, a reference to the blood of the lamb sacrificed to salvage firstborns from slaughter during the last of Egypt's plagues that preceded the Exodus.

Arabs lumped the beta star with the alpha cluster, which they called Alsa'd
Aldhabih, the lucky slaughterer. Chinese astrologers coordinated alpha, nu,
omicron, pi, and rho to make Nieu, the ox. The Romans considered Armus
the goat's heart; the rho star, Bos, they pictured on the goat's face. Castra,
the epsilon star, is a minor spot on the goat's abdomen.

Capricorn's position two centuries ago lent its name to the Tropic of
Capricorn, the southernmost arc where the sun stood overhead at midday.
On a globe, the arc passes through Argentina, South Africa, and Australia.
Capricorn's beta star, Dabih, is a double star composed of two asterisms,
one caerulean and one orangy-yellow, which form the goat's left eye.
Dorsum is a minor figure on the goat's spine. The minor delta star, Deneb
Algeti, and the gamma star, Nashira, dot the goat's tail. The constellation
also features two July meteor showers, a faint spherical cluster, and binary
stars, which converge from a mutual gravitational pull.

ASTROLOGICAL HISTORY AND TRAITS

Governing the twenty-nine days between December 22 and January 19,
Capricorn dates to the Chaldean and Babylonian zodiacs. To the latter, the
constellation represented Ea, god of subterranean waters. A fanciful Greek
myth depicts Capricorn with a fishtail. The story of Pan, a male Arcadian
god named for the Greek for *all*, describes how, during a war with giants,
he repeatedly changed into animal shapes to elude the monster Typhon. Just
as Pan leaped into the Nile River, his upper half changed into a goat; his
lower half became a fish and swam out of Typhon's reach.

To the Greeks, Capricorn was also Amaltheia, the goat that nourished
Zeus. According to Hyginus's *Poetic Astronomy*, Amaltheia received a horn
from the sacred goat of Zeus, who filled it with an inexhaustible abundance
of fruits and vegetables. Additional horn myths include a tale of Hercules's
twelfth labor, during which he presented to Plutus, god of the underworld,
the horn of Amaltheia overflowing with fruit. In Roman times, Theogenes
proposed that Augustus adopt the horned goat as an emblem. Representing
his role as commander-in-chief, Capricorn appeared on the banners and
standards of his personal legions. Capricorn became a transitional figure on
the Gregorian calendar. Like Janus, the two-faced Roman god, he surveyed
the end of one year and the beginning of another. For this reason, the goat
sign represents gravity and sobriety, two emotions that assist self-assess-
ment and the making of New Year's resolutions. The goat's upturned head
stresses its progressive, hard-charging nature, which assures that its feet
continue to move up the rubbled path. An earth sign, Capricorn begins the

process of decay or dissolution, which Pisces completes. The sun sign answers to Saturn, the hard-edged, pessimist whose divinity is represented by omega, the last letter of the Greek alphabet and a symbol of doom.

According to astrologers, Capricornians tend to be drudges and crepe-hangers, perennially anticipating disaster. Because of ominous traits, they are accused of mean-spiritedness and inhibition. As is true of zodiacal stereotypes, this conclusion is obviously overgeneralized. Because Capricorn is a water sign associated with fresh and salt water, it profits from a conciliatory connection that tempers Saturn's harshness. The sign's broad amalgam of personality traits coordinates humility and thrift with earnest dedication to task.

As students, Capricorns traditionally thrive in the past. Their keen interest in genealogy, tradition, and past events and heroes gives them a toehold in the present, where they apply what they have learned about human tendencies and accomplishments. A devoted researcher and scholar, the archetype enjoys a challenge and excels at harmonizing seemingly inconsistent details and accommodating obscure philosophies. Altruistic from childhood, the goat sign hones promising talents and prepares for a life of service. On the negative side, the type epitomizes self-discipline and embodies the stodgy, humorless grind characterized in English slang as the goat, a pejorative referring to the expendable person sacrificed for the good of the group.

Traditionally, Capricorns dominate their neighborhoods, professions, careers, and marriages. Martyrs by nature, they relish a hard task, such as city planning, guiding tours, settling quarrels, unraveling a mystery, or conducting legal inquiries. Ambitious and adaptable, they detest tedious details that detract from the larger purpose. By focusing on a goal, they establish a useful spot as mediator or broker. Thus, the type works well in large amorphous or bureaucratic operations.

On the affective side, Capricorns are thought to take pains in selecting friends, business partners, and lovers, usually from among Taurians, Virgoans, or Librans. As companions and colleagues, goat archetypes flourish at holidays, birthdays, and anniversaries. An inborn sense of propriety is said to make them knowledgeable parliamentarians and advisers on protocol or procedure. They allegedly enjoy influencing and directing their inferiors by giving advice on love, goading a slacker, or cheering an elderly or sick relative.

The type's negative traits include a tendency toward pleasing superiors. In this capacity, Capricorn becomes a sycophant, snob, or abettor of illegal or ignoble activities. At the worst, the archetype never hesitates to cozy up to the brass, thus earning a reputation for boot-licking. Another side of Capricorn's upward mobility is an intensification of the war of the sexes. To gentle a forward woman, the male Capricorn attempts to reduce a female colleague or family member to a needy suppliant. Elevated to the status of patriarch, he flaunts supremacy, thus muddling relationships by becoming bossy, sexist, and judgmental.

Unhurried in romance, the standard Capricorn is described as late to marry, but even slower to divorce or abandon a lover. Once allied with a suitable mate, Capricorn remains true to the commitment, yet may starve a thriving relationship by withholding love or money or by ignoring a mate's emotional or sexual needs. As a parent, the goat sign exults in teaching children through advice and good example. However, when setting up goals for the offsprings' future, the archetype may choose social status, prestige, wealth, or impressive genealogy over love and happiness.

The astrologer's key to understanding Capricorn is to analyze the strength of religion and tradition in the personality. Overall, the stereotype is devout, reverent, and consistent in observing ritual. When spiritual drift threatens, the goat grows sententious and postures for the sake of self-aggrandizement. Faced with true paradox, Capricorn is inept, confounded by a deeper level of social or religious interpretation than precepts can explain. In these embarrassing situations, Capricorn confronts a shallowness in self that is likely to dismay or depress.

Physically, Capricorns are thought to lack a single unifying quality. They tend to be dark of skin and hair, appealing in expression and gesture, and engaging in casual conversation. Males are thin-bearded, narrow-chested, and slender. Capricorns age well, sometimes peaking after contemporaries and remaining vigorous into their nineties. If inhibited or cut off from their chief joy, goats fall into a decline that precipitates bodily ailments and despair. Astral medicine advises palliatives suited to a herd animal—fresh air, broad-based diet, and social interaction.

Traditionally, Capricorn's weak spot is skeletal and may twinge from overwork, lifting, or a chill. Given a trick knee, arthritis, or gout, the type lapses into invalidism and coughs or groans piteously. To avoid losing out at work, the dependable goat prefers to balance a briefcase on a lapboard rather than rest and follow orders. Astral healing maintains that herbal supplements of knapweed, cinchona, elder, plantain, and black hellebore prevent the typical goat-weakeners: anemia, rheumatism, cough, and deafness. The best diet makes the most of leafy plants, onions, parsley, watercress, rye bread, eggs, prunes, and cottage cheese plus mineral supplements of calcium phosphate. Also, milk is far better for the type than wine or other forms of alcohol.

SYMBOLISM IN ART AND RELIGION

Art depicts Capricorn as a curved arc of bright stars, the sacred token of the moon goddess called Cybele or Selene and a promising sign to wayfarers. Its myths provide a concrete shape on which artists invent imaginative patterns. On arras, heraldic shield, or pub sign, fantasy turns the seagoat into a crocodile, dolphin, and sea serpent. To the Chinese, the goat represented goodness and peace; Hindus, Sumerians, and Teutons concurred that it symbolized energy, divinity, and power. To Christians, the goat was the obverse of deity: it embodied lechery and venality, both damnable sins. Jews also saw the goat as a lewd figure.

A strongly feminine symbol, the horn in advertising and iconography has come to represent nurturing, maternity, and strength. The symbol appears on a wide variety of common items, including dried fruit, Italian bread, and Fruit of the Loom underwear. Animated advertisements for briefs and T-shirts feature brightly colored fruits dancing out of a cornucopia to upbeat music. Roman art developed the goat's horn into the cornucopia overflowing with fruit and vegetables, the emblem of Ceres, the Roman goddess of grain. The abundance that tumbles out of the hollow serves as the symbol of Thanksgiving, when families gather to share the earth's bounty and to pray for health, happiness, and fertility. A full-length statue of Fortuna, goddess of luck, stood at the port of Ostia, the warehouse city west of Rome on the artificial harbor built by the Emperor Claudius. In her right hand, she clutched a rudder; in her left, the horn of plenty. The graceful upright horn was etched with acanthus leaves and featured grapes and fruit. A parallel figure in bronze found near Capua displays a pensive Vesta, goddess of the hearth, with her head inclined to the right. In the crook of her left arm is the vertical horn of plenty, symbol of the festival of Vesta held each June to celebrate a full harvest. At a Roman settlement at Smyrna, Bupalus's statue of Tyche, the Greek goddess of fortune, shows her holding Amaltheia's horn. Another statue in Achaia represents Tyche holding a cornucopia.

To the Romans of the first century A.D., Capricorn was the sun sign of Augustus Caesar, the empire's first ruler. In the Gemma Augustea, a sardonyx cameo carved in Greek style about 15 A.D., a panoply of gods groups Poseidon, Demeter, and Apollo. The trio, by their attendance, appears to countenace the Emperor's deification. Enthroned in classic style, the emperor represents Zeus-Jupiter and shares a dais with Dea Roma, the city's patron goddess. Fortuna, the embodiment of luck, holds a festal wreath over his head. Above the grouping floats a circular planet containing the fish-tailed Capricornus.

In verse, the alliance of Pan with Capricorn fleshes out meager goat lore with vivid details. Pan grew up on the pastures of Arcady with his companion Zeus. Hermes, Pan's father, delighted in the boy's boisterousness and sweet smile. A cave-dweller and patron of herders, Pan appears with his mother Dryope in Homer's *Hymn to Pan*:

> About the dear son of Hermes, Muse, sing to me,
> The goat-footed, two-horned lover of noise, who roams,
> Through tree-filled meadows in the company of dancing
>   nymphs.
> They tread down the peaks of sheer rock
> Calling on Pan, the shepherd god, unwashed,
> With splendid hair, who has as his lot every snowy
>   hill-crest
> And the peaks of mountains and rocky paths.
> (Homer 1995, 153)

Ovid's *Metamorphoses* follows Homer's description with added information about Pan's pursuit of the maiden Syrinx into a bed of reeds, from which he cut panpipes to enhance his flirtation. The odes of Pindar describe Pan as a goat-footed sybarite, light of heart, who played upon the syrinx or panpipes while he pursued an ever-changing slate of females. From his name derives *panic*, a psychological state arising from sudden irrational fear and loss of composure, an emotion described in E. M. Forster's *Story of a Panic*.

Herodotus injects his *Histories* with a late-blooming myth that can be dated to the Battle of Marathon in 490 B.C. According to his story, Athenian generals needed to send a message to Sparta. They chose a herald named Pheidippides, who reported that he met the god Pan on Mount Parhenium, above Tegea:

> Pan, he said, called him by name and told him to ask the Athenians why they paid him no attention, in spite of his friendliness towards them and the fact that he had often been useful to them in the past, and would be so again in the future. The Athenians believed Pheidippides' story, and when their affairs were once more in a prosperous state, they

built a shrine to Pan under the Acropolis, and from the time his
message was received they have held an annual ceremony, with a
torch-race and sacrifices, to court his protection. (Herodotus 1961,
397–398)

This remarkable event coincides with one of Greek history's memorable
folk heroes. After Pheidippides arrived in Sparta the next day, he summoned
his hearers to Athens, which had already lost Eretria to the Persians.
Pheidippides raced back from Sparta with a reply and, after delivering it,
fell dead from exertion. In legend, he is called the Runner of Marathon; in
modern lore, his name has been corrupted to a more euphonious Philippides.

The honor list of Capricornians includes two composers—Franz
Schubert and Wolfgang Amadeus Mozart. The former wrote engaging
melodies based on folk tunes; the latter produced an unadorned style of
music that makes use of every note. Literature has profited from similar
styles, the most influential being Francis Bacon, pioneer of the essay. His
collected works, like Mozart's compositions, are spare, concise, and elegant. Two other notable Capricorns are writers Gertrude Stein and James
Joyce. Stein is irrevocably linked to her sardonic pronouncement, "A rose
is a rose is a rose." Joyce, a master of fiction, refined his reflections on
growing up Irish in *A Portrait of the Artist as a Young Man*, a classic autobiographical novel. In the same vein, eighteenth-century statesman Alexander
Hamilton and presidential nominee Adlai Stevenson honed public orations
to reveal an economy of words and a sharp focus on substance.

By nature given to weighty, muscular prose, the Capricorn writer is said
to excel at metaphor and to frame a theme through sonorous, majestic
prosody. A worthy example is Jack London's fiction, particularly *The Call
of the Wild*, *The Sea Wolf*, and "To Build a Fire," a short story about a failed
attempt to survive extreme cold. The story appears alongside adventure tales
detailing the straightforward actions of sailors, miners, and mushers. London builds heavily philosophic themes, particularly strife with nature and
the differences between animals and humans in their ability to survive
hardship or disaster. The rigors of living in the wild, wresting a living from
the earth and sea, or taming wild creatures generated London's larger-than-
life characters, who succeed by extremes of self-control.

Military leaders displaying the best of Capricorn's influence include
three generals—Stonewall Jackson, Robert E. Lee, and Joan of Arc. Jackson
and Lee formed a strong camaraderie that carried them through the first part
of the Civil War. After Jackson was accidentally shot by Confederate forces,
Lee mourned his passing and regretted that he could no longer rely on

Jackson's loyalty and genius for battlefield strategy. One of the most unusual Capricorn leaders is the French maiden general, Jeanne d'Arc or Joan of Arc, an early fifteenth-century visionary who claimed to have received messages from St. Margaret, St. Catherine, and the archangel Michael. Born in 1412 in Domrémy, France, Joan of Arc responded to a divine call and led France to military victory. During the Hundred Years' war, she assisted in crowning Charles VII at Rheims. Cheering soldiers venerated her as the Maid of Orléans.

In 1430, Joan's luck changed. Burgundian troops captured her and ransomed her to the English. She underwent interrogation and torture, but refused to reply to charges that she was a sorceress dressed in men's armor to lure their souls to perdition. At age nineteen, she was burned at the stake. Myth claims that white butterflies surrounded her staff and that a white dove ascended from her pyre into heaven. A quarter century after the execution, an ecclesiastical court found her innocent. She was canonized in 1920. The story of the charismatic virgin was the inspiration for Heinrich Schiller's *The Maid of Orléans*, George Bernard Shaw's *Saint Joan*, and Jean Anouilh's *The Lark*.

AQUARIUS

ASTRONOMICAL FACTS

The eleventh sign of the zodiac is the water-bearer, Aquarius [uh • kway' ree • uhs]. Abbreviated Aqr, it is the tenth largest constellation. Usually pictured as a man bearing a tall amphora or urn, the symbol derives from the Latin for water carrier. The astral shape appears to pour water into Fomalhaut, one of the sky's most important navigational stars. It dots the mouth of Piscis Austrinus, the southern fish. A focus of the autumn sky in the Northern Hemisphere and the spring sky in the Southern Hemisphere, Aquarius borders Aquila, Capricornus, Cetus, Delphinus, Equuleus, Pegasus, Pisces, and Sculptor. It contains an identifiable cluster of stars easily viewed, especially during October around 9:00 P.M. Of fifty-six stars in the constellation there are seven highlights:

alpha star	Sadalmelik, the king's lucky star
beta star	Alsa'd Alsu'ud, luckiest of the lucky
gamma star	Sadalachbia, lucky star of the tents
delta star	Skat, the shin bone
epsilon star	Albali, the swallower
theta star	Ancha, the hip bone
kappa star	Situla, the bucket

The Arabs viewed two of Aquarius's stars in one cluster, which they called Alsa'd Albula, the good fortune of the swallower. The grouping of the gamma, alpha, zeta, eta, and pi stars they named Alsa'd Alahbiyah, the lucky star of hiding places. The Hindu identified the lambda star as Catabhishaj, the hundred physicians. The Chinese saw Alsa'd Alsu'ud as Heu, the void, and blended the epsilon star with mu and nu to get Mo, the woman. A fanciful twist allied Sadalmelik with the epsilon and theta stars of Pegasus for the Chinese constellation of Gui, the steep.

A notable part of Aquarius is the lemony twinkle of the alpha star, Sadalmelik, which adorns the waterman's right shoulder. A sign of rain, Alsa'd Alsu'ud, also pale yellow, appears on Aquarius's left shoulder. The delta star, Skat, is a minor star on the waterman's right leg. In addition to these single stars, Aquarius features two nebulae—Saturn and Helix. The latter is the closest nebula to earth and is visible through binoculars. The constellation coincides with six meteor showers, which appear in the house of Aquarius once in May and July and twice each in August and September.

ASTROLOGICAL HISTORY AND TRAITS

Governing the thirty days between January 20 and February 18, Aquarius dates to Babylonian astrology and is connected with water because the sun enters the constellation at the beginning of winter's rainy season. In Babylonian lore, Aquarius ruled a part of the sky known as Sea, which contained four water signs—Capricornus, Eridanus, Hydra, and Cetus. In Greek mythology, the water bearer first reflected the myth of Deucalion, the Noah figure who survived a cataclysmic flood. A more permanent connection was established with Ganymede, a gorgeous princeling, the son of Laomedon of Troy. At Zeus's direction, an eagle abducted Ganymede, who became cupbearer of the Olympian gods and served them nectar, which, along with ambrosia, made up the divine diet. Because he was a royal child, Zeus compensated Ganymede's father with magnificent horses.

Despite the obvious connection to water, Aquarius is an air sign. It is governed by Uranus, an unpromising omen for the unwary, but an impetus to genius when it combines with a balanced nature, illumination, and clear judgment. In keeping with its emblem, the Aquarian traditionally pours a generous stream of emotion and is capable of loving a variety of people, animals, and social causes. According to astrologers, Aquarius influences friendship, aims, and hopes and denotes a gentle, mild-mannered, undemonstrative personality that avoids criticism. An individualist, the Aquarian seeks an unconventional way. Deficient in concentration and slow at reading, the type appears to dilly-dally, yet absorbs ideas from a wide range of sources to apply to problems and ambitions.

Sometimes emotional and given to gestures rather than words, the stereotypical Aquarian accepts and sympathizes with outsiders, particularly people of different social classes, races, and religions. The true archetype avoids ostentation in favor of down-to-earth honesty. Astrologers see in Aquarius the intellectual spark and idealism of the scientist or charity organizer and predict success in law, labor organization, theater, religion, and mediation.

Because Aquarians are allegedly inclined toward acquiescence, they earn a reputation for slow-wittedness, impracticality, and inefficiency. A hypersensitive group, they overstate small crises as calamities and boldly champion the poor, hungry, and disenfranchised. In making decisions, Aquarians are said to bide their time to study an issue or to consult experts. In matters of taste, they allegedly are eager to learn from others rather than to set trends. These traits produce a personality type that irritates others because they seem to waste time and lack initiative.

Characterized as large in body and girth, the Aquarian is nonetheless deft of movement and quick to perceive abstract logic. Emotionally serene and tranquil, the water bearer avoids boasters, scrappers, and fighters. This non-confrontational attitude earns Aquarians the label of cowards, particularly when they pursue the greater good or ponder an abstract element of warfare, such as the sufferings of the noncombatant. In armed conflict, they are unfocused fighters who lack pugilistic skill or the blind fury that motivates a true killer, like Homer's Achilles or the desperadoes of western movies and television.

Zodiacal typing pictures the Aquarian as a steady, even-tempered companion who blends well with Librans, Geminians, and Arieans. At parties and friendly gatherings, the archetype stands aloof from frivolity. The Aquarian makes tactless comments and shares intimacy and affection without fear of provoking jealousy in others. As a wooer, the archetype deflates the beloved by forgetting to display affection and loyalty. A late bloomer, the Aquarian prefers a long engagement and marries late, often to a best pal, who reaps the benefits of genuine love. As described by Paul in I Corinthians 13:4, the Aquarian style of love is "not puffed up" and seeks the partner's true happiness.

Traditionally, parenting comes easily to the Aquarian, who dislikes infant care, but enjoys rearing children. The unconventional water bearer dismays rigid authoritarians by placing mild demands on offspring and by establishing a nondirective style of correction. In anticipation of a lasting dynasty, the parent prefers progressive education that teaches children to think for themselves rather than to parrot memory work. At home, the Aquarian parent rules the domain and expects to be catered to by mate and children.

According to astral health lore, the Aquarian enjoys a sound constitution, yet is characteristically uncomfortable in drafty rooms on rainy days. The Aquarian's profile and proportioned physique tends toward the dramatic, as demonstrated by actors John Barrymore and Clark Gable. Inclined toward fragile skin, blue or gray eyes, rosy cheeks, and understated mannerisms, the type speaks softly and conceals laughter. Usually mannerly, the

Aquarian may astonish others by boldly defending the vulnerable or defying crudeness, discourtesy, or other signs of ill-breeding.

Overall, the robust Aquarian is said to live a vigorous life until overwork or accident compromises well-being. Although the headstrong water bearer is likely to seek unconventional treatment or self-medication, the Hermetica of Egypt advises the ailing Aquarian to try simple herbal compounds of valerian, tansy, balm, and ladies' slipper to relieve leg cramps, flu, edema, flatulence and diarrhea, or goiter. The best diet for the Aquarian avoids alcohol and stresses salads of radish, spinach, chard, and celery and fruit treats rich in apples and strawberries.

The zodiacal flow from Aquarius ties directly into Pisces, the dual fish sign. Thus, astral symbolism creates a smooth transition from one house to another. However, unlike the paired fish, who are joined by a tether, Aquarius's flow represents dissolution, setting free, dissolving, or decomposing, a sign of liberation from the body to the spirit. A mystical link to the supernatural, Aquarians are thought to have powers of communicating with the mind's unconscious forces.

SYMBOLISM IN ART AND RELIGION

Although the sign of Aquarius is less common in art than its zodiacal comrades—particularly Virgo, Capricorn, Gemini, Taurus, and Pisces—gushing water became a standard unifying horizontal in the art of the Chinese, Celts, Semites, and Amerindians and in the classic, Christian, Medieval, and Renaissance periods. An ambiguous sign, the water bearer traditionally allied with both death and renewal and attached to cycles of death and regeneration, particularly in agriculture and the tending of vineyards and orchards. To the Inca and Maya, water symbolized primeval chaos; to Buddhists, the flow concretized the historical and emotional flux that besets humankind. The Chinese paired water with fire or sunshine, an elemental example of yin circumventing yang. Cultists, including the Maori, Celts, and Sumerians, connected lakes, wells, and fountains with spontaneous magic and the source of supernatural power, for example, the Lady of the Lake and maidens who attend the fallen king on his barge in Arthurian lore and the pensive figure in Alfred Tennyson's "The Lady of Shalott." The mystical song of the latter drifts "down to tower'd Camelot," causing weary reapers to proclaim her a fairy (Tennyson 1949, 12).

In Greco-Roman mosaic, bas-relief, and sculpture, water imagery prefigures another type of emergence—the birth of Aphrodite from the sea and the power of Poseidon over the Mediterranean, a correspondence similar to the Hindu myths of Agni, Vishnu, and Varuna, all water powers. In ritual scenarios, the male servant representing Aquarius typically pours water from his jug to the east, the direction of Pisces, the last figure in the zodiac. When Roman ceiling art casts Ganymede in the role of urn bearer, the slim-limbed boy struggles against Zeus, who bears him inexorably to a love-nest on Mount Olympus.

Interpreted by Christian apologists as the soul rising to heaven, a calmer, cherubic Ganymede reflects the human expectation of joy in the afterlife. The garment he wears is often the Greek chiton or a simple drape. His head bears a graceful fillet of flowers or a corona woven of myrtle, the magic healing herb. His composure seems appropriate to languid, recumbent gods and goddesses at the heavenly table or to the Christian vision of heaven as a serene escape from earth's upheavals.

Egyptians associated Aquarius with the god Hapi, the rainy season, and the yearly flooding of the Nile River, a propitious event that carried fertile river sludge to the parched land. In bas-relief, processionals place the water bearer alongside musicians, priests, and the sacred asp, symbol of Isis and fecundity. This set piece recurs in Roman art and attests to the widespread cult of Isis, one of many foreign deities in polytheistic Rome. To early Jews, water represented Genesis, in which the spirit of Yahweh moved across the deep. It also characterized Exodus and the leader Moses, epic progenitor of a ceaseless flow of law and justice from the Torah. Christianity continues to stress the living water of baptism, a cleansing, sanctifying, and refreshing gift of God—a token of grace and salvation. In Islam, the Koran declares that Allah's throne resides on water, the source of mercy and divine revelation.

In medieval times, more imaginative Aquarian symbolism appeared in the form of a sea maiden, which permeates heraldry with implications of a long and successful line issuing from a mythic union with a sea creature. Some 1,200 fountains in Rome date from the Renaissance and express the city's delight in free-spurting plumes of water and relaxing baths. The focus of Roman water art tends toward such fantasy figures as naiads, Tritons, and mermaids rather than the staid, servile Aquarius. The traditional water bearer recurs in a complex drawing of the contorted figure juggling towel and water jar, an illustrated constellation in Theodorus Graminaeus's *Arati Solensis Phaenomena et Prognostica* (Aratus's Solar Phenomena and Prognostications), published in 1569.

From ancient times, Aquarius has been labeled the perfect natal sign. In verse, the Roman poet Marcus Manilius claimed that "the good, the pious, and the just are born when first Aquarius pours out his urn" (Cavendish

1970, 111). In myth, this emphasis on freedom and breaking of bonds takes the form of love relationships between humans and water sprites, such as nereids, the wavy-haired mermaids, and the Rhine sirens called Lorelei. Literary depictions of Ganymede stress the shift of the shepherd boy's life from the Trojan plains to Olympus. The rapid transfer to heaven occurred while Ganymede was playing with Argos, his dog. Zeus's eagle Aquila swooped down, snatched up the boy, and deposited him at the throne. Ganymede asked one favor—to return to his people a dependable water supply; Zeus agreed and made rain, to even out the flow and spare humanity the misery of floods and droughts.

In Apollonius's *Argonautica*, the poet introduces Ganymede as a victimized water bearer. A pastoral setting places his lord in the orchard:

> with Ganymede, whom Zeus had established in heaven to dwell with the immortals because the boy's beauty filled him with desire. The two of them were playing with golden knucklebones, as young friends will. Greedy Eros' left hand was already full and he held the palm against his chest as he stood upright. The complexion of his cheeks bloomed with a sweet flush. Ganymede, however, squatted nearby, silent and downcast; he only had two knucklebones left, and he constantly threw one after another without achieving anything in his fury at Eros' crackling mockery. Very soon he lost these as well and went off empty-handed and distraught. (Apollonius 1995, 69)

Athena scolds her son Eros for taking advantage of Ganymede, who seems unaware of the precarious role of boy favorite of Zeus, the chief philanderer among the Olympian divinities.

The theme of the snatched boy serving at court animates William Shakespeare's *A Midsummer Night's Dream*, a popular stage fantasy that pits Oberon and Titania, the king and queen of fairies, in a domestic tiff over Titania's lovely changeling:

> For Oberon is passing fell and wrath,
> Because that she, as her attendant, hath
> A lovely boy, stolen from an Indian king—
> She never had so sweet a changeling—
> And jealous Oberon would have the child
> Knight of his train, to trace the forests wild;
> But she perforce withholds the loved boy,

Crowns him with flowers, and makes him all her joy.
(Shakespeare 1958, II, i, 20–27)

Titania claims to treasure the child because he is the offspring of her former handmaiden:

His mother was a vot'ress of my order;
And in the spiced Indian air, by night,
Full often hath she gossiped by my side,
And sat with me on Neptune's yellow sands,
Marking the embarked traders on the flood;
When we have laughed to see the sails conceive
And grow big-bellied with the wanton wind;
Which she, with pretty and with swimming gait
Following (her womb then rich with my young squire)
Would imitate, and sail upon the land
To fetch me trifles, and return again,
As from a voyage, rich with merchandise.
(Shakespeare 1958, II, i, 125–36)

Upon the servant's death, Titania fostered the boy. She explains, "for her sake do I rear up her boy, And for her sake I will not part with him" (Shakespeare II, i, 137–139). Obdurate against the pleas of her covetous husband, Titania, who broke with Oberon over the child's abduction, postures with an overstated maternal air. During the magical night in the forest, a fairy transfers the boy to Oberon's fairyland bower.

An example of Aquarian altruism lies at the center of poet Robert Browning's "My Last Duchess," a powerful verse drama in which a brutal egotist explains why he killed his wife. The Duchess's generosity and openness to all levels of society both astound and dismay her proud husband, who considers her a valuable possession not to be squandered on underlings. The Duchess's misunderstanding of her worth to a noble genealogy precipitates her husband's rage, a preface to murder. As the Duke phrases it, "I gave commands; then all smiles stopped together" (Browning 1949, 290). The sole reminder of her joyous embrace of life is the portrait that the Duke selfishly keeps covered until he has occasion to show her off to a guest.

In Egypt, Aquarius, a water spirit, bore two water jars, one on each shoulder. The duality inherent in the symbol coincides with the double wavy line, the ideograph by which astrologers abbreviate the house of Aquarius. Water symbolizes fluidity, vitality, and the life source, particularly to desert peoples. Psychologically, the flow represents the emersion of repressed thoughts from the unconscious to the conscious mind. In 1966, Gerome Ragni popularized the astrological significance of Aquarius in a song from *Hair*, a popular stage play, which predicts: that peace will guide the universe when the moon in the seventh house and Jupiter and Mars, coincide. His foretelling of "the dawning of the age of Aquarius" looks ahead to the alliance of Aquarius with the sun in 2200 A.D. New Age folklore connects this heavenly pattern with tranquillity, harmony, and peace on earth.

16
PISCES

ASTRONOMICAL FACTS

Pure Latin term for fish, Pisces (pih' seez or py' seez), abbreviated Psc, is the last of the zodiac's twelve signs. The fourteenth in size, the constellation borders Aquarius, Aries, Cetus, and Triangulum. Pisces, also called the Circlet, is a dim cluster of fifty stars that reach the fourth magnitude. There are five major stars:

alpha-one star	Alrisha, the cord
alpha-two star	Okda, the knot
beta star	Fum al Samakah, the fish's mouth
eta star	Alpherg
omega star	Torcularis Septentrionalis, northern wine press

The constellation, which lies between Aries and Aquarius south of Andromeda and near Pegasus, resembles a V with a triangle on the end of the shorter leg and a ring on the opposite leg. Alpherg, a focus in Pisces, is a double star accenting the tether that joins the two fish. The Greeks saw Alpherg as the head of the monster Typhon, which lies near the northern fish's tail. Pisces contains meteor showers in September and October and reaches the night sky's zenith in November. Established in the first century B.C., Pisces, called the First Point of Aries, contained the vernal equinox. The Hindu identified its zeta star as Revati, the rich.

ASTROLOGICAL HISTORY AND TRAITS

Governing the period between February 19 and March 20, Pisces may cover twenty-nine or thirty days, depending on the dispersal of an extra day to flesh out a leap year every four years. The dual sign of two fish is influenced by Jupiter and Neptune and attuned to the primordial waters from which creation sprang. It balances the beginning of destruction in Aquarius with a waning of power, which provides closure and finality, for example, to a flood or tide.

According to Ptolemy's *Almagest*, the fish sign originated in ancient times in the Egyptian zodiac, which named the figure the Pi-Cot Orion or Prolonged Fish. In Greek mythology, the joined fish relates to the escape of Aphrodite and Eros from Typhon. By jumping into a river, the two transformed themselves into fish and swam out of the monster's reach. In both Indian and Greek lore, the fish is the savior of humanity, whose life is imperiled by a cataclysmic flood, a parallel to the Judaic myth of Noah and the ark, a symbol of Church doctrine, which floats believers atop roiling waters, the liquid evil that covers the earth. Christian astronomers attached the fish imagery to Christ's selection of disciples, who came from a fishing community. In Matthew 4:19, Christ designates them as his first ministers, whom he called fishers of men.

As a group, Pisceans are stereotyped as pleasure-lovers who follow lofty ideals and attempt to draw others into their carefree attitude. Typically, they are emotive folk who refuse to answer to reason. A talented, weak-willed lot, they respond to imagination and mental stimulus and succeed in the arts, education, or the church, but fail in the business end of careers. Incapable of balancing their checkbooks or squaring tax returns, the standard Piscean is said to call on a consultant for advice in the simplest matters, from insurance to mortgage payments, or to let chaotic elements seek their own level and resolve themselves. Powered by vivid fantasies and vague periods of woolgathering, fish folk may escape inner turmoil to reside in a haven of the imagination.

By nature attuned to others' needs, Pisceans are said to make good-natured, sympathetic journalists, teachers, librarians, veterinarians, and nurses. Their lack of focus precipitates drift from the task at hand to any triviality that relieves them of making decisions. The fish sign predisposes the type to overacting and histrionics, the result of an inability to accept reality. The archetype hates the military, sports, and other forms of regimentation because Piscean makeup excludes competition and restriction. Because they pursue wishful thinking and easily part with money, they are prime targets of shysters, con artists, and unscrupulous relatives.

In zodiacal interpretation, the fish's dualism creates a streak of versatility, which unsympathetic outsiders may interpret as wishy-washiness. Outsiders are often amazed at a sudden burst of resilience or creative excellence, for example, the unforeseen success of Santiago, Ernest Hemingway's luckless fisherman in *The Old Man and the Sea* or the escape of the doubt-wracked protagonists in Margaret Atwood's *The Handmaid's Tale* or Lois Lowry's *The Giver*. The same duality precipitates untenable sympathy for pariahs and unfounded revulsion at harmless neighbors. Obstructions in the path of the Piscean's career include indiscretion and slovenliness. A popular winner of hearts, the archetype never lacks for friends, but often loses supporters. If life becomes too grim, the Piscean is said to withdraw from strife by retreating to the shore for fishing and contemplation, joining a monastery, erecting a house on a hill, or traveling to an undisclosed destination. Two literary masterpieces that draw on Pisces's penchant for escapism are Zora Neale Hurston's *Their Eyes Were Watching God* and Toni Morrison's *Beloved*, the near-tragic story of a plantation slave who flees her role as a breeder of more slaves.

In matters of love and survival, astrologers maintain that Pisces applies intuition and natural psychic powers, which counter self-destructive romanticism. Though unassuming in dress and behavior, devoted fish such as Jane Eyre yearn for a dashing, overpowering suitor. To enhance a lackluster romance, the type is capable of selecting the perfect sweetmeat or nosegay and composing a poetic *billet doux* to accompany it. St. Valentine may have had this sign in mind when designing the first love messages. At odd moments, the archetype receives strong extra-sensory signals from a potential lover, a power exhibited by the protagonist of Charlotte Brontë's *Jane Eyre* when she realizes that Edward Rochester, her former employer, needs her:

> It did not come out of the air, nor from under the earth, nor from overhead. I had heard it—where, or whence, for ever impossible to know! And it was the voice of a human being—a known loved, well-remembered voice—that of Edward Fairfax Rochester; and it spoke in pain and woe, wildly, eerily, urgently. (Brontë 1981, 401)

The call redeems Jane Eyre from a loveless marriage to St. John Rivers, a religious drudge. True to her Piscean nature, she flees Rivers and searches out Edward. Her otherworldly powers enable her to restore his failed vision and to produce a male heir.

In such storybook marriages as Jane's to Edward Rochester, the stereotypical Piscean adapts well to home and works willingly in the kitchen, yet skimps on regular chores that keep a love nest clean, orderly, and inviting. Housework centers the Piscean in domesticity punctuated by deep reading, meditation, gardening, and musical performances. The astral personality is strong in nurturance, particularly of hungry sparrows, stray cats, and neglected urchins, but is equally endowed with anxiety and misgivings about self and family. As a parent, the fish dotes on its young. When others accuse the fish's child of wrongdoing, there is hell to pay for the accuser. During private difficulties, the Piscean may lash out at a mate with harsh words or may slap a sassy child, then pour out affection to neutralize rancor. Overall, children profit from having a Piscean parent and grow up rich in security and trust.

The soft hair, gentle eyes, ready smile, and smooth complexion of the stereotypical Piscean betoken basic strength and health compromised by inherent fragility of frame, displayed in a forward head, widow's hump, and scoliosis or lordosis. The weakest of the type is notorious for psychosomatic ills and tends toward melancholia, schizophrenia, and madness, the curse of Jane Eyre's nemesis, Bertha Rochester. Problems with corns, flat feet, bunions, and fallen arches may not crop up until mid-life. Into old age, the Piscean affinity for wide-eyed incredulity and wonder drops years from the personality. Friends of all ages feel at home with the Piscean, whose soulfulness and candor welcome confessions and solicitations of advice. Deeply religious, the fish embraces a respect for God and belief in an afterlife, yet acknowledges a wide range of theological possibilities.

Pisces rules mosses and ferns, which grow near springs and rivulets, as well as seaweed and algae, natural companions for a water sign. A diet rich in dried beans, spinach and lettuce salad, and frequent snacks of nuts, figs, dates, raisins, and fresh fruit may relieve menstrual distress, inflammations, weakness, gout, ulcers, colitis, edema, and hemorrhage. Astral healers do not advise alcohol, even a sip of wine. According to the Egyptian Hermetica, beneficial herbal concoctions for the ailing Piscean should contain peppermint, saxifrage, vervain, and moss.

SYMBOLISM IN ART AND RELIGION

In art, the fish move in opposite directions to depict past and future, arrival and departure, and the beginning and end of cycles, especially the solar calendar. Romans decorated homes, wall murals, floor mosaics, jewelry, and pottery with fish shapes. They counted laps at the Circus Maximus with a clever line of bronze fish that the referee upended one by one. On a clay amphora found at Rome's Villa Julia, simple Etruscan designs feature lotus blossoms twining on the neck. The motif develops into a seascape with Triton, the fantailed god, bearing a fish in each hand. A Tarquinian burial vault built in the sixth century B.C. depicts a propitious pair of dolphins. They precede the prow of a ship in gladsome leaps at the surf. Seabirds flutter aloft as though linking the scene to a heavenly blessing. From the same era comes a red-lined cup depicting an ebullient myth in which Dionysus turned his ship into a vine-crowned fantasy barque. After seven crewmen leaped overboard, he changed them into dolphins, which balanced the bounty of vine and sea.

An energized seascape from first-century A.D. Ostia, Rome's warehouse district, decorates the Baths of the Seven Sages in black and white. One mosaic presents fish shapes dashing alongside Neptune's chariot, which is pulled by four horses. Fanciful sea creatures and human swimmers cavort on the periphery. Winged Cupids harness and drive two dolphins. The imaginative juxtaposition of horses with seahorses, eels, fish, and crustaceans harmonizes with the tastes of a sophisticated clientele.

The motif of frolicking dolphins derives from the story of the singer Arion, a luckless passenger on a Mediterranean vessel crewed by thieves and assassins. When the sailors hoist him to the gunwales, he sings a piteous melody that strikes the hearts of nearby dolphins. They swim under him and ferry him to shore. When the ship arrives in port, the crew meets retribution in the form of Arion and the authorities, who execute the sailors for attempted murder.

Other paired fish occur in a Roman myth about Venus and her son Cupid. Waylaid by Typhon, a fire dragon, they flee to water, the element that Typhon must avoid. Venus, the love goddess born of sea form, escapes easily. She and Cupid are changed into fish and slip under the dark Mediterranean waters. To keep together, she tethers herself to her son. According to Al-Sufi, the Persian astronomer, the yoked pair were mirrored in the sky by Pisces.

Because the equinox moved to the west into the sign of Pisces, the Christian used the Greek *ichthous* or fish as an anagram for Christ, which they derived from the phrase: *Iesous Christos Theou Uios Soter* (Jesus Christ, Son of God, Savior). An image of everlasting life in Christian symbolism, the fish summed up the spiritual goal of Christianity. Prominently arranged on a third-century A.D. cask found in Konia, Turkey, the fish harmonize with columns, pediments, and arches, all classical elements. As an unassuming marker for a safe house, the symbol welcomed followers of the new religion to fellow converts. The fish emblem remains strong in European religious celebrations, which feature fish-shaped chocolates, pastries, breads, trinkets, good luck talismen, and chrismons. Fundamentalist Christians favor the fish emblem as a bumper sticker or on jewelry and T-shirts.

Like the Orphic mysteries that grew out of the dismemberment of the singer Orpheus, Pisces governs occult rituals and secrets. The Christian concept of earthly death followed by spiritual resurrection links the fish with hope. The sign represents mystic fusion or epiphany, the sudden realization of a concept or image, in particular, the end as a prologue to a new beginning. For Christians, the end is penitence and a rejection of the old life. The new life results from a burial in water or baptism, a sacrament conferring hope of redemption and resurrection.

The converse of fish imagery is a funereal association with putrefaction and disintegration, often symbolized by the suffocating airlessness of the tomb at Maundy Thursday services, skeletons in Good Friday processions, skulls, crows, and vultures. Compounding the concept of the fish as a symbol of regeneration is Christ's promise to make his disciples fishers of men. These spreaders of the gospel, or "good news," uplifted the downtrodden with promises of everlasting life and salvation for followers of Christ's teachings. The imagery extends to church architecture, in which the nave, derived from the Latin for *ship*, assembles the elect of Christ.

Appendix I

A TIME LINE
OF DEVELOPMENTS IN
ZODIACAL STUDY

25,000 B.C.	Early humans note phases of the moon by notching mammoth tusks and reindeer antlers.
2750 B.C.	Sargon of Agade charts solar eclipses and oversees the composition of *The Day of Bel*, an astrological handbook.
2449 B.C.	Chinese astronomers identify the constellation Capricornus.
ca. 2150 B.C.	Job, the sufferer in the Old Testament, refers to the constellations.
2073 B.C.	China's first emperor sacrifices to the seven planets.
1800 B.C.	Celtic astrologers construct Stonehenge.
ca. 1750 B.C.	Babylonians divide the year into twelve lunar months.
1375 B.C.	Pharaoh Ikhnaton commissions a hymn to the sun.
ca. 1350 B.C.	Sumerians worship the sun, moon, and Venus, whom they call Ishtar.
ca. 1000 B.C.	Babylonians learn cast horoscopes based on five planets—Ishtar, Nergal, Marduk, Ninib, and Nebo.
ca. 900 B.C.	Greeks acquire Mesopotamian calculations of equinoxes and phases of the moon.
ca. 700 B.C.	Babylonians begin to shape their zodiac.

ca. 650 B.C.   King Ashurbanipal expands the royal library at Nineveh to include the Creation Legend documenting astral positions.

ca. 600 B.C.   Mediterranean rulers seek guidance from astrologers. Also, Thales of Miletus, a Greek astronomer, introduces Phoenician astrology.

ca. 550 B.C.   Anaximander describes the universe geometrically. Anaximene depicts the stars as nailed to a crystal overlayer that rotates about the earth.

ca. 539 B.C.   Chaldeans use asterism to predict human fate.

ca. 530 B.C.   Pythagoras theorizes that heavenly bodies move in concentric circles and produce a celestial harmony.

ca. 500 B.C.   The table of Cambyses contains a codified zodiac.

ca. 475 B.C.   Eustemon of Athens writes a weather almanac that links forecasts with Aquarius and other constellations

ca. 450 B.C.   Folklorist Pherecydes of Athens uses mythology to account for the setting of the constellation Orion as Scorpio rises. Oenopides discovers the ecliptic.

419 B.C.   Babylonians identify the constellations as Aries, Gemini, Leo, Libra, Scorpio, Sagittarius, Capricornus, Aquarius, and Pisces plus Pleiades, Praesepe, and Spica, which were later changed to Taurus, Cancer, and Virgo.

409 B.C.   Babylonians produce the first horoscope.

400 B.C.   Egyptians interpret mathematical calculations of the positions of constellations.

ca. 350 B.C.   Eudoxus of Cnidus, author of *Phaenomena*, composes a verse description of constellations.

331 B.C.   Alexander the Great conquers Chaldea.

ca. 310 B.C.   Heracleides hypothesizes that the earth rotates, planets move about the sun, and stars remain fixed.

300 B.C.   Euclid applies geometric axioms to astronomy.

ca. 280 B.C.   Berosus, priest of Marduk, writes *Babyloniaca*, a compendium applying star knowledge to healing.

ca. 275 B.C.   Babylonian astronomer Kiddinu explains equinoxes.

ca. 250 B.C.   Eratosthenes calculates the earth's circumference.

ca. 250 B.C.	The Greek poet Aratus writes *Phenomena*, which explains how star groups are named.
ca. 225 B.C.	Eratosthenes composes *Catasterisms*, a collection of forty-four zodiacal myths.
220 B.C.	Carneades warns that astrology violates reason.
ca. 150 B.C.	Hypsicles composes *On Rising Times*, which calculates the appearance of zodiacal figures.
139 B.C.	Rome's college of auguries ousts the *Chaldei*.
120 B.C.	Hipparchus compiles a catalogue of 800 stars.
ca. 100 B.C.	The Farnese Globe positions constellations.
70 B.C.	Greeks cast natal horoscopes. Geminus publishes *Introduction to Astronomy*, a scientific description of the heavens.
ca. 45 B.C.	Cicero composes *On Divination*, which argues that astrology is ignorant superstition.
33 B.C.	Augustus Caesar temporarily bans horoscopy.
30 B.C.	Thrasyllus interprets Augustus's horoscope.
ca. 15 A.D.	Manilius publishes *Astronomicon*, which links the zodiac and human character.
ca. 50	Strabo writes a geography text that proclaims the accuracy of the Chaldean zodiac.
52	Claudius evicts soothsayers from Rome.
ca. 100	The Maya evolve cyclic star interpretation.
127	Juvenal publishes *Satire VI*, which lampoons women for dependence on astrology.
140	Ptolemy completes *Tetrabiblos*, which defends the casting of horoscopes, and *Almagest*, which formalizes Ptolemy's astral interpretations.
ca. 150	The *Planisphere of Geruvigus* maps constellations as seen from Earth.
ca. 190	Galen publishes the *Prognostication of Disease by Astrology*, which links disease and healing with the zodiac.
397	Augustine's *Confessions* claim that astrology violates Christian doctrine.
ca. 400	Catholic doctrine rejects zodiac study as heretical.

700	Islamic astrologers practice astral prognostication.
ca. 950	Arabic documents record astral calculations.
ca. 1200	Astrology separates into specialized fields.
ca. 1250	Johannes Campanus systematizes zodiacal houses.
1275	Chinese astrologers advise Kublai Khan on matters of state.
1400	Aztecs worship Quetzalcoatl, the feathered serpent representing the planet Venus.
1437	Ulush Beg duplicates Ptolemy's star studies.
ca. 1450	Printed astrology textbooks, almanacs, and tables become available. Johann Müller translates Ptolemy's *Almagest* for use in ephemerides.
1536	Peter Bienewitz carves forty-eight constellations in a woodcut.
1540	Alessandro Piccolomini publishes *De le Stelle Fisse*, a compendium of star charts.
1543	Copernicus publishes *De Revolutionibus Orbium Caelestium*, disproving the heliocentric universe.
1555	Nostradamus's prophecies are published.
1595	Pieter Dircksz Keyser adds twelve star clusters to the southern constellations.
1603	Johann Hondius places Keyser's constellations on a globe. Johann Bayer publishes *Uranometria*, which charts the thirteen new southern constellations.
1619	Johannes Kepler reconciles planetary motion with modern astrology in *Astronomia Nova* and *Harmonice Mundi*.
1647	William Lilly predicts the London Fire, plague, and decapitation of Charles I.
1664	Robert Hooke discovers Mesarthim, Aries's gamma star.
1666	The French Academy of Sciences bans Colbert's astrology.
1687	Isaac Newton publishes *Principia Mathematica*, a modern astronomy text.
1690	Hevelius identifies nine new constellations.
1729	John Flamsteed catalogues 3,000 stars.
1763	Nicolas L. de Lacaille locates fourteen constellations.

1781	William Herschel finds Uranus in Gemini's boundaries.
1784	French astronomer Charles Messier numbers fifteen objects in Sagittarius and eleven in Virgo in his *New General Catalogue*, a compendium of nebulae.
1800	Johann Elert Bode maps the monthly shift of constellations.
1801	Giuseppe Piazzi discovers Ceres, the first asteroid.
1814	Piazzi publishes a star catalog.
ca. 1820	Goethe studies astrology.
1824	Robert Cross Smith introduces popular horoscopy.
1828	Raphael of England writes *The Manual of Astrology*.
ca. 1835	The Romantic movement revives astrology.
ca. 1850	William Parsons Rosse locates the Crab Nebula.
1863	F.W.A. Argelander publishes *Atlas des nordlichen gestimten Himmels,* which catalogs 324,198 stars.
ca. 1875	Alan Leo issues a medieval astrology text and pamphlets on astral predictions.
1898	Svante Arrhenius links human life, weather, and the lunar cycle.
1930s	Horoscopes reach the public through magazines, newspapers, and annual handbooks.
1930	Clyde W. Tombaugh spots Pluto in Gemini.
1930	Eugène Delporte's *Délimitation Scientifique des Constellations* standardizes constellation boundaries. The International Astronomical Union completes a definitive list of stars.
1939	Nazis apply Nostradamus's predictions to a master race.
1940	A. L. Tchijevsky links sunspots and human life.
1941	Maki Takata connects a solar ray and blood serum.
1948	Frank Brown establishes the theory of biorhythms.
1950	Giorgio Piccardi studies the effects of the cosmos on chemical analysis.
1957	Satellites disclose interactions between solar bodies.
1960	Research correlates heredity and the planets.
1963	Maarten Schmidt defines quasars.

Appendix II

A COMPARATIVE CHART OF ELEMENTS OF THE CONSTELLATIONS OF THE ZODIAC

	Aqr	Ari	Cap	Cnc	Gem	Leo
directly overhead						
(month/day)	8/25	10/30	8/8	1/30	1/5	3/1
highest altitude						
(month/day)	2/24	4/31	2/5	8/1	7/8	8/31
brightness	5.715	6.344	7.489	4.545	9.148	5.491
brightness ranking	8th	7th	5th	11th	3rd	10th
area in sq. deg.	979.85	441.39	413.95	505.87	513.76	946.96
ranking in area	2nd	11th	12th	9th	8th	3rd
number of stars	56	28	31	23	47	52
number of major stars	6	4	7	5	13	12
	Lib	Psc	Sco	Sgr	Tau	Vir
directly overhead						
(month/day)	11/8	3/29	12/4	1/6	6/2	10/12
highest altitude						
(month/day)	5/9	9/27	6/3	7/7	11/30	4/11

	Lib	Psc	Sco	Sgr	Tau	Vir
brightness	6.505	5.622	12.480	7.493	12.292	4.481
brightness ranking	6th	9th	1st	4th	2nd	12th
area in sq. deg.	538.05	889.42	496.78	867.43	797.25	1294.43
ranking in area	7th	4th	10th	5th	6th	1st
number of stars	35	50	62	65	98	58
number of major stars	5	4	12	13	15	13

Appendix III

GEOGRAPHICAL AREAS LINKED WITH SUN SIGNS

Astrologers who apply zodiacal care to history find patterns in the topography and rule of geographical locations.

Sign	Countries, Continents	Islands, Mountains	Cities
Aquarius	Afghanistan		Bremen
	Russia		Hamburg
Aries	England		Florence
	Denmark		Marseilles
	Germany		Verona
	Syria		
Cancer	Africa		Algiers
	Holland		Amsterdam
	Scotland		Cadiz
			Genoa
			Milan
			Venice
Capricorn	Albania	Orkney Islands	Oxford
	Bulgaria		

Sign	Countries, Continents	Islands, Mountains	Cities
	East India		
	Greece		
	Mexico		
Gemini	Belgium		Cordoba
	United States		London
			Nuremberg
			New York
			Versailles
Leo	Chaldea	Alps	Philadelphia
	France		Prague
	Italy		Rome
Libra	China		Antwerp
	Japan		Frankfurt
	West India		Lisbon
			Vienna
Pisces	Portugal		Alexandria
			Seville
Sagittarius	Arabia		Avignon
	Hungary		Cologne
	Spain		Narbonne
	Yugoslavia		Toledo
Scorpio	Morocco		Ghent
	Norway		Liverpool
Taurus	Mideast	Cyprus	Dublin
	Russia	Samos	Leipzig
			Parma
Virgo	Switzerland	West Indies	Babylon
	Turkey		Jerusalem
			Paris
			Toulouse

Appendix IV

PLANETARY CORRESPONDENCES

Planet	Jewels	Metals	Herbs	Governance
Sun	diamond ruby carbuncle	gold	almond celandine juniper rue saffron	business executives authority figures
Moon	pearl opal moonstone	silver	chickweed hyssop purslain moonwort	workers public figures
Mercury	quicksilver	quicksilver	calamint endive horehound marjoram pellitory valerian	intelligentsia business leaders

Planet	Jewels	Metals	Herbs	Governance
Venus	emerald	copper	artichoke foxglove fern sorrel spearmint	good will ambassadors social leaders
Mars	bloodstone flint	iron	aloe caper coriander crowfoot gentian ginger honeysuckle pepper	military leaders weapon makers
Jupiter	amethyst turquoise	tin	anise balm myrrh lime linden nutmeg jessamine	judiciary investors and financiers
Saturn	garnet black stones	lead	aconite fumitory ivy medlar moss aloe senna	executives of state the poor
Uranus	chalcedony lapis lazuli	radium		transportation workers
Neptune	coral ivory	lithium platinum		social workers demagogues
Pluto	beryl jade	tungsten plutonium		organized labor idealists

Planet	Color	Flavor/Smell	Form/Shape	Sense	Pathology
Sun	orange gold yellow	sweet pungent	circle curve arc		fever disease of the spleen, heart, spine
Moon	white pearl opal iridescence	odorless tasteless	skewed lines		inflamed mucosa endocrine imbalance
Mercury	slate-gray	astringent	short lines	sight	nerve ailments
Venus	cerulean mint	warm sweet	curves	touch	blood impurity
Mars	carmine	astringent pungent	straight lines angles	taste	infection
Jupiter	purple deep blue	fragrant	curves	smell	indigestion
Saturn		cold sour	short lines	hearing	melancholia rheumatism skin disease
Uranus	streaks mixtures	cold astringent	broken lines		swelling
Neptune	lavender	seductive	curves		glandular ailments
Pluto	luminous shades	aromatic	straight lines sharp angles		arthritis acidosis

Appendix V

ZODIACAL PATHOLOGY

One of the lesser regions of sun sign application stereotypes human tendencies toward physical disturbance and illness or dysfunction.

Sign	Eating Habits	Symptoms	Afflictions
Aries	hurried, finicky	excessive force, hot, dry skin, inflammation	sleep disturbances, brain irregularities, vertigo, inflamed eyes and gums, scalp disease, fever, fainting
Taurus	overeater, simple palate, loves potatoes	brooding, anger, intractibility, love of luxury	laryngitis, tonsillitis, throat polyps, bronchitis, swollen glands, goiter, stroke
Gemini	small meals, likes buffets	restlessness, nervousness, dark moods	asthma, pneumonia, anemia, consumption, tuberculosis, blood and pulmonary disease, neuritis
Cancer	high water content, tends to gain weight	torpor, suspicion, vengefulness, overeating	alcoholism, gastritis, flatulence, indigestion, sclerosis, hiccups

Sign	Eating Habits	Symptoms	Afflictions
Leo	needs pampering	arrogance, obsession, impulsiveness	heart irregularity, angina, ataxia, spinal weakness, fever, spleen dysfunction
Virgo	picky, dyspeptic	hypercriticism, self-absorption, hypochondria	poor nutrition, bowel complaints, constipation, appendicitis, colic, peritonitis, parasites
Libra	prefers ornate place settings	hypersensitivity, melancholia, jealousy	lumbar pain, nephritis, diabetes, uremia, renal dysfunction
Scorpio	Spicy, likes condiments and hors d'oeuvres	nettlesomeness, dominance, destructiveness	venereal disease, fistula, uterine disease, urethritis, prostatitis, rhinitis, hernia
Sagittarius	red meat	accidents, restlessness, lack of focus	sciatica, rheumatism, hip degeneration, motor dysfunction
Capricorn	controls diet, eats health food	dry mucosa, hesitancy, crystallization	dislocated joints, knee degeneration, eczema
Aquarius	salt, multicultural cuisine, natural foods	suicidal, hyper-sensitivity, tics, anxiety	edema, leg cramps, varicose veins, skin disease, neuralgia
Pisces	bubbly drinks, low spice, casseroles	sensitivity, weakness, flab, secretiveness, addictive behavior	deformed toes and arches, gout, tumors

BIBLIOGRAPHY

PRIMARY SOURCES

Aesop. *Aesop's Fables*. Los Angeles: Troubador Press, 1986.

Apollonius. *Jason and the Golden Fleece*. New York: Oxford Press, 1995.

Aratus, trans. G. R. Mair. Loeb Classical Library. Cambridge, Mass.: Harvard University Press, 1989.

Aristotle. *The Works of Aristotle*. 2 vols. Oxford: Clarendon Press, 1930.

Augustine. *The City of God*. London: Penguin, 1984.

————. *The City of God*. www.cs.bc.edu/~Kwashim/city—of—god. html, November 11, 1996.

Brontë, Charlotte. *Jane Eyre*. New York: Bantam, 1981.

Browning, Robert, "My Last Duchess." In ed. James Stephens, et al. *Victorian and Later English Poets*. New York: American Book, 1949.

Carroll, Lewis, "Jabberwocky." In ed. Walter Loban, et al. *Adventures in Appreciation*. New York: Harcourt Brace & World, 1958.

Catullus, trans. Francis Warre Cornish. Loeb Classical Library. Cambridge, Mass.: Harvard University Press, 1893.

Chaucer, Geoffrey. *The Works of Geoffrey Chaucer*. Boston: Houghton Mifflin, 1961.

Cicero. *De Natura Deorum*. Boston: Ginn & Heath, 1885.

————. *De Senectute*. London: Macmillan, 1926.

————. *Marcus Tullius Cicero: Seven Orations*. Boston: Silver Burdett, 1912.

————. *Selected Orations*. Boston: Allyn & Bacon, 1904.

————. *Select Orations*. Chicago: Benjamin H. Sanborn, 1915.

————. *Select Orations of Marcus Tullius Cicero*. Philadelphia: Eldredge & Brother, 1880.

Copernicus, Nicolaus. *On the Revolutions of the Heavenly Spheres*. Chicago: Encyclopedia Britannica, 1963.

Dante Alighieri. *The Divine Comedy*. New York: Washington Square Press, 1966.

————. *The Inferno*. New York: New American Library, 1982.

Flaubert, Gustave. *Madame Bovary*. New York: Signet, 1964.

Galen. *On Medical Experience*. http://web/.ea.pvt.k12.pa.us/medant/Gal Natl.htm, November 18, 1996.

Gilgamesh, trans. Danny P. Jackson. New York: Farrar, Straus and Giroux, 1992.

Godolphin, Francis R. B., ed. *The Latin Poets*. New York: Modern Library, 1949.

Greer, John Michael, ed. *Corpus Hermeticum*. www.memoria.com/caduceus/ hermetica/index.html, November 11, 1996.

Grene, David, and Richmond Lattimore, eds. *Greek Tragedies, Volumes 1–3*. Chicago: University of Chicago Press, 1960.

Hamilton, Edith. *Mythology*. Boston: Little, Brown, 1942.

Herodotus. *The Histories*. Baltimore: Penguin, 1961.

————. *Persian Wars*. New York: Modern Library, 1942.

Hesiod, trans. Richmond Lattimore. Ann Arbor: University of Michigan, 1973.

Holy Bible. Grand Rapids, Mich.: Zondervan, 1978.

Homer. *Homeric Hymns*. Newburyport, Mass.: Focus, 1995.

————. *The Odyssey*. New York: Harper & Row, 1967.

Hugo, Victor. *Les Miserables*. New York: Fawcett, 1961.

Hyginus. *Hygini Fabulae*. Leyden, Holland: A. W. Sythoff, 1933.

Josephus. *Complete Works*. Grand Rapids, Mich.: Kregel, 1960.

Jung, Carl G. *Man and His Symbols*. Garden City, N. Y.: Doubleday, 1964.

————. *Memories, Dreams, Reflections*. New York: Pantheon, 1963.

Juvenal. *The Satires*. New York: Oxford University Press, 1992.

————. *The Satires of Juvenal*. Boston: Allyn & Bacon, 1892.

————. *The Satires of Juvenal*. New York: American Book, 1890.

Kepler, Johannes. *Epitome of Copernican Astronomy: The Harmonies of the World*. Chicago: Encyclopedia Britannica, 1963.

Ovid. *Metamorphoses*. Cambridge: Harvard University Press, 1984.

————. *Selections from Ovid*. Boston: Ginn, 1891.

Petronius. *The Cena Trimalchionis*. Oxford: Clarendon, 1925.

————. *Satyricon*. New York: Book Collectors, 1934.

Plato. *The Republic*. In *Great Dialogues of Plato*. trans. W.H.D. Rouse. New York: Mentor, 1956.

————. *Timaeus*. http://the-tech.mit.edu/Classics/Plato.timaeus. body.html, November 15, 1996.

Pliny. *Natural History*. Cambridge, Mass.: Harvard University Press, n.d.

Plutarch. *Plutarch's Lives*. New York: P. F. Collier & Son, 1909.

————. *Plutarch's Lives of the Noble Greeks*. New York: Dell, 1963.

Ptolemy. *The Almagest*. Chicago: Encyclopedia Britannica, 1963.

Qabalah. www.memoria.com/caduceus/qabalah/index.html, November 11, 1996.

Shakespeare, William. *Henry IV*. New York: Washington Square Press, 1960.

————. *Julius Caesar*. New York: Washington Square Press, 1959.

————. *King Lear*. New York: Washington Square, 1957.

————. *A Midsummer Night's Dream*. New York: Washington Square, 1958.

Stevenson, Robert Louis. *Treasure Island*. New York: Airmont, 1962.

Stewart, Mary. *The Crystal Cave*. New York: Fawcett Crest, 1970.

Tennyson, Alfred, "The Lady of Shalott." In *Victorian and Later English Poets*. ed. James Stephens, et al. New York: American Book, 1949.

Tu Fu, "Night in the Watch-Tower." In *World Masterpieces*. gen. ed. Eileen Thompson. Cambridge, Mass.: Prentice-Hall, 1991.

"United Nations Charter," *Encyclopedia Americana*, Vol. XXVII. Danbury, Conn.: Grolier, 1987.

Virgil. *Eclogues, Georgics, Aeneid I-VI*. Cambridge, Mass: Harvard University Press, 1967.

————. *Virgil's Works*. New York: Modern Library, 1950.

SECONDARY SOURCES

Allen, Richard Hinckley. *Star Names: Their Lore and Meaning*. New York: Dover, 1963.

Asimov, Isaac. *Words from the Myths*. New York: Signet, 1969.

Bakich, Michael. *The Cambridge Guide to the Constellations*. New York: Cambridge University, 1995.

Bartlett, John. *Familiar Quotations*. Boston: Little, Brown, 1992.

Bell, Robert. *Dictionary of Classical Mythology*. Santa Barbara, Calif.: ABC-Clio, 1982.

————. *Place-Names in Classical Mythology*. Santa Barbara, Calif.: ABC-Clio, 1989.

————. *Women of Classical Mythology*. Santa Barbara, Calif.: ABC-Clio, 1991.

Bernbaum, Ernest, ed. *Anthology of Romanticism*. New York: Ronald Press, 1948.

Biedermann, Hans. *Dictionary of Symbolism*. New York: Facts on File, 1992.

Blitzer, Charles. *The Age of Kings*. New York: Time, 1967.

Bowder, Diana, ed. *Who Was Who in the Greek World*. New York: Washington Square Press, 1982.

————, ed. *Who Was Who in the Roman World*. New York: Washington Square Press, 1980.

Bowra, C. M., et al. *Classical Greece*. New York: Time, 1965.

Boyce, Charles. *Shakespeare A to Z*. New York: Facts on File, 1990.

Brown, Norman O. *Hermes the Thief: The Evolution of a Myth*. New York: Vintage, 1969.

Capt, E. Raymond. *The Glory of the Stars*. Thousand Oaks, Calif.: Artisan Sales, 1976.

Carpenter, Rhys. *Folk Tale, Fiction and Saga in the Homeric Epics*. Berkeley: University of California Press, 1958.

Casson, Lionel. *The Ancient Mariners: Seafarers and Sea Fighters of the Mediterranean in Ancient Times*. Princeton, N.J.: Princeton University Press, 1990.

Cavendish, Richard, ed. *Man, Myth & Magic*. New York: Marshall Cavendish, 1970.

Ceram, C. W. *Gods, Graves, and Scholars: The Story of Archaeology*. New York: Alfred A. Knopf, 1968.

Chute, Marchette. *Geoffrey Chaucer of England*. New York: E. P. Dutton, 1946.

"Cicero on Divination and the Gods." www.111.perseus.tufts.edu/~ellen/omens.html, November 11, 1996.

Cirlot, J. E. *A Dictionary of Symbols*. New York: Dorset Press, 1991.

Clark, R. T. Rundle. *Myth and Symbol in Ancient Egypt*. London: Thames & Hudson, 1978.

Cooper, J. C. *An Illustrated Encyclopaedia of Traditional Symbols*. London: Thames & Hudson, 1978.

Cumont, Franz. *Astrology and Religion Among the Greeks and Romans*. New York: Dover, 1960.

Devereux, Paul. *Secrets of Ancient and Sacred Places: The World's Mysterious Heritage*. London: Blandford, 1992.

Dolan, Chris. *The Constellations and Their Stars*. www.astro.wisc.edu/~dolan/constellations/html, October 3, 1996.

Duff, J. Wight, and A. M. Duff. *A Literary History of Rome in the Golden Age*. London: Ernest Benn, 1960.

————. *A Literary History of Rome in the Silver Age*. London: Ernest Benn, 1964.

Durant, Will. *The Story of Civilization: The Life of Greece*. New York: Simon & Schuster, 1939.

Edwards, Paul, ed. *The Encyclopedia of Philosophy*. New York: Macmillan, 1973.

Encyclopedia Britannica. (CD-Rom) Chicago: Encyclopedia Britannica, 1997.

Evslin, Bernard. *Heroes, Gods and Monsters of the Greek Myths*. New York: Bantam, 1968.

Feder, Lillian. *The Meridian Handbook of Classical Mythology*. New York: New American Library, 1970.

Fischer, Carl. *The Myth and Legend of Greece*. Dayton, Ohio: Pflaum, 1968.

Flaceliere, Robert. *A Literary History of Greece*. New York: Mentor, 1962.

Forbes, J. T. *Socrates*. Edinburgh: T. & T. Clark, 1913.

Fox-Davies, A. C. *A Complete Guide to Heraldry*. London: Thomas Nelson, 1969.

Frazer, Sir James George. *The Golden Bough*. New York: Macmillan, 1947.

Gardner, John. *The Life and Times of Chaucer*. New York: Alfred A. Knopf, 1977.

Gauquelin, Michel. *The Cosmic Clocks*. New York: Avon Books, 1967.

Gill, Sam D., and Irene F. Sullivan. *Dictionary of Native American Mythology*. Santa Barbara, Calif.: ABC-Clio, 1992.

Gleadow, Rupert. *The Origin of the Zodiac*. London: Jonathan Cape, 1968.

Goldschneider, Gary. *The Secret Language of Birthdays*. New York: Penguin, 1994.

Grant, Michael. *Ancient History Atlas*. New York: Sanford J. Durst, 1971.

——— . *Myths of the Greeks and Romans*. New York: Mentor, 1962.

Graves, Robert. *The Greek Myths*. London: Penguin, 1960.

——— . *New Larousse Encyclopedia of Mythology*. London: Prometheus Press, 1970.

Gregory, Richard, ed. *The Oxford Companion to the Mind*. New York: Oxford University Press, 1987.

Grimal, Pierre. *Dictionary of Classical Mythology*. London: Penguin, 1990.

Guerber, H. A. *Myths of Greece and Rome*. New York: American Book, 1921.

Hadas, Moses. *Ancilla to Classical Reading*. New York: Columbia University Press, 1954.

Halc, William Harlan. *The Horizon Book of Ancient Rome*. New York: American Heritage, n. d.

Hallam, Elizabeth, ed. *Saints: Who They Are and How They Help You*. New York: Simon & Schuster, 1994.

Hammerton, J. A., ed. *Wonders of the Past: The Romance of Antiquity and Its Splendours*. Vols I–IV. New York: William H. Wise, 1933.

Hammond Historical Atlas of the World. Maplewood, N.J.: Hammond, Inc. 1984.

Heifetz, Milton D., and Will Tirion. *A Walk Through the Heavens: A Guide to Stars and Constellations and Their Legends*. Cambridge: Cambridge University Press, 1996.

Heindel, Max, and Augusta Foss Heindel. *Astro-Diagnosis: A Guide to Healing*. Oceanside, Calif.: Rosicrucian Fellowship.

"Hermes Trismegistus: The Archaic Underground Tradition." http://marlowe.win-sey.com/~rhand/streams/scripts/hermes.html, November 11, 1996.

"The History of Space Exploration: Gemini Spacecraft." http://nauts.com/hist-pace/vehicles/histgemini.html, November 26, 1996.

Hodgkins, Adrian. *Britain's Kings and Queens*. Eastleigh, Hants: Pitkin Pictorials, 1994 (pamphlet).

Hooke, S. H. *Middle Eastern Mythology*. Baltimore: Penguin, 1963.

Howatson, M. C., ed. *The Oxford Companion to Classical Literature*. New York: Oxford, 1991.

Howell, Michael, and Peter Ford. *The True History of the Elephant Man*. London: Allison and Busby, 1980.

In the Image of Man: The Indian Perception of the Universe Through 2000 Years of Painting and Sculpture. New York: Alpine Fine Arts, 1982.

James, Peter, and Nick Thorpe. *Ancient Inventions*. New York: Ballantine, 1994.

King, Henry C. *Pictorial Guide to the Stars*. New York: Thomas Y. Crowell, 1967.

Kramer, Samuel Noah. *Cradle of Civilization*. New York: Time, 1967.

Larrington, Carolyne. *The Feminist Companion to Mythology*. New York: Pandora, 1992.

Leeming, David Adams. *The World of Myth*. New York: Oxford, 1990.

Lemesurier, Peter. *Gospel of the Stars: A Celebration of the Mystery of the Zodiac*. New York: St. Martin's, 1977.

Levitt, I. M., and Roy K. Marshall. *Star Maps for Beginners*. New York: Simon & Schuster, 1992.

Lurker, Manfred. *The Gods and Symbols of Ancient Egypt*. London: Thames & Hudson, 1984.

Lynch, John, ed. *The Coffee Table Book of Astrology*. New York: Viking, 1967.

Lyttelton, Margaret, and Werner Forman. *The Romans: Their Gods and Their Beliefs*. London: Orbis, 1985.

MacKendrick, Paul. *The Mute Stones Speak: The Story of Archaeology in Italy*. New York: Mentor, 1960.

MacNeice, Louis. *Astrology*. Garden City, N. Y.: Doubleday, 1964.

Magnusson, Magnus, ed. *Cambridge Biographical Dictionary*. Cambridge: Cambridge University Press, 1990.

Mantinband, James H. *Dictionary of Greek Literature*. Paterson, N.J.: Littlefield, Adams, 1963.

——— . *Dictionary of Latin Literature*. Paterson, N.J.: Littlefield, Adams, 1964.

"McDonnell Gemini Spacecraft." www.am.upsafb.af.mil/museum/space, November 26, 1996.

McEvedy, Colin. *The Penguin Atlas of Ancient History*. London: Penguin, 1967.

Mikolaycak, Charles. *Orpheus*. New York: Harcourt Brace Jovanovich, 1992.

Miller, James, et al. *Literature of the Eastern World*. Glenview, Ill.: Scott, Foresman, 1970.

Milton, Joyce. *Sunrise of Power: Ancient Egypt*. Boston: Boston Publishing, 1986.

Montagu, Ashley. *The Elephant Man: A Study in Human Dignity*. New York: E. P. Dutton, 1979.

More, Daisy, and John Bowman. *Aegean Rivals*. Empires Series. Boston: Boston Publishing, 1986.

Morford, Mark P. O., and Robert J. Lenardon. *Classical Mythology*. New York: Longman, 1977.

Moyer, Linda Lancione, and Burl Willes. *Undiscovered Islands of the Mediterranean*. Santa Fe, N.M.: John Muir Publications, 1992.

Murison, Charles Leslie. "The Death of Titus: A Reconsideration." http://137.122.15/Docs/Directories/AHB/AHB9/AHB-9–3f/html, November 11, 1996.

Neal, Bill. *Gardener's Latin*. Chapel Hill, N. C.: Algonquin Books, 1992.

O'Donnell, James J. "Augustine's City of God." http://ccat.sas.upenn.edu/~rs/4/augustine.html, November 11, 1996.

Parker, Sybil P. *McGraw-Hill Concise Encyclopedia of Science & Technology*. New York: McGraw-Hill, 1989.

Perowne, Stewart. *Roman Mythology*. London: Paul Hamlyn, 1969.

Pierce, James Smith. *From Abacus to Zeus*. Englewood Cliffs, N. J.: Prentice Hall, 1991.

Pinsent, John. *Greek Mythology*. London: Paul Hamlyn, 1969.

Progoff, Ira. *The Symbolic and the Real*. New York: McGraw-Hill, 1964.

Radice, Betty. *Who's Who in the Ancient World*. New York: Penguin, 1984.

Rawson, Hugh, and Margaret Miner. *The New International Dictionary of Quotations*. New York: New American Library, 1986.

Riggsby, Andrew M. "Cicero Homepage." www.dla.utexas.edu/depts/classics/documents/Cic.html, November 11, 1996.

Robson, Vivian E. *The Fixed Stars and Constellations in Astrology*. New York: Samuel Weiser, 1969.

Rose, H. J. *Gods and Heroes of the Greeks*. New York: Meridian, 1960.

————. *A Handbook of Greek Literature*. New York: E. P. Dutton, 1960.

Rosenberg, Donna. *World Mythology*. Lincolnwood, Ill.: Passport Books, 1992.

Rosenberg, Donna, and Sorelle Baker. *Mythology and You: Classical Mythology and Its Relevance to Today's World*. Lincolnwood, Ill.: National Textbook, 1984.

Seltman, Charles. *The Twelve Olympians*. New York: Crowell, 1962.

Severy, Merle, ed. *Greece and Rome: Builders of Our World*. Washington, D. C.: National Geographic, 1977.

Shulman, Sandra. *Astrology*. New York: Hamlyn, 1976.

Slater, Philip E. *The Glory of Hera: Greek Mythology and the Greek Family*. Boston: Beacon Press, 1968.

Smith, Eric. *A Dictionary of Classical Reference in English Poetry*. New York: Barnes and Noble, 1984.

Snodgrass, Mary Ellen. *Auctores Latini*. New York: Amsco, 1993.

————. *Roman Classics*. Lincoln, Neb.: Cliffs Notes, 1988.

————. *Voyages in Classical Mythology*. Santa Barbara, Calif.: ABC-Clio, 1994.

Staal, Julius D. W. *The New Patterns in the Sky: Myths and Legends of the Stars*. Blacksburg, Va.: McDonald and Woodward, 1988.

Stearns, Patty LaNoue. "Star-grazing," Charlotte (N.C.) *Observer*, January 29, 1997, 1–3E.

Stewart, Desmond. *Early Islam*. New York: Time, 1967.

Sullivan, Jack, ed. *The Penguin Encyclopedia of Horror and the Supernatural*. New York: Viking, 1986.

Tester, Jim. *A History of Western Astrology*. New York: Ballantine, 1987.

Thorndike, Lynn. *A History of Magic and Experimental Science During the First Thirteen Centuries of Our Era*. New York: Columbia University Press, 1964.

Tripp, Edward. *The Meridian Handbook of Classical Mythology*. New York: Meridian Books, 1970.

Understanding Astrology: The Influence of the Stars on You and Others. London: Octopus, 1973.

Van der Heyden, A.A.M., and H. H. Scullard, eds. *Atlas of the Classical World*. London: Nelson, 1959.

Vendler, Helen Hennessy. *Yeats's Vision and the Later Plays*. Cambridge, Mass.: Harvard University Press, 1963.

Wechsler, Herman J. *Gods and Goddesses in Art and Legend*. New York: Washington Square Press, 1961.

Wedeck, H. E. *Dictionary of Astrology, Astrological Concepts, Techniques, and Theories*. New York: Citadel Press, 1973.

Wilkinson, Herbert. *Livy's Legends of Ancient Rome*. New York: Macmillan, 1906.

INDEX

Page numbers in **boldface type** refer to the chapters on the Zodiac signs.

About the Author

MARY ELLEN SNODGRASS is an award-winning author of reference works and English and Latin textbooks. Her work *The Encyclopedia of Utopian Literature* (1996) was cited as an Outstanding Reference Book by the American Library Association and received citations from *Choice* and *Library Journal*. She is also the author of the *Choice*-award-winning *Voyages in Classical Mythology* (1994) and of *Japan and the U.S.: Economic Competitors* (1993), which received an award from the New York Public Library. In addition to publishing 52 works, she was Chair of the English Department at Hickory High School in North Carolina and a columnist for the *Charlotte Observer*.